COURTING DISASTER

Manchester University Press

COURTING DISASTER

Reading Between the Lines of the Regency Novel

Zoë McGee

Manchester University Press

Published by Manchester University Press
Oxford Road, Manchester, M13 9PL

www.manchesteruniversitypress.co.uk

British Library Cataloguing-in-Publication Data
A catalogue record for this book is available from the British Library

ISBN 978 1 5261 8885 4 hardback

First published 2025

Typeset
by New Best-set Typesetters Ltd

In loving memory of Mike Michael

Contents

Introduction 1

Part I: Consent

1 Clarissa, or The Perfect Victim Myth 15
2 Cecilia, or Credit and Credibility 35
3 Jane Doe, or Misreading the Room 63

Part II: Innocence

4 Ophelia, or Resisting the Unknown 83
5 Camilla and Eugenia, or What You Don't Know Can Hurt You 101
6 Evelina, or The Value of Virginity 119

Part III: Violence

7 Anon., or The Context of the Courtroom 141
8 Mary, or Violating Convention 156
9 Theodora and Dorothea, or The Bystander Effect 181

Part IV: Marriage

10 Elinor, or Honouring Engagements 205
11 Fanny, or The Price of Refusal 228
12 Anne, or Negotiating the Future 257

Conclusion 273

Appendix 277
Acknowledgements 280
Notes 283
Bibliography 310

Introduction

> I believe any woman for whom the feminist breaking of silence has been a transforming force can also look back to [...] a shock of recognition at certain lines, phrases, images, in the work of this or that woman, long dead, whose life and experience she could only dimly try to imagine.
>
> – Adrienne Rich[1]

It all started with me and my friends laughing. And while we laughed about a lot of things, this was one of the times when the laughter was more of a desperate attempt not to scream into the void. With the start of the university term had come consent workshops, and with consent workshops had come the people (generally men) who were loudly and petulantly offended at being invited to them. According to one student who caught the headlines in 2015, it was outrageous that the organisers had invited him, because they should have been able to tell that he wasn't a rapist. Never mind that seven in ten university students were experiencing sexual violence, or that statistics show that one in seven were raped during their degree.[2] Others vowed that although women might say no to sex, they actually wanted to say yes – or their bodies said yes for them. And we laughed, because at that point what else could we do? If all rapists came with badges then maybe it would be a little easier to avoid them. Maybe then they wouldn't have been people we knew, and maybe then we wouldn't have got hurt.

In the midst of all this hopeless laughing, a conversation from a favourite book of mine crept into my head and wouldn't leave. This insistence that women did not know what they wanted and weren't serious in their refusals? That right there is the first proposal scene in Jane Austen's *Pride and Prejudice* (1813), the one where the odious and highly entitled Mr Collins insists to Elizabeth that – no matter what she might have to say on the subject – she definitely does want to marry him. I had read Austen many times, ever since I first picked up a copy of *Pride and Prejudice* by accident as a kid and proceeded to carry it around to try and make myself look smart. This time, however, I was looking for something specific. Did these kinds of conversations happen elsewhere in her books? Or was this moment of consent discussion – so similar to the ones happening around me – a one-off? I knew that this was something I wanted to dig into more deeply. I went on to write a PhD on consent and eighteenth-century novels.

This book is about consent, and about stories, and about how stories have the capacity to change the world by changing what's inside people's heads. Why words are powerful, and why unspoken words are powerful too. I believe the way that we make sense of the world is by telling ourselves stories about it. We give things a shape that helps us to understand them, that fits with all the other things we think we know. We get used to the shape that things have in our heads. And then when something comes along that doesn't fit with the way those stories work, we struggle, because it's a story that goes against the ones we already know. All this includes giving a shape to things like rape. We build stories about who the people who harm us can be, how they act, and how victims are 'supposed' to act. There's a plotline for how we think people behave in the aftermath of sexual violence. What innocence looks like, what guilt looks like. When enough individuals tell themselves the same-shaped story, it becomes a dominant social narrative. *This is the way we all see this thing.* And that, crucially, has a huge impact on whether individuals talk about or report their experiences of sexual violence, and on the kinds of responses they receive. I believe that the ways in which we understand crimes – as judges, as jurors, and as a general public – are dramatically shaped by the way a crime fits into our personal and social narrative of what that crime 'typically' looks like and what kind of harm we think it causes.

If the story we tell is that rape is committed by strangers attacking randomly at night, those who are attacked by close friends or family are demonstrably less likely to report it. They will be concerned that it is not 'real' in some way, that it doesn't count as a rape because it doesn't look like the story they know of what rape is. They worry that people will blame them (or they blame themselves) because in the story we often tell, victims don't know the perpetrator. They worry that people will think that since they knew them, they should have been able to avoid getting assaulted. Or they should have known that they were with a dangerous person in the first place, because they knew that person and should have known what they were like. And at that point, why were they choosing to spend time with a dangerous person? And the narrative of their rape or assault gets reshaped into a misunderstanding, or regrets the morning after, or, or, or. Anything but an actual assault. All this despite the fact that acquaintance rape is by far and away the most common form. The landmark NUS 'Hidden Marks' survey, which profiled university students in the United Kingdom, found that the majority of all perpetrators of sexual violence were known to the victim – and more specifically, that it was more common for the victim to know their attacker when the crime they experienced was serious sexual assault.[3] RAINN, the largest anti-sexual violence organisation in the United States, reports that a rapist is known to the victim in eight out of ten cases.[4] The likelihood of it being a stranger is significantly lower compared to the likelihood of it being someone the victim knows.

If we tell ourselves that sexual violence only happens to women, then a man speaking up about this having happened to him must fight with the competing narratives that somehow he is either – both

– not a 'real' man or did not suffer a 'real' assault. We end up with men carrying an additional kind of shame that makes them less likely to come forward. Men are supposed to celebrate sex, so why are they making such a fuss about it? Men should be able to fight off an attacker, so clearly they must have wanted it. Maybe if they were a better, manlier man, this wouldn't have happened to them. Men are more likely to be raped than to be falsely accused of being a rapist, but the story of false allegations is disproportionately loud.[5] We have a social narrative which tells men to beware of people – particularly women – making false accusations against them, but not one which takes the sexual assault of men seriously.

This book talks a lot about the eighteenth century, and the elephant in the room is that the eighteenth century is not very good at allowing anyone other than wealthy white men to talk. The female authors I write about use their novels to speak about consent in part because they were not really permitted to address it directly. But they did still have a means of publicly talking about it, even if they had to use the fact that they're writing fiction as a shield of plausible deniability. There are also people who often get left out of the dominant social narrative – both in the eighteenth century and today. Disabled people, people from racially marginalised groups, members of the LGBTQ+ community, neurodivergent people, working-class people. The more of these groups a person falls into, the more barriers there are to their voices, their stories, and their experiences being heard. When thinking about consent advocacy and social narratives around sexual violence, it's vital to remember who isn't being heard, and to keep in mind that that does not mean those narratives do not exist. Some of these eighteenth-century authors include characters in their books who are servants, who are people of colour, who are disabled, who are queer-coded (again with plausible deniability). But that is not the same as those people being able to openly write for themselves, and it does not automatically follow that those characters are well written or well handled. Individual authors recognise levels and degrees of oppression, but in keeping with their not having one unified 'female' voice, they do not present one unified discussion. It is perhaps one of the things I find most striking about their advocacy for the importance of meaningful consent; it is something that all of these writers seem to agree on, despite their other differences.

Fiction, novels, stories. It's easy to simply say that they aren't real. That because the characters do not live and breathe and walk around, the book is not something to take seriously. But books have writers, and books have readers. What authors write, how they write it, who they write it for – all of these things are anchored in the real world that they and their readers live in. Their words can have real-world impacts, beyond the intentions and even lifespans of the authors. Sometimes writing books and crafting narratives is the only way people can get their stories and their messages out there. That certainly was the case if you were a woman wanting to talk about consent and you lived a couple of hundred years ago. It still can be now. When I think about these novels, what I'm often thinking about is what readers might take from them. I'm thinking about what gets presented as normal danger, by which I mean what kinds of threats are written about as though they exist and are not unusual to encounter. What behaviours are the markers of the bad guys? What does the storyline say about the way things ought to be? While the characters and the scenarios they find themselves in are made up, they always exist in conversation with the world the author was living in and writing for.

I should pause here to say that gendered terms are complicated, and the ways that we think and talk about gender and sex have changed over time. A lot of the material from the eighteenth century (and from far more recent periods) is cisgendered and uses binary pronouns, and so this discussion is dominated by that binary. Given that, it feels important to take a moment to acknowledge that trans men and trans women, as well as non-binary and gender-fluid people, are often put to one side in these discussions, or falsely assumed not to have existed. Particular to the topics covered in this book is a level of cis-assumption where 'men' are understood to have penises. This is heightened when talking about the former legal requirement that penetration during rape be done with a penis. It is also linked to the fact that the majority of sexual violence offences are perpetrated by cis men, resulting in a penis = man shorthand. Gender is one more thing we have a dominant social narrative for; working with material that follows that dominant narrative is not the same as endorsing it.

Courtship novels like Austen's – novels that focus on a young woman finding a husband – are ideal for consent-based discussions. They focus on the transitional moment when the heroine is intending to move from being under the authority and jurisdiction of her father and family, to being under that of her husband. In the eighteenth century the idea of marrying for love was increasingly popular, and so the choice of husband was – in theory, if not in practice – supposed to belong to the young woman herself. Marrying for financial or social advantage didn't go away of course, it just became the part you weren't supposed to mention out loud. Choice is integral to consent – if you have no choice about something, you can't consent. That's why we don't hold people responsible for the things they do with a gun to their heads. Eighteenth-century society didn't allow young women to make many significant choices about their lives; having a say in who they married was supposed to be the big one. The novels which centre around the courtship process therefore spend a lot of time questioning how free the women really were to make those choices, frequently focusing on the types of coercion or familial pressures that were used to reduce their capacity to consent. (If there's one thing eighteenth-century society loves a daughter to be, it's obedient.) Signing the marriage contract was not something to be taken lightly. Legally, it gave husbands an enormous amount of control over their wives. Married women didn't exist in the eyes of the law. They were literally 'covered' by their husband (the term is *femme couvert* and applied to every wife but the King's, on the basis that he was too busy running the country to have to worry about petty matters like managing his wife). Being *femme couvert* meant that you weren't a property owner, because any houses or land would be transferred to your husband unless there were specific legal protections or allowances in place. For the landed classes, who made their money from their estates, this meant that married women didn't have a specific income – they would generally live off money given to them by their husband. And whatever class you were, any money you did earn – such as through writing – didn't belong to you, it belonged to your husband. Financial freedom was therefore extremely limited, and this is another strand of the argument for what we might call meaningful consent that populates these courtship novels.

Femme couvert also meant that children belonged to the father, and a woman who wanted to separate from her husband would not be legally entitled to keep her children with her. She had no legal right to a say in how the family's money was spent. *Femme couvert* meant that married women couldn't bring cases to court, because in the eyes of the law they didn't exist. So if a wife wanted to seek some kind of legal redress, she didn't just need her husband's permission, she needed him to be in the courtroom filing the case. And, crucially, by signing a marriage contract, a woman legally signed over sexual consent to her husband. That one lasted for a long time – much longer than people realise. Marital rape only became recognised as a crime in the UK in 1992, and it still isn't recognised in every country worldwide. There was an active expectation that eighteenth-century marriage would involve sex and would lead to the wife having children. Contraceptive options were limited, childbearing carried very significant risks to the life and health of the mother, and venereal disease was rife and easily communicated – meaning that there were additional risks to consider quite apart from the fact that the wife wasn't legally given a say in whether she wanted any sex to happen. Choosing a husband was therefore also choosing a sexual partner to whom you gave the legal power to hurt you for the rest of your life if he wanted to. It's so terrifying a concept that philosopher Mary Astell wrote a whole treatise – *Reflections on Marriage* – about how the institution was fundamentally unsafe all the way back in 1694. She described getting married as 'Elect[ing] a Monarch for Life', saying that

> She must be a Fool with a witness, who can believe a Man, Proud and Vain as he is, will lay his boasted Authority, the Dignity and Prerogative of his Sex, one Moment at her Feet, but in prospect of taking it up again to more advantage; he may call himself her Slave a few days, but it is only in order to make her his all the rest of his Life.[6]

Charlotte Smith, a poet and novelist born in 1749, wrote often about the constraints imposed on women by their legal obligations to husbands and fathers. She was 15 when her father's reckless spending led him to force her into marrying Benjamin Smith, the violent son of a wealthy merchant in the East India Company. Charlotte herself had no choice in the matter – her father agreed to the proposal on her behalf, and she later would describe the event as turning her into a 'legal prostitute'.[7] Her husband was also bad with money, and Charlotte spent much of her life negotiating with his creditors, moving in and out of debtors' prison with him, and selling her writing to pay off his debts. When she eventually left her husband, he retained his rights to the profits she earned from her literary work, and by the end of her life she was living in poverty, selling her personal library in a bid to afford food and coal. All this means that novels which focus on this moment of negotiating marriage – a plotline we often characterise as frivolous today – are never just discussing who a person is attracted to. They're fundamentally arguing about a lifetime of treatment, rights, and freedoms. This is what's at the core of this book: the fact that novels about marriage are always novels about consent.

Having said that, most of these novels don't have an explicit quotable mission statement about the importance of meaningful consent (meaningful consent being quite simply when someone understands what they are consenting to, and has the freedom to make the choice). A lot of what is being shown by the authors comes in the gaps of the texts – the implications (which would have been understood by their readers), the power dynamics of the scenes, the context of who is speaking, the polite euphemisms, the things actively left unsaid. That's why this book contains a lot of spoilers! The novels are too long to explain everything that happens in them, but here you'll find summaries of key plotlines and character dynamics, so as to give you a sense of the power structures and tensions at work. If we break down how we think about consent being given, on a very simplistic level you end up with consent coming from words and consent coming from actions. I start by thinking about the words, and what it looks like when your word carries power in the context of a novel. Who gets to give their word, and who needs to have someone else backing them up before they can follow through on their decisions? This involves a lot of thinking about money, and ideas bound up in credit and credibility – it's no coincidence that those words are so linguistically close.

I then move on to talking about behavioural consent, or consent that is read from actions. A victim's behaviour is often very closely scrutinised in cases of sexual violence, no matter the time period, and it gets used to suggest that they did actually consent to what was done to them. In the eighteenth century there were a lot of rules for how women were supposed to behave, and how they were supposed to be. Innocence was a desirable quality for young unmarried ladies, but it's something that is valuable precisely because it's vulnerable. Ultimately, a lot of that boils down to the fact that most 'proper' female behaviour was socially coded as a kind of consent. In the middle of this book we'll take a break from digging into novels to look at who reported rape to the law courts, and what their testimony can tell us about how people spoke about sexual violence. We'll look at what factors influenced the chances of a guilty verdict, as well as understanding who *wasn't* being served by the courts. Some of those unheard voices are the subject of the next section, where we'll look at how some of the novelists who did write more explicitly about sexual violence handled it. Rape is shown to have a cost – both personal and social – and one that is only exacerbated by the way society tends to welcome perpetrators back into the fold, but ostracises victims. Finally, we'll look at the best-known and latest author in this book – Jane Austen – and the way in which her novels build and draw on these earlier works to advocate for the importance of meaningful consent. Peppered throughout you'll also find stories from our own time – bringing home the fact that though the world has changed, some of the conversations we're having about consent remain the same.

When I was working on the early stages of what would become this book, a victim impact statement from an American rape trial went viral on the internet. Chanel Miller, then identified by the protective alias Emily Doe, wrote powerfully and eloquently about the harm Brock Turner had caused her. All around the world people were reading this statement, words from a complete stranger, and weeping at their screens. She had not been permitted to read the full statement to the court during the trial – the judge presiding over Miller's case allowed her only four minutes to speak, and she was not allowed to face her assailant to deliver it. But her decision to release the full statement through a trusted journalist ended up being an incredibly powerful act of taking back narrative control. Not only did it finally allow her to air the words she had wanted to say, but it reached millions of people all around the globe (more than 15 million people had viewed the article in the first week alone). It was read out in full on CNN and international television news. It was read on the floor of the state senate to successfully advocate for specific law changes in California, ending the requirement for legally recognised rape be carried out with a penis. And then there were letters. Lots and lots of letters. Women writing to say that her words had given them the courage to take their children and leave the abusive households they had been living in. Unknown voices crediting her with saving their lives or those of their children. Women telling her that they now understood that what had happened to them was not their fault. Her words, this act of writing and sharing, tangibly changed the world: it changed laws and it changed lives.

It resonated very powerfully with me. Sexual assault had been a significant part of the university experience for most of the women I knew – of course it resonated. One point in particular spoke to me: Miller wrote about the power and privilege of constructing narratives in sexual violence cases, about the way in which her being unconscious meant that her assailant was allowed to 'write the script' of the attack.[8] I carried that around with me, and although I was supposed to be writing strictly about the eighteenth century, I ended up quoting her in my dissertation. Not just because her words about competing narratives and the privilege of social capital were important, and just as valid when applied to two hundred years ago, but because I wanted whoever read that essay about the eighteenth century, and marriage, and bonnets, and muslins, and imaginary lake-diving scenes, to remember that questions of consent always have a human cost. That the real people reading and writing those books were navigating real risks.

But if quoting Miller offered the opportunity to humanise the eighteenth century and bring it closer to us, it also highlighted that we haven't moved as far away from it as we would hope. The judge presiding over Miller's case gave Brock Turner such a lenient sentence that it was later used as grounds to remove him from the judicial roll.[9] Though it was only days after Miller made her statement public that I included her words in my essay, Turner had finished serving his sentence before I got that essay back from the markers. Though only linked circumstantially, there is no world in which the turnaround time on an essay should be slower than the process of making restitution for a serious assault. The judge had Turner's narrative over Miller's – a story that said that here was a talented young man who didn't deserve to have his life derailed for what

Turner's father grossly referred to as 'twenty minutes of action'.[10] But changing those narratives, and changing those stories, is a core part of how we fight back against sexual violence. They're how we take back control of our own lives, how we heal from trauma, and how we work to make the world a better place. We do it through hashtags, through impact statements, through whisper networks. But we also do it through novels, and have done ever since they were invented. We use the sharing of stories – fictional and otherwise – to try to change the world. And that's really what this book is about.

PART I

CONSENT

1

Clarissa, or The Perfect Victim Myth

> Writing and sharing these stories helps us feel less alone but, more than that, comparing experiences of oppression and hardship and hurt makes it possible to believe that the problem might not be with us, as individuals.
>
> – Laurie Penny[1]

> Let me not thus be cruelly given up to a man my very soul is averse to […] why should I be denied the liberty of *refusing*? That liberty is all I ask.
>
> – Samuel Richardson, *Clarissa*[2]

When you don't know what to do, ask a book. Courtship novels are guides to behaviour – both proper and improper. Only turn someone down for a dance if you're not going to do any more dancing that evening. Don't get confused and think that the man abducting you from your family home has your best interests at heart. Be very, very careful of carriage rides. These eighteenth-century characters exist in a world where 'the right thing to do' is complicated, and where their behaviour can be wildly misread. They are stuck trying to balance competing and contradictory claims of duty, loyalty, and morality. Don't offend your father by disagreeing with him, but also don't marry the guy who makes your skin crawl. There are dilemmas and tensions, and people misunderstand each other all the time. Think you'll prove to your one true love that you've accepted their cruel rejection of you by showing that you're not committing the cardinal sin of brooding? Well, it turns out that that was a test to see if you're serious enough for them, and they now think you're a massive flirt who never cared about them in the first place. Oh, and the old man you were chatting to because he's too old to have any romantic notions? He begs to differ, and he's pretty sure you're into him too. (The miscommunication trope is an eighteenth-century favourite, and when you miscommunicate over 800 pages, you *really* miscommunicate.) These novels were a great improvement on the conduct manuals that had previously been the socially acceptable literature for young women and girls to read and get ideas about life. Where conduct manuals focused on how to be a good daughter, a good wife, or a good servant, the novels had a different idea in mind.

If a traditional conduct manual attempts to teach a girl how to avoid being raped or seduced, a novel seeks to educate people about why that rape and seduction is wrong. How the most significant causes of sexual violence are not aspects of the victim's behaviour, but the actions of the person carrying out the abuse (we're sadly still teaching this class today). Novels can demonstrate what a threat can look like, and who it can come from, so that people have half a chance of recognising when they are in a dangerous situation. And they open legal and social practices up to wider debate. We use novels to this day to challenge and question ideas. To make people aware of things, and feel things, and connect with perspectives that they otherwise might not. That's not the job of every novel – novels have many purposes, and sometimes we just need entertainment for its own sake, especially when it feels like the world is descending into apocalyptic chaos… But writing and storytelling are a big part of how we fight against sexual violence. To understand how we get there it's important to go back to the beginning. Not the beginning of the story – that would be impossible. But we can and should go back to the beginnings of the novel, because it's the start of the conversation that all of these books are having with each other.

Novels were newly invented in the eighteenth century. Credit for the first novel is usually given to Daniel Defoe for his 1719 work *Robinson Crusoe.*[3] And what you'll find with Defoe's work, and with many of the early novels, is that they aim to be believable, marketing themselves as true stories told to the author by the hero of the story, and then written down. This also served as an excuse for anything impolite or shocking in the books – after all, the author wasn't making it up, they were just writing down the story as it was told to them. They couldn't be blamed for its content... Having said that, novels often did have shocking things in them, as that was part of the entertainment value. Defoe's second novel, *Moll Flanders*, might well see Moll finding religion, but only at the end of a book's worth of sexual exploits and escapades. The book that really popularised the novel, however, was written by Samuel Richardson. Called *Pamela; Or, Virtue Rewarded* and first published in 1740, the book was an enormous and instant success. There was a real fashion for *Pamela* merchandise.[4] Snuffboxes were decorated. Key quotes would be written on fans and wafted alluringly across the ballroom. People would carry the book itself around with them on their walks so that everyone would know it was their favourite – or would think that it was, which would still make them look good.

One of the big things that Richardson did with *Pamela* was play up the idea of respectability. The inspiration for the novel came from the guide to letter writing that he was working on at the time, where he would compose model letters on particular themes. Being good at writing letters was an important skill in the eighteenth century, as letters would probably be passed around the whole family – and any visitors, friends, or neighbours who happened to visit – as a means of sharing news and entertainment. *Pamela* is written as a series of letters (also referred to as an epistolary novel), most of which are written by Pamela herself. Though the letters are well constructed, the novel moves past being a guide for how to write and presents itself as a guide for behaviour too. It sets itself up almost as if it were a conduct manual. Pamela is a 15-year-old servant girl who goes to be a maid in the house of the wealthy bachelor Mr B. Mr B decides very early on that he wants to have sex with Pamela, and spends much of the book attempting to seduce her. (As a quick guidance note, the eighteenth century calls things 'seduction' when the woman agrees to the sex, and 'rape' when she doesn't. This distinction isn't very stable, and we're going to come back to it a bit later on.) Pamela's virtue, however, protects her from his advances. Mr B gets frustrated with the failure of his seduction schemes and attempts to rape Pamela with the help of his housekeeper – but luckily Pamela faints and he finds himself unable to go through with it. Eventually, he's so won over by her goodness that he stops trying to force her into bed and starts trying to marry her instead. Wouldn't you know it, by the end of the novel they are husband and wife. Pamela receives a fortune that matches her goodness, Mr B becomes a better man who's worthy of her, and everything is settled to their mutual delight.

If I'm being honest, I don't love it. Pamela's virtue creates a big quandary for her, because she's supposed to stay a virgin, but she's also supposed to obey her master, and she spends quite a lot of time wrestling with this dilemma of how to do the right thing. That's frustrating if you don't happen to share the same scruples about obedience, and to me it doesn't feel like a real person's perspective, it feels like the perspective of the made-up idealised person that people who kept servants wanted their servants to be like. The other thing that bothers me is that Pamela's behaviour is meant to save her, but she's never really in control of what's happening to her. She's not the one who can affect whether she gets attacked or not. And while there's an argument that says she gets to rise in society because she's virtuous, it's outweighed for me by the fact that the man she's marrying wanted to rape her. I really struggle to get on board with the trope where the wannabe rapist is reformed by the power of his intended victim's virtue. There are some really dark elements to the novel, with its violence and Pamela's vulnerability as a servant who can't necessarily afford to lose her job, who is dependent on this man who initially just sees her as something to chase. There's a moment when we're told that Pamela hides her letters next to her skin so that Mr B won't find them, but then we hear from him about how he's taken them from her, and he's touching and handling the letters thinking about how close they've been to her flesh, and it's a very effective (and creepy) fetishisation of these letters. But then you also have the need for everything to end happily ever after, and a resolution that feels overly simplistic – and the two tones just don't mix together that well. It feels as though Richardson is trying to resolve two competing ideas, and hasn't quite worked out what it is that he really wants to say. But whatever you think of the book, in blurring this line between novels and conduct manuals Richardson really highlighted the potential novels had for changing people's minds. And his next book is the big one for talking about writing and consent.

It is a truth universally acknowledged that if you read any academic book on consent or rape and the eighteenth-century novel, it's going to talk about *Clarissa*. *Clarissa; or, The History of a Young Lady* (early novels love a double title) is a behemoth of a book. Published in seven volumes in 1748, it remains one of the longest novels ever written in the English language. Its word-count is around 33% longer than *War and Peace*. If you were looking for a book to use as a murder weapon, this would be the one. It's also an epistolary novel, written in letters between our heroine Clarissa Harlowe and her friend, and the villainous Robert Lovelace and his friend. The (highly, highly) abridged version of the story is that Clarissa is a wonderful girl with a terrible family who are trying to make her marry a man she doesn't like. They're petty and mean and nasty, and end up locking her in her room and forbidding her from seeing or talking (or writing) to her friends, until she agrees to marry the man they have chosen for her. Our villain, Robert Lovelace, is not that man. He was supposed to be marrying Clarissa's older sister, but after they fall out he sets his sights on Clarissa instead. Clarissa doesn't want to marry him either, but her family don't believe her. They become increasingly cruel and restrictive, and in the end the situation becomes so dire that Clarissa considers eloping with Lovelace just to get away from them. Though she isn't really sure that she wants to go through with it, she does agree to meet him in the middle of the night. Lovelace has his servant make a noise around their hiding place, convincing Clarissa that the family have discovered their plan, and terrifying her with thoughts of what will happen to her. He grabs her and runs her to his waiting carriage, in which the pair drive off. Clarissa isn't hugely keen on being run off with in this carriage, but even though she's telling Lovelace she doesn't want to go, he drags her off anyway. The upshot of the matter is that Lovelace gets Clarissa away from her family home and into his clutches. He keeps her as his prisoner for months.

Clarissa's family want nothing more to do with her. They think she has betrayed them and lied to them, and that she always intended to run off with Lovelace. Clarissa can't return to them herself, and they're not interested in coming to get her. Lovelace, meanwhile, embarks on a campaign to make Clarissa have sex with him. He doesn't believe that virtuous women exist, and so he wants Clarissa to agree to sleep with him to prove his point: even someone as pure as she is can't resist sin. Clarissa refuses him, wanting simply to live on her own in peace – the poor girl just wants to have a life somewhere where she's not being locked up by her family or harassed by this obnoxious man. This is baffling to Lovelace. Unsurprisingly he ignores her wishes. He claims that women will forgive men anything if they justify it as coming from their passion for them – or to put it another way, if he says he's just doing it because he loves her so much, she will accept all sorts of mistreatment. This has more basis in fact than we might like to believe, but part of that is because we say that this kind of behaviour is romantic. Take something like *The Notebook*, which was *the* weepie romance when I was growing up. Hanging off a Ferris wheel and threatening to kill yourself if you don't get a date gets worse the longer you think about it, but that's how the love story starts. Lovelace tries various schemes, including setting a fire so that he has an excuse to go into Clarissa's bedroom and rescue her while she's not wearing very many clothes.

Richardson actually got complaints about how racy this scene was. He publicly apologised for writing it in too much detail – Clarissa's not wearing very much, and Lovelace is very close to her and keeps trying to get her to sleep with him – it's pretty direct for a book that's supposed to be polite rather than bawdy. But he said he had to write it that explicitly so that readers knew exactly what happened – and crucially, exactly what *hadn't* happened. Clarissa and Lovelace definitely didn't have sex. He said that if he'd been more vague about it, more delicate and euphemistic, people might think that something had happened. And if they thought that Clarissa had relented to Lovelace, they might then use that previous sexual history to justify her rape later. That's sensible on Richardson's part, because even today the sexual history of victims gets used in court to try to show that they weren't raped because they had had sex before, or had had sex with the perpetrator before, or had had a lot of sex and therefore weren't the kind of person who can be raped.

Anyway, Lovelace's approaches become increasingly violent, and Clarissa continues to resist them, until it reaches the point where he threatens to rape her. Under this threat, he extracts a promise from her that she will forgive him for everything and that she'll marry him. Clarissa, thankfully, has absolutely no intention of fulfilling a promise that was extorted from her, and she proceeds to escape from the house at the earliest opportunity.

Lovelace is furious and vows his revenge. Eventually, after much scheming and strategising, he is able to get her back to the disguised brothel he had been keeping her in. Lovelace and the brothel madam drug Clarissa, and then Lovelace rapes her while she's incapacitated. He expects this to change Clarissa's attitude to him, but when she awakes she is still disgusted by him, and even more shockingly (to Lovelace that is) still has no wish to marry him. Her virtuous nature has not been damaged by the rape – forced sex has not given her an interest in a sinful life. She's still the same person that she was before. Lovelace realises that even though he has raped her, he hasn't been able to corrupt her. He decides that perhaps the problem was that she was unconscious during the first rape, and so she didn't have the opportunity to capitulate to him, so he plans to rape Clarissa while she's conscious to see if the awareness of his domination will fundamentally change her. Lovelace really is horrendous. When he tries, however, Clarissa threatens to kill herself, and this mystifies Lovelace. He doesn't want her dead. Clarissa once again manages to escape, but even then she can't get free of him. She lives in perpetual fear of him finding her again. She becomes increasingly ill from the stress of this (understandably, as constantly having to evade someone who wants to kidnap and torture you will take it out of a person) and it reaches a point where she's convinced that she's not got much time left. She puts her will together and dies in the full confidence that she will go on to a better life in heaven. Lovelace is killed in a duel with her cousin, and her family finally decide that maybe they had made a mistake about Clarissa after all. Whatever solace you take from the idea of Clarissa ending up in heaven, you can't label this ending a happy ever after.

So what makes *Clarissa* such an important book? Well, if you ask ten academics, you'll likely get ten slightly different answers depending on their particular interests and takes. If you're asking me, I think it comes down to a specific piece of rape law and a question about innocence. The definition of rape as a crime in the eighteenth century included the requirement that the woman resist with all of her strength. (It is gendered – rape of someone identified as a man would be tried as sodomy.) This was quite a nasty piece of legislation, as it meant that victims would not only have to prove that they had resisted, but that they had resisted *enough*. In Clarissa's case, Richardson has Lovelace drug her, and this is important because it means that Clarissa clearly cannot give her consent – not even under duress – because she is unconscious. No one can argue that she agreed, or that her behaviour indicated part-way through that she wanted it, or any of those problematic suggestions. She's blacked out unconscious, and not through any act of her own will (not that that would make a difference to the fact that she can't resist or consent). Richardson makes the fact that Clarissa cannot consent explicitly clear. But the condition for rape in law requires Clarissa to resist, and if she's unconscious she also can't do that. She can't do anything. She's out cold. By setting up the rape in this way, Richardson focuses the attention of his readers on this problem with rape law. Laid out in this enormous and very popular book, is a clear case where the act of rape has taken place, but it doesn't neatly fit within the definition of the crime.

Clarissa is not the perfect victim. Richardson himself wrote: 'I did not want her to be wholly blameless.'[5] He said that 'Clarissa was not drawn absolutely perfect, but as having something to blame herself for, tho' not in Intention.'[6] This doesn't mean that he's saying that Clarissa wanted to be raped, or that she deserved to be raped, or that she wasn't really raped because she somehow invited it. What he's saying is that if you take the whole book point by point, Clarissa doesn't always make the 'correct' choice. She wouldn't be a perfect model behaviour pattern for a young girl, despite her being a highly moral character. After all, she agrees to meet Lovelace alone in the dark, and she does consider eloping with him. If she hadn't done that, he wouldn't have been able to run her into the carriage and carry her off. That doesn't justify Lovelace. If she'd met him in the dark and he hadn't abducted her, she also wouldn't have been abducted. She didn't agree to any of what was done to her. It doesn't take away any of what Clarissa suffers. But that's kind of the big point. Richardson is challenging the idea that you have to be totally and 100% perfect in order to have the harm that is done to you recognised.

Maybe all that sounds obvious to you. But that's why it's important. It was important in the eighteenth century to write a behemoth of a book explaining that you don't have to be a saint to be the victim of rape, and it was important to make the point that you can't consent when you're unconscious, and it was important to make the point that even if the character is charming and rich, if he's a rapist he probably shouldn't be considered prime marriage material. But, and here's the weird bit, it's still important today. Partly, it's important to know that people were fighting for this then, because increasingly loud and problematic groups are right now trying to bring back a past that was frankly dangerous for a whole lot of people. I mean, of course it was – right now is dangerous too, even with lots of things being better. But it's also important because not *enough* things are better, and we're losing some of that hard-won ground. This is not a new fight. Getting to where we are now has taken time, blood, ink, sweat, and tears. And so when people push back against the – fairly basic – rights that we're upholding and say that they're just millennial snowflake nonsense (or whatever generational put-down is trending), we need to be able to metaphorically bop them on the head with a 700-page novel and prove them wrong. Regency dramas and their modern iterations are a whole lot of fun, but you would not want to go back to being governed by the laws of consent at the point of marriage, or a wife having no legal identity. That kind of power terrified plenty of real women back then, and it doesn't need to come back now.

So so what if Clarissa met Lovelace at night? She didn't ask to be raped. In the story she doesn't choose to be drugged, but if she had done that still wouldn't have justified his actions. Clarissa is innocent, but she doesn't look like a perfect victim. She left her family home and she can't prove it wasn't under her own steam. She didn't resist her rape. She made a plan to elope with the man who later harms her. It is impossible for a victim to participate in the act of being raped – it is by its very nature something which is done to them; the thing-ification is another part of the violence. But people often use contextual factors – what were they wearing? how much did they have to drink? how many people have they had sex with before? – in order to determine whether the victim contributed to the scenario. The fact that they can't consent to the rape remains the most important thing. It is never the victim's fault. But Richardson's point isn't whether we should do this contextual blaming or not. It takes the fact that society does just that – we still do that – and bypasses it. Sure, we could have a debate about whether you think the contextual factors mean that Clarissa (or any other victim) bears some responsibility. And we might well violently disagree on that. But we don't have to, because the fact remains that *it doesn't matter*. Even if you think that the victim has contributed to the circumstances, they remain just as harm-able as a 'perfect' victim.

And that's what's important about *Clarissa*. The book isn't spending its many (many, many) pages defending the fact that she was raped or trying to prove it happened. It doesn't try to make Clarissa look perfect. Even though she does display a fairly inhuman amount of patience and forbearance, there are factors there for people to get their teeth into and argue about regarding degrees of complicity and culpability. Because if there's one thing I've learned from years of research on consent, it's that there will always be people who want to pick and pick at everything until they can suggest that the rapist isn't responsible. This dissection of the actions and motives of the victim doesn't get applied to the perpetrator in anything like the same way. There's a lot of talk around the idea of being innocent until proven guilty, and the importance of that ruling. But the court of public opinion often misapplies it. Because when people say 'innocent until proven guilty', they take that to mean that we must assume that the alleged perpetrator is innocent until we can prove their guilt. So far, so good. But in order to do that, we have to listen with a point of view that says that they are telling us the truth – which means operating on the assumption that the alleged victim is lying.

For whatever reason, we don't always remember to apply that right to the alleged victim too. We don't stop treating the alleged perpetrator as innocent when we talk to the alleged victim because we're trying to maintain the innocence-until-proven-otherwise of the perpetrator. So trials are often conducted from a position where, in order to support the right of the alleged perpetrator not to have to prove their innocence, we treat the victim as if they were guilty of lying and require them to prove that they are not. Innocent until proven guilty is an important right, but the way we use it means that the victim is often denied it in practice. It's a monstrously unfair burden.

Richardson recognises that rape is awful even when the victim isn't perfect. And so, rather than write the world's most perfect victim, he writes something which moves beyond the conversation that gets bogged down in the potential culpability of that victim. Okay, the book seems to say, she did something she wasn't supposed to. She met a man at night who turned out to be a terrible person. She contemplated leaving her family. That doesn't mean she wanted to be raped, and it doesn't mean it didn't harm her. So let's talk about that bit. Let's talk about what Lovelace did that was wrong. Let's talk about what Clarissa feels afterwards. Let's talk about all the bits that don't get talked about because people are too busy dissecting the victim's actions in order to decide whether they deserve to have any sympathy. Let's talk about the fact that this clearly *was* rape, and how the law is wrong for not recognising it.

A big part of that necessitates focusing on the actions of Lovelace. This is something that Richardson would return to many times, amending the text of *Clarissa* over the years. This was, generally, because despite being an absolutely terrible person, Lovelace was also a dashing, dangerous, wealthy, and charming man – what the Regency period would term a rake. And rakes, like the twenty-first-century's bad boys, were attractive. A reformed rake, so the saying went, made the best husband. To put the problem simply, Lovelace was much too popular. Readers – many of them women – wrote to Richardson insisting that he reform Lovelace by the end of the book, have him learn his lesson, and marry Clarissa so as to live happily ever after. Rather than oblige them, Richardson doggedly went back, adding details and footnotes and extra text to try and make it abundantly clear that Lovelace is a bad man and not someone to swoon over.

The thing that I find most interesting about all of this is the way it highlights the mess that exists between ideas of courtship and violence. What I mean by that is that a lot of the behaviours that we think of or write about as desirable, or as indicating desire – and a lot of the ways that we demonstrate that we're interested in someone – can get very similar to the ways that people harass and harm. Historian Toni Bowers has an excellent book called *Force or Fraud: British Seduction Stories and the Problem of Resistance 1660–1760*, which breaks this down in detail.[7] The title refers to the two ways it was thought that women ended up having sex with men; by force, meaning physical violence and rape, or by fraud, which meant seduction and capitulation. She explains that

> 'Seduction' came to denote the gradual achievement of female complicity with presumably primary male desire, whilst 'rape' came to signify an act of sexualised force defined as such by female resistance. Increasingly, too, women's resistance had to be unmitigated and unrelenting – even to the point of death – for the event to qualify as rape and not seduction. The distinction between 'force' and 'fraud' crucially came to require a determination of whether the respondent, paradigmatically female, colluded in or resisted her own fall, and it posited collusion and resistance as necessarily exclusive acts.[8]

What changes with seventeenth-century fiction, Bowers explains, is not the introduction of a new term, but the recoding of existing ones. 'Rape' and 'seduction' used to be more interchangeable. People didn't necessarily have a strict definition as to what the difference was, and they wouldn't take issue with you switching between the two. However, as time went on, there was an increasing interest in defining the two as distinct and separate – almost developing them into different categories. Toni Bowers argues that this clear distinction between the two gets muddied by the fact that the seduction path is effectively the same as the rape path, up until the (apparent) consent or capitulation of the respondent. (The idea that, if you stop resisting, then your resistance was never genuine, totally fails to recognise the way that harm-reduction strategies work.) The distinction between rape and seduction, Bowers is saying, lies in whether the woman resists or not. And crucially, that 'or not' can be taken at any point – if you were to stop resisting so as to prevent your death, that rape might well be categorised as a 'seduction' instead. Which is another way of saying that the actions of a rapist and the actions of a seducer are essentially the same; what is seen as transforming the interaction is the female response to it. Blame is attached to women in seduction cases, because that lack of resistance – whether from desire or as a safety mechanism – is taken as complicity. Either you are party to your own 'fall' or you resist it – but if you don't resist enough or in the right way, then that resistance gets overwritten and doesn't count.

The most important thing that Bowers talks about – at least as far as this book is concerned – is the fact that courtship is supposed to be different to the rape-or-seduction category divide, but it really isn't. Courtship, she writes, was increasingly characterised as something mutual. But the power dynamics and the practices employed meant that it didn't function as something fundamentally distinct. At best it's part of a spectrum of submission, what she calls a 'subset of seduction'. Here's what she says:

> when force is at once gendered and eroticized, when sexual arousal and satisfaction are routinely linked with men's domination of women, a stable distinction between seduction and rape, like the idea of straightforward consent and resistance that distinction relies on,

> becomes problematic […] For when it is one person's unquestioned right to pursue and the other's job to resist or consent, the answering voice will remain secondary and subordinate […] the category 'rape' might well be understood as a kind of scapegoat for 'violence without seduction.' As the reserved location of violence, 'rape' allows for pretence that seduction/courtship is *not* a power play, that the gendered partners really are equal unless (or until) the man uses direct physical force.[9]

The power dynamics of courtship are highly gendered. Men are cast as the instigators and pursuers, as dominant forces, while women are expected to be reactive responders, who by saying 'yes' are also submitting. Though the stereotypically female role can be presented as a position of power, because she gets to say yes or no and therefore determine whether the courtship is successful, in practice it's secondary to the pursuit by the male. The responder in this scenario doesn't have the same opportunities to approach the person they are interested in. Their choice isn't a question of who they would like to marry; they are presented with an offer that they can accept or decline. The way that courtship roles were gendered means that seeking was something men did, and responding was something women did. There wasn't an equality of position where both parties could seek. As a result, consent is often misunderstood as a purely feminine matter. We only ask the question of consent of the female party because the man as the seeker is actively pursuing the interaction – which is seen as indicating his consent.

Obviously, coercion is possible for men in this scenario. They might not want to actively pursue a particular person, and might be being compelled to do so. They might feel obliged, or pressurised, or any of the other things that impact a person's ability to choose. But we tend not to ask the question of whether they are willing or not, because we assume that the person asking someone to do something wants them to do it. If I ask you to dance with me, you'll probably assume that I want you to. We focus on the question of whether the responder wants to do the thing or not because that moment of response is the moment of choice for them, whereas the seeker's decision making about the action happens earlier, at the point where they choose (or are forced) to ask the responder. We read seekers as consenting because we work on the general principle that they want what they are seeking. And because men are often cast in the role of seekers by society, we therefore don't think about consent as something that gets asked of men. We assume that if they're asking someone to marry them, they want the marriage to happen. It isn't always the case, but it's certainly the implication created.

This in turn means that the courtship is built around trying to make what the male instigator wants happen, which isn't terribly mutual. Bowers talks about how, because of these power dynamics, courtship (and seduction) operate within the 'shadow of rape' – a phrase which reminds us that the difference between rape and seduction here is whether physical force is used and, if it is, whether the woman stops resisting. It's a threat that is present even in apparently mutual narratives of courtship. Effectively, what we see is the idea that meaningful consent is impossible in a scenario where power is so unevenly distributed.

What Bowers doesn't spell out here is that the power of that responsive position to give or refuse consent is ultimately very dependent on the attitude that the seeker has to consent itself. To return to the example from Jane Austen I mentioned in the introduction of this book, when Mr Collins proposes to Elizabeth, she says no. Several times. In increasingly blunt ways. Does he listen? Absolutely not. He reinterprets her refusals as acceptances – she's just trying to increase his love by suspense, or she's refusing him because all women refuse at least once to show that they're elegant. He starts to flag a bit towards the end, finding it harder to explain away this woman doing everything but shouting 'I don't like you' at him, but he sticks to his guns. In the end, Elizabeth has to leave the room and get her father to explain the facts to him. The responder – in this case Elizabeth – has to borrow her father's authority in order to have her refusal acknowledged by Mr Collins. Mr Collins just won't listen to it from her. Her power to refuse consent is limited by Mr Collins's willingness to acknowledge her response. And she's lucky, because Mr Bennet backs her up. But if he had done what his wife wanted and insisted that Elizabeth marry Mr Collins, then she'd have been in an extremely tricky position where continuing to refuse could see her with nowhere to live and no money to live on. She needed Mr Bennet's backing to be able to refuse safely. So the position of responder has some pretty big limitations on its power.

Samuel Richardson, writing his *Clarissa*, makes this clear. In a scene I mentioned earlier, Lovelace starts a fire and nearly rapes Clarissa. She's trying very very hard to put him off. And he is deciding whether or not he's going to do it. (In that scene, he doesn't.) But Richardson is refreshingly clear about the fact that this is Lovelace's choice. He's ignoring what Clarissa wants, and there are no magic words she can say that will prevent him from doing it if he chooses to. She's at his mercy. She's doing all the right things to try to dissuade him, but ultimately, he is deciding whether he's going to treat her more like a person or a thing. I say it's refreshing to see that because it's blunt and it's honest. It is a terrifying prospect to acknowledge that if someone is going to attack you, that's a choice that they make and that you can't say the right things to stop them. They're the ones making the choice about attacking you, and while we like to keep that safety net around us that if we can do or say the right things then we can be safe, that simply isn't the case. It doesn't mean that the attack will be successful, or that the person won't change their minds. But the attack is their choice. The eighteenth-century laws around resistance – and particularly the conversations that happened in courtrooms – have this edge to them where they can imply that if you resist properly then nothing should happen to you. Therefore, if something happens to you, you didn't resist properly, and if you didn't resist properly you consented; and so, by flawed and circuitous logic, if something happened to you, you consented because it happened. Richardson is being blunt about the fact that resistance isn't enough to save you. And while it's a scary thing to hear, it's also an important one for readers to know.

When we start doing this dissection of what people could have done to be safe, trying to make perfect model characters who couldn't possibly have blame assigned to them, we start to blame real victims. Not being attacked doesn't make you better than someone who was attacked. It doesn't mean that you followed the rules and they didn't. Part of what Richardson's leveraging to get a reaction out of his audience with Clarissa is that she's a good girl from a good family; she's white, and genteel, and all the things that theoretically make her safe. She's the image of the perfect victim, and thus perfectly positioned to wring maximum sympathy out of her genteel white audience. Then she makes a mistake – depending on how you look at it – and winds up in the impossible position of having to resist while being drugged unconscious. She's no longer perfect, but Richardson doesn't want us to have any ideas that she deserved or wanted this. (That's partly why she has to die, to give the tragedy its final flourish.)

The perfect victim paradigm that Richardson was tackling is everywhere. Among other things, it impacts who ends up in the stories. The more marginalised the community your identity intersects with, the more likely you are to be attacked, and the less likely you are to get an eighteenth-century novel written about it. Today, it makes you less likely to get sympathetic media coverage, because the perfect victim is a pretty white cis woman, who's able-bodied and was doing something innocuous and unconnected to sex. The more of those perfect-victim boxes you fit into already, the more you want to believe that story, because it tells you that you don't deserve to be attacked and that what you're doing is making yourself safer. It also tells you that people from marginalised identities deserve to be attacked more, building upon and contributing to the racist perception that white skin equates to higher value and superior morality, the ableist perspective that sees disabled people as somehow worth less than the able-bodied, the bigoted view that demonises trans bodies for simply existing.

If we step away from *Clarissa* for a moment and think about the extensive coverage of Sarah Everard's murder in 2021, there was one line which came up again and again in the way people talked about and reported her story: she was just walking home. And part of that is because it was a terrible event, and part of that is because we all go home at some point and so it's relatable. It's something we all do. This terrible thing could happen to us, even if we don't do any of the things that we've identified as being 'risky'. On the one hand, this proves the point: you don't choose to be murdered. You don't choose to be raped. She wasn't doing anything that could be seen as dangerous, therefore this can happen to anyone (though there were still internet commentators suggesting that she should have done things differently). It happens to more women than we hear about – women like Sabina Nessa, who was also murdered while walking home. Her name is less familiar than Sarah Everard's, because Nessa was a woman of colour, and so wasn't seen by the press as fitting into the kind of perfect victim paradigm that makes for round-the-clock news stories. In her article for Al Jazeera, Professor Catherine Rottenburg wrote about how race, age, and class don't simply affect how much people's stories are covered, but also 'how they are framed; namely, whether the victims are portrayed as "innocent" or, conversely, shamed and blamed'.[10] Behind this shocked sentiment of 'just walking home' in the Sarah Everard case coverage is hiding the perfect victim sentiment, which says that you deserve this less if you're just walking home because you weren't doing anything that could be seen as wrong. It's not necessarily intentional, but it's still a reinforcement of the toxic idea that somehow everyday actions like the clothes you wear or the route you walk can influence how much you deserve to get murdered. And, as many articles have pointed out, this way of thinking, of measuring risk, of typifying behaviours into risky and safe, is all part of an equation where we ask that we are not the ones who get raped or killed. That it's someone else instead.

I don't mean we think that consciously. But because the decision to attack is coming from the attacker, if they are going to be motivated by sexy clothes and we're not in the sexiest clothes, then it won't be us. If they're going to go for the drunk person and we're less drunk, it won't be us. It's a grotesque version of tying your bike up somewhere where it's not the fanciest bike so that yours is less likely to be stolen. Wearing different clothes, walking different streets, drinking less – none of these fix the problem because none of them deal with the person doing the attacking. Their potential impact is on which victim gets the short straw, not on stopping there being a victim. So, they were just walking home? They should never have been harmed. But also, they were just out clubbing, they were just wearing a cute outfit, they were just looking for a one-night stand? Whatever they were just doing, they should never have been harmed. Because no one deserves to be raped. Because the idea of the perfect victim is a paradox.

This is what Richardson's getting at with *Clarissa*, and why it's so important to him that she isn't perfect. But he's not the only author who talks about this issue. Actually, novel writing was primarily a female profession in the eighteenth century. And you can bet that the women writing in this brave new genre had plenty to say on this subject.

2

Cecilia, or Credit and Credibility

> The violence in domestic violence is best understood as a subset of what is now often called coercive control, an attempt to dominate someone by means that are psychological – and may also be financial, physical, social, political – by preventing them from participating in the larger world and holding opinions of their own and exercising agency over their own bodies, lives, finances, truths.
>
> – Rebecca Solnit[1]

> Cecilia for some time hoped he was merely indulging his strange and sordid humour by an opposition that was only intended to teize her; but she soon found herself extremely mistaken: he was immoveable in obstinacy, as he was incorrigible in avarice; he neither troubled himself with enquiries nor reasoning, but was contented with refusing her as a child might be refused, by peremptorily telling her she did not know what she wanted, and therefore should not have what she asked.
>
> – Frances Burney, *Cecilia*[2]

Not having control of your own money is awful. Not having the option to earn your own money is also awful. Being financially trapped, basically, is awful. This is true today, and it was true in the eighteenth century. The eighteenth century was pretty rubbish generally when it came to women having access to their own money. As we talked about in the previous chapter, getting married removed a woman's independent legal existence, which meant that her husband would almost universally own everything she earned or brought to the marriage. That meant that if your husband had a gambling habit, or a drinking habit, or backed investments that you didn't agree with, you couldn't do anything about your money being funnelled away.

If you didn't get married? Well, you didn't have a husband for your money to belong to, but you did still have financial restrictions. And a big part of that was because there were limitations on the kinds of jobs you could do as a woman (spoiler: most of them were poorly paid). This would only get worse as you got older, because a lot of the jobs involved physicality – you try wrangling heaps of wet wool and petticoats around in a hot steamy room with a big stick for hours (otherwise known as doing the laundry) and you'll see what I mean. There wasn't a guaranteed safety net in the eighteenth century. No state pension. No retirement age. You could end up with something like a pension, but it would come from your employer at their discretion, and they weren't required to actually give you one. In some ways that all sounds far removed from today, but when my mother was around my age she couldn't open a bank account to store her own money without having that account authorised with a signature from either her husband or her father. The types of labour that are the worst paid are broadly the same today as they were in the eighteenth century. Today we group these under the five Cs (caring, cleaning, catering, cashiering – meaning retail – and clerical) – while clerical work wasn't a common option for women in the eighteenth century, the other jobs were and are characterised as 'women's work' and are still primarily performed by women.

Another big factor impacting eighteenth-century financial independence was the lack of reliable contraception. Women were far more likely to get pregnant unintentionally than they are now. Childbirth is still dangerous, but in the eighteenth century, before we had scans or properly effective sanitation, the mortality rates were far higher. And repeatedly bearing children year after year is exhausting on a body even when those children are wanted.

Then there's the fact that with more children, you need to do more work – more cooking, more washing – and you need to be bringing in more money for food. There's also the added factor that for many jobs (like being a servant) women were supposed to be unmarried. The understanding was that married women would be busy being pregnant, running the household, looking after the children, and doing work that was compatible with the first three. I should also point out here that children in the eighteenth century were more likely to be cared for by their mothers (or nannies and nurses if there was money in the family) but would belong to their fathers. So women seeking to leave their husbands would not have custody of the children. And that in turn limits how able people felt to leave difficult situations; firstly, you might not want to leave your children behind; secondly, you might want to take them with you but be afraid of the ramifications of the law catching up with you; and thirdly, you might struggle with the logistics of taking them with you and then needing to support both yourself and your children on the money from the limited job options open to you.

The important bit of what I'm saying – something my mum has always said – is that money equals choices. If you don't have access to money, you don't have choices. Money doesn't buy you happiness, but it can allow you to quit your job if your boss is awful to you. It can allow you to get a cab home when it's late, or order food if you're too tired, or buy better-quality things that won't need replacing as quickly. It can get you childcare, can buy you a house that no one can kick you out of, or let you rent somewhere that feels safe. It can let you walk into a shop and know that you can choose to buy something without worry or calculation. The heady freedom of just being able to. Maybe money doesn't buy you happiness, but it can buy things that make your life easier, better, and more fun. However much it is, it all contributes to your being able to choose. Every now and again on social media a discourse about running-away money surfaces, which is one of the biggest illustrations of money giving you choices that there is.

Running-away money is exactly what it sounds like: money that will enable you, should you ever need to, to get away from your living situation. Inevitably, when this discourse surfaces, some people find out about running-away money for the first time, and get very offended about the idea that they might be someone that people need to run away from. Others frame the idea of a secret supply of money as a betrayal of trust, and talk about how having entirely shared finances shows trust and open communication in a relationship. And the points that are usually reiterated by long-suffering netizens trying to help people understand can be summed up as follows:

1. Having running-away money doesn't mean that you are going to leave. It just means that you have the option to. Having the option to leave means that you can choose to stay. Not having the option to leave means that staying is something you have to do whether you want to or not.
2. Someone who has the capacity and means to leave you does not inherently love you less or trust you less. It means that they could leave you, but are choosing not to. I would say that that's a bigger sign of love and trust than someone who has no choice.
3. Running-away money isn't only for women. Historically, it has been most commonly documented with women, but that's partly because we only really documented things along the gender binary, and men were generally in control of the finances of the couple so they already had exclusive access to a fund. But that doesn't mean that men today can't or shouldn't have their own separate running-away money. Everyone should be able to get away from a bad situation.

The book I'm focusing on in this chapter is about a character who does have money, and who theoretically also has safety nets, except they aren't very good ones. She's actually a wealthy heiress. Her name is Cecilia, and the book is also called *Cecilia; or Memoirs of an*

Heiress (1782), so you can be confident that her being an heiress is important. In theory, Cecilia has a lot of choices. In practice, she doesn't have access to her money. That means she spends most of the novel being dependent on awful people. Also, when she stops having a fortune, she's in an even worse position. *Cecilia* was written by Frances Burney, one of the most respected novelists of her generation and, next to Austen, the author whose courtship novels are most commonly still read today. In this, my favourite of her novels, Burney uses Cecilia's inheritance and privilege to raise some really important points about money, independence, and consent.

Before I start digging into what Burney's points are and why you should care about them, here's what you need to know about the plot. Cecilia is orphaned just before she reaches legal adulthood and she inherits money and a valuable estate from her uncle. The money belongs to her immediately, but she isn't allowed to touch it until she's 21, so it's held in trust for her by a guardian. The estate, which is much, much more valuable, has a special condition attached to it. Cecilia's uncle was obsessed with the idea of leaving a legacy, but didn't have a son who would continue the family name. His brilliant solution was to stipulate that Cecilia's future husband has to take her surname when they marry. If he doesn't, the whole estate goes to Cecilia's male cousin. Taking the woman's name really wasn't the done thing at the time, but it's important to be aware that this isn't happening as a feminist statement of independence. It's happening because Cecilia's uncle wants his own name to live forever.

Cecilia doesn't actually have just one guardian overseeing her fortune. She has three, and they all have issues. Mr Briggs is a miser and hates spending money on anything. He lives in squalor because he doesn't want to wear the house out with cleaning it, and it wouldn't be hard to clean because he has hardly any furniture. This man throws a major tantrum when Cecilia has the audacity to sharpen a pencil. An unholy extravagance! Practically throwing money away! He's stingy to the extreme and completely unreasonable with money, and he doesn't think Cecilia should spend anything at all. Instead, she should be keeping it nice and safe until she can transfer it to her husband – and Briggs is keen to find her one who shares his parsimonious tendencies. Cecilia isn't so much the fortune's owner, in his mind, as much as she is a means of transferring it from her uncle to whatever husband she ends up with. No matter how reasonable her requests for financial access are, Briggs refuses to allow it, despite the fact that the money is actually hers. He just keeps insisting that she doesn't know what she wants. Mainly because she's female. (Honestly, it's intensely frustrating, and only a short step away from patting her on the head and telling her to go play with her dolls – but then dolls would be an unnecessary extravagance, so he's stuck with plain old patronising.)

Guardian number two is Mr Harrel, the husband of one of Cecilia's schoolfriends, and he has the opposite problem. He spends far too much. He spends all his money. He spends other people's money. He's very keen to spend Cecilia's money. And he doesn't really care about paying people back unless they're society gentlemen, which translates into lots of tradespeople carrying the bills for his expenses because he keeps not paying them. They aren't really people as far as he's concerned, so it doesn't matter if this means they end up starving. He sees Cecilia's fortune as a fund that's going to help him clear his debts, but he can't access it directly as Briggs can. Instead, he has to think of more creative ways of getting to it. In the short term, he gets Cecilia to borrow money from moneylenders in order to help him out of some immediate trouble. She isn't really supposed to be able to do that, because she's not legally an adult, but funnily enough the people charging vast quantities of interest are quite happy to bend the rules when there's a fortune they know they can be reimbursed out of. Harrel's longer-term plan is just to sell Cecilia. He finds a man who has money, and who he already owes money to, which is not difficult as he owes money to a lot of people. He promises this man that he can marry Cecilia. After all, Harrel is her guardian, so he should be able to make that happen. So he promises Sir Robert Floyer (shockingly not a nice man) that he can have Cecilia, and Sir Robert is therefore more than happy to cover expenses for Harrel. After all, he's getting an estate out of it, and that's a whole lot more valuable. Harrel has no problem with Cecilia spending her money, providing she's using it to get him out of trouble, but he doesn't really want Sir Robert to find out about this until after the wedding because he doesn't want Cecilia to look less valuable.

Finally, there is guardian number three, Lord Delvile. Lord Delvile is one of the most self-important aristocrats around – and that's saying something. His problem isn't that he spends too much or too little, but that he is obsessed with his own nobility. He's deeply offended that he's forced to share this guardianship position with two men who are completely and utterly beneath him in every way. It's hard for him, because as far as he's concerned pretty much everyone is completely and utterly beneath him in every way. Because he's so very important, he thinks Cecilia should do exactly what he says, and should be grateful that he has found the time in his busy schedule to bestow his advice on her. Her not following his advice is deeply offensive. As is her not having asked him for it. Basically, anything she does that implies that she can think for herself offends him on some level. But that makes sense, because he's an offensive kind of person. He has a son called Mortimer who is much nicer (though honestly still could use some work – more on that later), who falls in love with Cecilia. She falls in love right back. The only problem is, Mortimer knows that his father isn't going to think Cecilia is worthy of the great Delvile name – especially when marrying her would mean that the great Delvile name would actually disappear. Lord Delvile suspects none of this and finds an appropriately noble suitor for Cecilia to marry. Now that her husband has been decided on, there is only one course of action she can follow that he will be remotely accepting of. If she's not doing what he tells her, she'll get no support from him.

Despite their differing priorities and mutual loathing, her three guardians all agree that Cecilia isn't qualified to make any decisions about her own money. (To be honest, I could probably have stopped that sentence after 'make any decisions'.) This is for two main reasons. The first is that she's female, which all of these men believe makes her incapable of rationality. The second is that she doesn't want to do what they say, which they take as conclusive proof that she can't be trusted to make decisions. Neither of these two reasons have very much to do with Cecilia. They aren't objecting to a particular aspect of her personality, or to her actual ability as an individual to make choices. She's one of the most fiscally responsible characters in this novel – though admittedly that isn't that hard. They just object on the grounds that they've decided that all women are irrational, and because they want to get their own way. This is infuriating, both for the readers and for Cecilia, but the problem is bigger than that. I'm going to be talking about money and inheritance a lot in this chapter, and it's really important to make one thing clear straight away: the money is a big deal in its own right, but this is not just a conversation about money.

When these guardians decide that Cecilia – and women generally – don't have the capacity to make decisions about their money, they're saying it's because they don't have the ability to make judgements. And if you can't make judgements, you can't consent. The conversations happening in this book about money are important in their own right, but they are also being used to talk about sexual consent. Part of that is because the money is attached to Cecilia. These men can only access it through her. And the biggest way they can trade on her money for their own profit is by marrying her off to someone. Marriage comes with expectations of sex, and because marital rape wasn't illegal, it also comes with a legal handover of consent to your husband. When they are trying to trade Cecilia, they are absolutely selling sex with her as part of the bargain. And the other part? Well, it's all to do with promises.

The money in Burney's novel isn't something any of the characters hold in their hands. It's largely abstract. The arrangements that are made with it – credit, contracts, and debts – are a series of promises. And as far as I'm concerned that's where things get really interesting. Promises in the eighteenth century have a lot to do with the idea of 'giving your word' or your 'word of honour'. Honour is really important as a concept, and it's a commodity that has value but that theoretically can't be traded. It's heavily linked to reputation (are you actually good for the money, do you actually pay back your debts) as well as noble status and birth (sure, you might pay everyone back, but you're a farmhand, so society isn't going to be impressed by your honour). It sits at the intersection between credit and credibility; how much people trust you and believe in you based on your word and finances. It's something people were and are extremely touchy about. Duels were fought over insults to honour. And duels were both illegal and dangerous. So honour is this kind of nebulous concept that people are very attached to and defensive of, and it's also something that has a slightly different usage when it's applied to men and women in the eighteenth century. Because when people talk about honour for women in that period, they often mean sexual honour. 'Defending her honour' is basically a synonym for maintaining her virginity. The kind of honour used to make promises and contracts is more commonly attributed to men. And that's where we come back around to consent and judgement and Cecilia's money and Cecilia's guardians. Because throughout this novel, with all its different examples of borrowing money, spending money, promising to pay people, creating debts, and trading heiresses, this question of honour comes up again and again and again. And, more specifically, who is allowed to have honour. Who gets to give their word and have that word acknowledged for what it is.

Early in the novel, Cecilia decides that she is going to buy some books. Books were often expensive items, but they also retained value after being bought, and having a library added value to an estate. Cecilia reasons that by buying the books she's gratifying herself in the short term, but that it's a legitimate use of some of her fortune because it's going to remain with the estate. It's part of her legacy as the estate owner, and it's also Burney reminding her readers that Cecilia is a good person because she likes books, and characters in books liking books is usually a sign that they're a good and trustworthy person. (Plus, it's her money and she wants to buy a thing.) The key point is that she thinks about the purchase and weighs up the appropriateness of the spending. It's not a whim. So Cecilia goes to the bookseller and orders her books. She promises to pay the bookseller when they're delivered, and off she goes to ask her guardians to give her the money. She asks Mr Harrel first, because she lives with him and his wife, her former schoolfriend. He can't access her bank account – luckily – but she's asking Harrel because he owes her money. She'd had the money to pay for the books, but he had needed to borrow it and he promised to pay her back. He makes lots of vague excuses about why he doesn't have the money right now, but eventually resorts to just running out of rooms when she walks in. She very quickly works out that she isn't getting her money back, and she's not going to be able to pay for her books that way.

She then goes to Mr Briggs, who as I mentioned earlier doesn't think people should spend money full stop. When she asks for her money, he tells her that she shouldn't have spent it, and starts giving her advice about how to take the books back to the shop. Cecilia's not happy about this because she wants the books, and because doing that would be dishonest and would end up cheating the bookshop owner. She gave him her word that she would pay him, after all, and he's laid out all the costs of the paper and printing and binding. But Briggs doesn't care about Cecilia's word of honour. He insists that she doesn't really know what she wants and therefore he won't give her the money. He knows better. Nothing she can say makes him listen to the fact that she has made a decision and she isn't actually asking him for permission. Burney puts a lot of emphasis on the point that Briggs's refusal has nothing to do with the transaction itself. He doesn't have a specific dislike of books, though he does think they – like everything else – are a waste of money. It comes down to the fact that he believes that young women don't know the value of money, and that he thinks it's his job to make sure that the fortune Cecilia's uncle left her gets put into 'proper hands' – aka those belonging to her future husband. His function is not to help to guide her to make good decisions with her money, but to pass it on from the dead man to the imaginary man without it having a chance to accidentally get to Cecilia and be spent, or something equally disastrous.

Cecilia then asks Lord Delvile to talk to Briggs on her behalf. Quite apart from being highly offended that she would even dare to suggest he act in such a demeaning role (perish the thought), he has another objection. And it's very important that they address it before they get around to actually listening to Cecilia. His issue is that he thinks she shouldn't have run up this bill in the first place because it's for books. As far as Lord Delvile is concerned, a young woman like Cecilia has no business buying books. She's clearly not going to read them, and when she marries the kind of man that he approves of, he will come from a family that will have a library already. And then she can flick through as many of their books as she likes. Just like when she spoke to Briggs, Lord Delvile's main focus is on whether Cecilia should have promised to pay the bookseller in the first place. He doesn't get around to her actual point – that he help her access her own money – because he spends the entire time deciding whether or not he approves of her choice. To Lord Delvile, the most important question in the interaction is whether he would have given permission if she had thought to consult him first. Once again, Cecilia might as well be talking to a wall.

Between all three of her guardians, Cecilia's word gets undermined. She's made a promise to the bookseller that she fully intends to make good on. She has the money to do it with. But because the three men who have control of her life refuse to treat her like a rational individual who makes considered choices, she finds herself stuck. When she makes choices that the guardians agree with, they treat her as though she can make decisions. Harrel thinks she has top-quality reasoning when she agrees to sign a loan with the moneylender. At that point, she's fully capable of making decisions which relate to her finances. Lord Delvile applauds her wisdom when she tells him she doesn't want to marry nasty Sir Robert Floyer (the guy Harrel is trying to sell her to), and thinks she's got every right to have a say in who she marries. Right up until he finds out she doesn't want to marry his candidate either. She's a consenting adult when she does what they want, and an incapable child when she doesn't. What Burney really highlights with this guardianship situation is the way that it's not someone's word that counts, but whether they are able to enforce it.

Cecilia's word never gets to stand on its own. It's not enough that she wants to do something – for it to actually happen she needs to get at least one of the male characters on board. And the male characters are only okay with her doing something if it's what they want too. Live there, marry him, do this or do that. Her ability to consent is compromised because she isn't able to refuse. It's like with running-away money. Without the ability to leave, choosing to stay isn't a meaningful choice because there aren't any other options. The thing that Burney shows over and over again in her novel is that Cecilia, this example of a rich, privileged, well-educated woman, is consistently restricted by limited and irrational men on the basis that she isn't thinking clearly. There's frustration in that, and humour in the irony, but there's also the very clear message that Cecilia actually is totally capable. This in and of itself may not sound hugely groundbreaking, and it's not like the eighteenth century hadn't heard of capable women. But Burney is drawing attention to the restrictions that sexism imposes on the freedom of women, and the power women had to consent. Sure, Cecilia can make a promise to a bookseller, or tell someone she doesn't want to marry him. But if nobody listens? It's kind of irrelevant. She can say yes or no to things and it might look like consent, but it doesn't function like consent because it's not meaningful. It's not actually her who is being listened to. It's whichever male figure has the power in that moment who gets to decide whether Cecilia's consent stands or gets erased.

The callbacks to this ideology are why I find today's growing aestheticisation of tradwives difficult. Tradwives are women who practise and embrace traditional gender roles within marriage. Women who celebrate living in a relationship that upholds a status quo that they say is both traditional and natural, with a male breadwinner and a female homemaker. One of the core points of feminism is that all genders should be free to make choices. By critiquing the choice these women make, and insisting that women choose to work outside the home, we can easily replicate the same kind of limitations on choice we set out to challenge. My issue is not with someone choosing to be a housewife or homemaker. There's nothing wrong with either, and both are far harder than people assume. My issue is with the idea that it's somehow natural and right for one gender identity to be submissive to another – regardless of how you're dividing the domestic labour. Especially the natural part. Budgets, bank accounts, credit cards, and the division of financial assets are not things that exist in nature. They are things we've made up, and then decided who gets to be in charge of them. The same is true of most jobs. You might choose to divide the labour between partners by saying 'right, you go do the labour that brings in money over there, and I'll do the labour that keeps the domestic side of things working over here', but neither of you has an inherent or biologically predetermined right to be in charge of your collective finances. Online, the tradwife aesthetic is predominantly white – and leans on imagery of and nostalgia for a way of life from a time when people of colour were even more actively discriminated against than today. Journalist Sian Norris has written extensively about the way 'much of trad wife culture, is a fear of the so-called "great replacement" – a baseless conspiracy theory that believes white people are being "replaced" by migrant people from the global south, while feminists repress the white birthrate via abortion rights'.[3] This natural and right rhetoric is also quite specifically around women in a relationship with and being submissive to men: a relationship that doesn't fall into the cishet framework is by implication unnatural. So it's less a choice to do the housework and more an advocacy of white supremacy and heteropatriarchy.

It's important to be sceptical about advocacy for submission in relationships. Marital rape was only criminalised in the UK in the 1990s. It still isn't criminalised everywhere. Men's rights activists and alt-right online groups argue for the right to rape women on private property, or suggest that sex is generally something women owe to men. Sex within marriage is considered a conjugal right – something that does not allow for consent or free choice. Sex and gender-based submission and marital rape are so closely linked together ideologically that it's irresponsible to preach the inherent rightness of one party in a relationship being automatically in charge. If you accept the premise that the tradwife lifestyle is a choice that should be respected, it's important also to ask what happens if you change your mind about what you want. Part of why doing housework is disenfranchising is not because there's anything wrong with the work itself, but because it's underappreciated and it doesn't have earning power, so there's a reliance on receiving money from your partner even as you also contribute labour to the partnership. If you decide that you want to leave, are you going to be able to? And if you decide you don't want to have sex, is that going to be a problem? The eighteenth century's marriage laws meant that it was very easy to end up trapped in the ownership of a careless or dangerous person. Part of what was so oppressive about them was that you couldn't get out of the situation. If you want to divvy up the way decisions are made in your household that's one thing. But buying in to a narrative where it is natural and right for one person to be in sole command, and surrendering your authority to that person, does carry a danger. And so whatever your view on who makes the decisions – and honestly, however nice your partner is – you need to leave yourself a way out.

One of the most useful tools I've found for reading critically – whether that's online rhetoric or the unsaid things in eighteenth-century novels – is the idea of speech acts. Speech acts are, simply, all the different things that happen when someone says a thing. Philosophy professor Rae Langton tells us that there are three levels that things get said at; the *locutionary*, the *illocutionary*, and the *perlocutionary*.[4] To explain what these three levels do, I'm going to borrow Langton's example of a wedding ceremony. The locutionary level (or act) is the literal words said. On the locutionary level, I say the words 'I do' out loud. The illocutionary act is what you do *in* saying those words, which is another way of saying it's the action that gets achieved when you say the words. So in our wedding example I say 'I do', which is the locutionary bit, and *in* saying those words I marry my partner, which is the illocutionary part. The final one of the three is the perlocutionary, and that's an action or reaction that is caused *by* doing either – or both – of the other two bits. *By* saying the words 'I do' and therefore marrying my partner, I make my partner happy. Or foil the schemes of a family member who was determined that I should marry somebody else. Every time we say something, or a character says something, it has these multiple levels of meaning.

We use these different levels all the time without thinking about them or what they're called. We especially do this when it's important that certain things remain unsaid. In those situations, you have to manage to create the outcome you want (the perlocutionary) by saying the right words, even if those words themselves are not exactly what you really mean. Take a scenario that played out a lot for various friends of mine: you're out at a bar, or a club, and a man approaches you. You might not be entirely sure what his motivation is – maybe he just wants to make a new friend? – but you know you're not interested in him sexually or romantically. So you slip (or indeed, awkwardly wedge) into the conversation that you have a boyfriend. Whether you actually have a boyfriend is irrelevant in this scenario. What matters is that *in* saying this (the illocutionary bit), you make it clear that you're not interested in anything romantic or sexual. And *by* saying that (the perlocutionary bit) you're telling him that it has nothing to do with him personally. Ultimately, the locutionary act of saying the words 'I have a boyfriend' replaces the locutionary act of saying 'No, I'm not interested.' Both are a form of rejection, but by implying that you are 'taken' and not free to pursue anyone, it can increase how safe you are, or feel you are, in saying no. It turns it into 'Oh, I'm not available' rather than 'I don't like you', and that sounds less personal and decreases the chance that the rejection will make the man angry. Even if you're not concerned that the person approaching you might get angry, this particular excuse of having a boyfriend provokes fewer follow-up questions. It's often simpler and safer – and in my friends' cases it tended to reduce the amount of follow-up quizzing they got from the guy in question (a small tip: if a person says they aren't interested, insisting that they justify why so that you can 'prove' that their lack of interest is wrong is not going to make them want to spend time with you). Just as with Cecilia, your refusal is supported by a (potentially made-up) guy, and for some people that phantom male voice carries more weight than your word. If you want to refuse this person and have them listen to you, whatever you choose to say to them, you're going to try to say it in a way that they will hear. Even if you don't actually have or want a boyfriend.

Sometimes people don't understand your speech act. Sometimes they ignore it. Langton goes on to talk about what happens when speech acts fail. Sometimes, she says,

> a woman tries to use the 'no' locution to refuse sex and it does not work. It does not work for the twenty percent of undergraduate women who report that they have been date raped. It does not work

> for the twenty-five percent of all final-year schoolgirls who report that they have been sexually forced. Saying 'no' sometimes doesn't work, but there are two ways in which it can fail to work. Sometimes the woman's hearer recognises the action she performs: i.e. he recognises that she is refusing. Uptake is secured. In saying 'no,' she really does refuse. By saying 'no,' she intends to prevent her hearer from continuing his advances. But the hearer goes ahead and forces sex on the woman. She prohibits, but he fails to obey. She fails to achieve the goal of her refusal. Her refusal is frustrated. 'Perlocutionary frustration' is too meek and academic a label for what is simply rape.
>
> Sometimes, though, there is a different phenomenon of illocutionary disablement. Sometimes 'no,' when spoken by a woman, does not *count* as the act of refusal. The hearer fails to recognise the utterance as a refusal; uptake is not secured. In saying 'no' she may well intend to refuse. By saying 'no' she intends to prevent sex, but she is far from doing as she intends. Since illocutionary force depends, in part, on uptake being secured, the woman fails to refuse [...] She says 'no.' She performs the appropriate locutionary act. She means what she says. She intends to refuse. She tries to refuse. But what she says misfires. Something about her, something about the role that she occupies, prevents her from voicing refusal. Refusal – in that context – has become unspeakable for her. In this case refusal is not simply frustrated but disabled.[5]

What Langton is saying here is that there are two different ways that speech acts fail to work in the way we mean them to. One of them sees your listener understand your refusal – recognise it for what it is, comprehend your meaning – but choose to ignore it. So while you have not failed to refuse consent, the outcome that was supposed to happen (the person stopping and not doing the thing you've expressly said not to do) doesn't happen. The second way is where the listener hears the refusal, but won't acknowledge it or accept it for what it is. So, an example of that would be the tired old line about how the person did say 'no', but their body said 'yes' and so the 'no' apparently didn't count. Or, in the example from *Pride and Prejudice* we talked about back in the introduction?

The one where Lizzie is telling Mr Collins very explicitly that she doesn't want to marry him? Well, he cannot conceive of a reason why she should say no to him. After all, he has the patronage of Lady Catherine de Bourgh. He's due to inherit the house when Lizzie's dad dies. And she ought to be grateful to him for being his almost-first-choice (her prettier sister not being available). He knows that he's much cleverer than her, because she is merely a member of the fair sex, who are largely ornamental and need the protection of wise and benevolent clergymen to tell them what to do. So if he cannot think of a reason, then she definitely can't think of one, because there's no way she could think of something that he hasn't thought of ('I don't like you' being a leap of comprehension far beyond him). Since there's nothing he can come up with, she can't actually mean to refuse him. So although she sounds extremely sure that she doesn't want to marry him, Mr Collins steadfastly attempts to categorise Lizzie's blunt rejections as flirtations.

This second failure of speech acts happens quite a lot in *Cecilia* (it is, for one thing, a very long book). But there's an example when it happens with the guy we're supposed to root for as the love interest – Lord Delvile's son Mortimer – and it's a good example of how it can be dangerous. Mortimer is convinced, completely and utterly convinced, that Cecilia is engaged. Sometimes he thinks she's engaged to a penniless poet, and other times to Sir Robert Floyer, the man her guardian is intent on selling her to. At no point is Cecilia engaged to either of these men, and at no point does she want to be. There are, though, a couple of circumstances that make it look like she might be, and chief among them is the fact that Mr Harrel is going around telling everyone that she's engaged to Sir Robert. He also invites him to come to their house as if they were courting, and tries to plan a little trip to the country for all of them as well. His plan – in many ways brilliant in its simplicity and accuracy – is that if they act as though Cecilia and Sir Robert are engaged, it's going to convince society that they are. And if society is convinced that you're engaged to someone, the easiest thing is to go along with it. There's less chance of scandal, or of being seen as damaged goods, and the weight of social expectation can be a pretty effective form of peer pressure. So we can forgive Mortimer for thinking that Cecilia's engaged, because both her guardian and Sir Robert are going around telling everyone it's the case, and he can see some behaviours that look like the sort of things that happen when a couple are courting. But my sympathy for him runs out around the time when I remember that whenever Cecilia tries to explain that she isn't engaged, he doesn't believe her. More than that. He has these internal monologues where he gets very confused about why someone so truthful in every aspect of their life is choosing to lie about this one specific thing. And she's so good at lying about it! It's almost exactly like she's telling the complete truth!

It is easier for Mortimer to believe that Cecilia is acting out of character and lying than that Harrel – a man who constantly makes promises he doesn't keep – is making things up. This doesn't come from an automatic trust of Harrel; it's more that Harrel's words confirm Mortimer's personal beliefs and suspicions. Mortimer believes that Cecilia is engaged to someone else, and he's not open to the idea that he might have misunderstood the situation (after all, he is a very clever boy). Though he is more sympathetic than most of the novel's male characters, even he fails to acknowledge or consider the possibility that he might be wrong. When presented with Cecilia's explanations and Harrel's assertions, Mortimer finds those most compelling which support and confirm his own beliefs. His approach to this situation privileges the male word as having more intrinsic reliability than the female, regardless of the personalities involved, and he places more inherent trust in his own instincts than Cecilia's honour.

I said that this was dangerous, so let's take a look at the stakes. Mortimer does a pretty good job of making these clear in the speech he gives when he finally (finally!) gets it through his head that there is no engagement. He says

> sometimes I thought you repented your engagement. I concluded, indeed, you had been unwarily drawn in, and I had even, at times, been tempted to acknowledge my suspicions to you, state your independence, and exhort you – as a *friend,* exhort you – to use it with spirit, and, if you were shackled unwillingly, incautiously, or unworthily, to break the chains by which you were confined, and restore to yourself that freedom of choice upon the use of which all your happiness must ultimately depend. But I doubted if that were honourable to the Baronet.[6]

So firstly, Mortimer describes Cecilia as being in 'chains', 'confined', 'shackled', all of which sound awful and make the point that being forced or tricked into marriage is a form of imprisonment. He gets it. He thinks that she's engaged, but that she didn't want to be. 'All her happiness' will depend on the person she chooses to marry – and given how much power over her a husband would legally have, this is a pretty legitimate concern. Who she marries is a pivotal question in Cecilia's life. Again, he gets it. He acknowledges that Cecilia should get to make the choice about who she marries, which in turn shows that he thinks she's capable of making judgements. He's not dismissing her as a silly little girl who needs to do as she's told. Instead, he's saying that she has the right to have her choice upheld, and beyond that, that she has the right to change her mind. From a meaningful consent perspective this is really significant: he's saying that she could have been forced into a situation that she may have given verbal consent to, and that that force may not have been physical. He acknowledges that coercion exists, and that if Cecilia was coerced then she didn't give meaningful consent. According to this speech, she has the power to save herself and 'break the chains'; her 'freedom' is something which she can 'restore to yourself'.

This suggests that Cecilia's word is powerful. By saying that there are circumstances which make it acceptable for Cecilia to call off the engagement, we can see that Mortimer thinks of Cecilia as someone who keeps her word. He's suggesting reasons that might make it okay for her to break a promise, not implying that her promises have no substance behind them. All of that is very nice, and the sentiment that her word should be enough to free her from a situation she had been coerced, blackmailed, or tricked into is honestly refreshing – but it isn't remotely backed up by Mortimer's actions. After all, if her words had all this power, surely he would have actually listened to what she was telling him. And if even our hero, who believes Cecilia's word has this great power to free her, will not listen to her repeatedly telling him that she is not engaged, what chance does she actually have of getting that across to a coercive foe? Mortimer's character here may seem to say lots of the right things, but his actions don't match his words.

Despite his great concern that Cecilia has been trapped by a terrible man, Mortimer, faced with this scenario, does precisely nothing. He thinks about doing something. More specifically, he thinks about actually asking Cecilia what's going on – forgetting, it would seem, that he usually ignores all of her answers – and then begging her to sort the whole thing out. He's deeply concerned for her and her future happiness, but not enough to take even this (really very limited) step. Instead, he sits back and keeps quiet. And this is for one simple reason – eight little words – which are somehow more powerful and important than the entire rest of the speech: he 'doubted if it were honourable to the Baronet'.

In the grand scale of Mortimer's moral compass, Sir Robert's honour weighs in as more important than all of Cecilia's future happiness. It's not clear whether Mortimer simply means that he would insult Sir Robert's honour if he suggested that he's the kind of person who would entrap Cecilia, or whether he feels that getting himself involved in Sir Robert's business would count as working directly against the man (which would be dishonourable for him to do). Either way, Mortimer seems to be operating on an honour spectrum, where certain kinds of honour are more important than others. Specifically here, where the honour of a man – however odious he might be – is more important and valuable than the honour of the woman he's in love with. (The fact that Sir Robert is rich and a noble also doesn't hurt.) It's worth emphasising here that Mortimer is simultaneously able to believe that Sir Robert is exactly the kind of dishonourable person who would trap or trick Cecilia into an engagement, potentially ruining her entire life, while also seeing him as someone whose honour is nonetheless more valuable than that of the woman he's in love with. He won't even ask the question of whether she's okay, because offending Sir Robert is a bigger concern to him. All of which raises the question of what kinds of behaviour can impact a man's honour if forcing Cecilia into marriage – and a sexual relationship and legal ownership – against her will doesn't seem to matter. Much in the way that Harrel thinks the only debts that count are the ones that he owes to gentlemen, Mortimer acts as though a man's treatment of women isn't relevant to the status of his honour. In this scenario, Mortimer's *asking* whether Sir Robert is mistreating Cecilia has more of an impact on Sir Robert's honour than whether he *actually* is. And this is something we see again and again in these Georgian novels, and indeed all the way through history. When everyone knows someone is doing something shady, but that bad thing has not been acknowledged in public by the right people, there isn't a big fallout from it. It takes public acknowledgement from the right voices before a bad actor's reputation is impacted, even if what they were doing was common knowledge.

Before I go on to press more on this point about the difference between things being common knowledge and being publicly acknowledged, there's one more character in *Cecilia* who I want to bring up. His name is Monckton, and in many ways he is the most loathsome character in the whole novel. Monckton is someone Cecilia has grown up with – she has known him ever since she was a child and she looks up to him as a guiding figure. A guardian – but quite unlike the three she's been saddled with. What Cecilia does not know, though, is that Monckton is actually a terrible and predatory person. As a young and attractive man, he married an older woman for her money, expecting her to die quickly and leave him hot, rich, and single. Unfortunately for him she proved to be quite healthy, and is still alive when the novel takes place many years later. This small fact has not put a stop to Monckton's plans: he intends to marry Cecilia and have both her and her estate all to himself. Cecilia suspects none of this – like I say, she has known this man since she was a small child, and she has no idea that he has a sexual or a financial interest in her. Throughout the novel, Monckton gives Cecilia financial advice, the better to preserve what he sees as his future estate. At one point, when he hears that Cecilia has signed a shady deal with a moneylender, he panics about the thought of those interest rates eating into his beautiful fortune and buys the debt off the moneylender himself. This means that, technically, Cecilia is in debt to him. He's relieved that the drain on the estate will be minimal, she's delighted at being rescued by someone she thinks is just being kind to her, and the whole exchange ends with Monckton having his claws dug a little deeper into Cecilia. She trusts him completely.

But there comes a time when Cecilia makes a promise that Monckton doesn't like. Harrel, the guardian who can't keep his hands out of his pockets, has once again spent far too much, and this time he's actually worried about it. He tries to get Cecilia to pay the debt for him, which she very justifiably does not want to do. It's a lot of money this time, and she knows he'll never repay it, and quite frankly she thinks Harrel is a waste of space. But then he locks himself in his room and threatens to kill himself if she doesn't agree to pay out the money. In the end she agrees, though she isn't remotely happy about it. She feels as though Harrel compelled the promise out of her with his threats of self-harm. Suicide had a pronounced religious element in the eighteenth century, as it was seen as a serious sin, so Cecilia is trying to protect both Harrel's life and his soul. Harrel is absolutely trying to coerce

Cecilia into paying his debts for him – he knows that asking her won't work, and he's come up with a plan that succeeds. But what's more interesting here than just the simple coercion is the way that Monckton reacts to it – and then blames Cecilia for it having happened in the first place.

When Cecilia tells Monckton what has happened, he is appalled. His lovely money promised away! He immediately suggests that Cecilia break her vow to Harrel. After all, he says, there's no dishonour in breaking your word when that word was forced out of you in the first place. 'An oath so forced', he tells her, 'the most delicate conscience would absolve you from performing.'[7] Again, this *seems* to be picking up on some of those core elements of meaningful consent that require a person to actually have a free choice. In practice, what Monckton is really saying is that he would support Cecilia in breaking her promise because she would be taking the course of action that he wants – and keeping her money safe for himself. It's not a disinterested view of her rights, it's another example of a male character supporting Cecilia in doing the thing that works out best for them personally. It's also interesting because when he says that people wouldn't blame Cecilia for breaking this particular promise, he's largely right. No one would reasonably assume that she was keen to destroy the value of her inheritance (these debts are really really big). Even the people who don't want her to make decisions about her inheritance merely think that women are bad at handling money, not that she would deliberately seek to lose it (for one thing, that would require more purposeful thought).

But if we were to transpose this scenario into a sexual context, the response would be less clear cut. A lot of rape myths focus on ideas of the victim's willingness or enjoyment, the suggestion that they wanted it really. Why am I talking about this? Because just as nasty Sir Robert poses a sexual threat to Cecilia with his scheme to marry her, so does Monckton. He wants to have sex with Cecilia and he wants to get his hands on her fortune, and throughout this book Cecilia's money and body and estate are all kind of one thing. So all the conversations about her money, and how freely she gives it away, even when they are actually only talking about money in the story, are having an extra conversation with the reader about sex too. Female honour is often seen as being the same thing as sexual purity – a treasure to maintain much like a fortune – and Monckton is intent on preserving and owning both. But where no one would believe that Cecilia wanted to have her money coerced from her, Burney offers us the secondary reading that if Cecilia had had her virginal treasure coerced from her, people would be a lot keener to blame her.

When Monckton realises that Cecilia is going to keep her word and pay Harrel's debts, he quickly switches to blaming her. He calls the whole thing a 'trick, which had not your generosity been too well known, would never have been played'.[8] Suddenly, it's entirely her responsibility to make sure that no one tricks her. She ought to have acted in a way that would discourage anyone from trying to do this in the first place. (She should have worn different clothes, she should have walked down a different street, she shouldn't have had a drink.) This fits with the way Monckton talks explicitly about women and sex, saying that women are 'readily duped'. According to him, they're waiting to be tricked – eager for it – and the responsibility is entirely on them. Generosity is usually a positive quality, but here Monckton weaponises it. He twists it, making it stand for being easy to manipulate, and emphasising the sexual connection (being 'generous with one's favours' was a common euphemism for having a lot of sex). If Harrel can extract what he wants from Cecilia, Monckton implies that other men will be able to do the same. Her generosity is 'too well known' so she has a reputation for this already… If Cecilia hadn't had a reputation for being generous, then Harrel wouldn't have tried to extort money from her – and therefore the whole thing is her fault because she allowed herself to end up in a situation where a man thought he could take money from her. Monckton's logic here is a true feat of ideological gymnastics, but sadly one that is still common in victim-blaming narratives.

What I find really striking about *Cecilia* is how candid Burney is throughout the whole book about how little Cecilia's voice matters. She manages to create an independent and thoughtful heroine while demonstrating that even when she makes decisions, it's not really her who is getting to make them – it's the people endorsing her. The question is not just who gets to speak, but who gets to be listened to. And I think this really hits true for me because it's something that's fundamental to Georgian polite society, but also to the way we do things today. In *Cecilia*, everyone knows Harrel has debts – or at least everyone whispers about it. Those debts are life-altering for the people he owes money to. We see the wife of one of his tradesman creditors come to plead for their money because her children can't eat. She's reduced to begging for what she's entitled to, trying literally to survive in a society with no welfare safety net. Meanwhile Harrel is out hiring more tradesmen he's not planning to pay, dismissing any attempt Cecilia makes to get him to take this woman's needs seriously, suggesting she's looking for a handout or charity. Harrel doesn't care about his debts to tradesmen, because tradesmen don't count as real people to him. He doesn't see the debts as things he has to pay back until they're to people of his own social class. Not even that – until they're to *men* of his social class. He's quite happy to leave Cecilia unrepaid. It's only when he can't pay back a gentleman that he sees his word – his honour – as having been engaged. And his despair over his inevitable disgrace is because his inability to pay his debts is going to become publicly acknowledged in society. What was an open secret is about to become openly acknowledged.

Society is very good at ignoring things that it isn't supposed to know about or see. What changes whether something is an open secret or a publicly acknowledged fact is who is doing the telling. One of the most prominent news stories in recent years was the Harvey Weinstein scandal. And a major element of the story was the question of whether there had been an institutional cover-up, with at least sixteen executives testifying that his abusive behaviour was known at both Miramax and the Weinstein Company.[9] Weinstein's behaviour was something everyone knew, but nobody talked about – except that, as Rebecca Solnit rightly points out, if everyone knew, then people were talking. It's just that they didn't count as the right people. Weinstein's abuses were going on for over thirty years and his predatory tendencies were known about by a lot of people; he had a lot of victims and a lot of enablers. Female assistants working with Weinstein were warning each other to sit on armchairs rather than sofas so it would be logistically harder for him to approach them. They were advising each other to wear multiple pairs of tights or big winter coats to work as a form of protection, an attempt at a preventative measure. People *were* talking. People knew about the abuse, people were talking about the abuse, but it wasn't stopped. An article running in the *Guardian* at the time the story was live quoted Professor Liz Kelly, the director of the Child and Women Abuse Studies Unit at London Metropolitan University, saying 'Women did speak about it. He used his position of authority to mute their voices. It is unrealistic and inaccurate to expect this to be stopped by the people it's happening to.'[10] After all, the easiest way to make complaints go away is to make the person complaining go quiet. That's especially true if they're people who don't have the same kind of financial and social capital – call it what it is, the same power – as the person harming them.

It's almost ironic, then, that a critical element of what helped journalists Jodi Kantor and Megan Twohey break the story about Weinstein was the presence of NDAs and the evidence of financial payouts: things that bound people from speaking out, things that documented that they had tried. Those documents represented a history of people making allegations that the company was fully aware of, but only appeared to care about when the story broke and came under the wrong kind of media and mass scrutiny. The victims of Weinstein were vital in this process. Whether it was their whisper-networking and solidarity, their speaking up and generating a paper trail that became evidence, or their going on the record with journalists – all of that talking gave voice to what was happening. But the sad truth can be summed up by this line from Twohey and Kantor's account of their groundbreaking piece: 'The thirty-three-hundred-word article triggered an immediate crisis for the Weinstein Company.'[11] Not Weinstein's actions. Not the abuses he perpetrated. But the fact that this information was suddenly and prominently public. It was a PR problem, not a moral one. If it had been about the behaviour, something would have been done years before.

It's an old truism that money talks. It also silences. The question of who gets listened to and who gets ignored is one that's always answered by power – no matter if you're someone who wants the financial control to manage your own life, or if you're trapped in an abusive workplace where you're likely to lose whether you speak up or not.[12] Burney's writing shows us an example of a society that makes women less powerful through reduced financial access, and that treats their consent and their words as irrelevant because of that limited power. When you represent a gender as incapable of making judgements, and you restrict their access to their finances, you're reducing their capacity to consent on two fronts. There's both an ideological unfitting and a practical disenfranchisement. It's vital that we don't walk ourselves back into a narrative where it's unnatural for women to make choices or to handle our own money. We are already too good at holding open secrets around those in positions of power. We are already too good at ignoring victims. Socially, we still link credit with credibility in a way that means the bigger your bank account, the more likely you are to get to shape the social narrative. If we want things to be better, we must make sure we don't lose the ground we've got.

3
Jane Doe, or Misreading the Room

> In rape cases it's strange to me when people say, Well why didn't you fight him? If you woke up to a robber in your home, saw him taking your stuff, people wouldn't ask, *Well why didn't you fight him? Why didn't you tell him no?* He's already violating an unspoken rule, why would he suddenly decide to adhere to reason? What would give you reason to think he would stop if you told him to?
>
> – Chanel Miller[1]

> Women know that much if not most sexism is unconscious, heedless, patronizing, well-meant, or profit-motivated. It is no less denigrating, damaging, or sex-specific for not being 'on purpose'.
>
> – Catherine MacKinnon[2]

When we think about consent, we often think about it being given in words. But there's also a type of consent that is inferred or read from behaviour. If you lean in to kiss someone, and then they lean and complete the kiss, you haven't exchanged words but you're both confident that the other person is on board. It's something that we use all the time, but it's also heavily reliant on interpretation – and so it's easy to get wrong. It's also something that it's easy to assign meaning to when there isn't any, reading intention into tiny little things that the person hasn't thought about. When it comes to cases of sexual violence, the victim's behaviour is often picked over, with people looking for any behaviours that might suggest they consented to what happened. It leads to rape myths like the one that says the victim's clothes impact whether they are raped or not. A short skirt is interpreted as the wearer being flirty and interested in sex, so wearing a short skirt is seen as looking for sex, which gets transformed into the skirt being an invitation for sex – and so suddenly by wearing that skirt, you've apparently consented. Why were you wearing that if you didn't want it to happen? Why did you go there? Why didn't you fight him? In its 2018 campaign Let's Talk About Yes, Amnesty International reported how

> More than 1 in 4 people in the EU believe that sexual intercourse without consent may be justified in certain circumstances, such as if the victim is drunk or under the influence of drugs; is voluntarily going home with someone, wearing revealing clothes, not saying 'no' clearly or not fighting back.[3]

These rape myths are pervasive. Behavioural consent also gets offered up as a counterpoint to verbal non-consent – for example when a person asserts that a victim 'really wanted' the encounter because, although they said no, their 'body said yes'. Somehow, their behaviour (or their clothing choice, or the look in their eyes, or their presence at a location) means that they agreed.

When we think about this in terms of the eighteenth century, behavioural consent is made more complicated by the fact that when you dig into the social code of acceptable behaviours for women, they all ultimately involve consenting. We're no longer in the same position – female obedience isn't as socially valued as it was – but we are seeing an increased call to move back to those days. The term 'incel' is a shortening of the phrase 'involuntary celibate', referring to men who want to be having sex but aren't succeeding at finding sexual partners, and who blame women for this. They feel that they deserve the attention of women, making comments like 'I wanted to kill them slowly, to strip the skins off their flesh. They deserve it. The males deserve it for taking the females away from me, and the females deserve it for choosing those males instead of me.'[4] The feeling of being denied something they are entitled to creates dangerous amounts of anger. Then there's a whole community of so-called Nice Guys who complain that they have done all the right things but still not been chosen by women as sexual or romantic partners. (Nice Guys is in capitals because this type of person is so prevalent online that it's become a meme.) You get the sense of a perceived contract where the etiquette states that if they take certain actions, the woman is supposed to have sex with them. Do all the right things, this rhetoric says, and you should win your chosen prize. When these men don't, they get angry.

In 2014 self-identified incel Elliot Rodger murdered six people and wounded fourteen others, before killing himself.[5] He left behind a 141-page document that the BBC described as highlighting 'his deep-rooted loathing of women, fuelled by an intense frustration over his virginity', as well as 'retribution' video-uploads to his channel explaining his motivations.[6] He was 'virtually canonised' by the incel community for this killing spree, and dubbed 'Our Supreme Gentleman'.[7] For a more detailed breakdown of this case, and the manosphere in general, I'd recommend Laura Bates's book *Men Who Hate Women*, which examines the online alt-right in more detail, and makes clear how those threats move into the physical world.[8] But when the men in these communities call Rodger 'supreme gentleman', they're harking back to historical periods like the eighteenth century, when being a gentleman meant having power. They're invoking their perceived social superiority. They're invoking being someone women should submit to. What's being viewed with false nostalgia are the times when it was much harder for women to have independence and make their own choices. Where all female behaviours could be read as consent.

Behavioural consent isn't inherently bad. We read or get confused by people's behaviour and what it means all the time; it's a constant stream of signals that we interact with when we interact with each other. Sometimes we say things which are very clearly not what we mean (this is why, for example, you might use safe words during sex). It is, however, something that can be fraught with misreading. We all have biases that impact how we interpret things, and behaviour is no different. In the context of sexual violence, there is a legal question of whether, if you make a reasonable mistake about whether someone is consenting, you should be liable for raping them if you get it wrong. This, and what it would take for a mistake to be reasonable, are questions which legal philosophers have been wrestling with for decades. When I was researching this, I found an article which had generated a lot of impassioned responses called 'Date Rape, Social Convention, and Reasonable Mistakes' by Douglas Husak and George Thomas.[9] Reading this article made me intensely angry. Not because Husak and Thomas were trying to blame women for rape – they weren't – but because these writers, who were clearly well intentioned, were talking about reasonable behaviour from a point of view that completely ignored a lot of the realities in the world that actively affect how we behave. They argue that 'consent to sex is typically given and withheld nonverbally', and that as a result, social conventions about which behaviours generally suggest that someone is consenting become key to deciding whether a crime has taken place. And while this essay, and the follow-up piece they wrote nine years later responding to the criticism their original article had generated, are not at the cutting edge of consent discussions today, to me they are representative of the mistakes people regularly make about behavioural consent in day-to-day life.[10] I'm going to use these essays to break this down so that as we move through the rest of this book, we're carrying this conversation with us – particularly when we're being asked whether victim behaviour impacts their responsibility.

Husak and Thomas start by arguing that the crime of rape requires *mens rea*, meaning a 'guilty mind'. Their view is that you can have acts of rape that don't have a criminal 'rapist' because the person who did the rape has made a reasonable mistake.[11] You need both the act of rape, and to understand that you are doing it, for it to count as a crime. It highlights a key difference in the way that English and US law approach rape cases. The American approach says that you can commit the *act* of rape, but might not be liable for the *crime* of rape. The two things are separate. English law says that if you aren't liable for the crime, then you also haven't committed the act.[12] The act and the crime are one. Husak and Thomas think that

> on virtually any occasion in which the defendant's belief about consent is unreasonable, the victim will have expressed her unwillingness to have sex in one way or another [...] Thus it is difficult to imagine a case in which a jury can be persuaded that a defendant has made an unreasonable mistake while unaware of the risk of making this mistake.[13]

This view places a lot of faith in juries, which really doesn't take into account the pervasive influence that damaging rape myths have been shown to have on them.[14] Nevertheless, on the basis of this view, Husak and Thomas suggest looking at those circumstances where a defendant might have honestly made a mistake – a 'reasonable' mistake. They take the idea that we use behavioural consent in non-sexual scenarios as well, saying that there are times when the way someone acts implies that they have agreed to something. To paraphrase one example, a person who gets into a taxi and asks to be taken to the airport hasn't explicitly *said* that they will pay the driver, but because the way taxis work is that you pay a fare to get taken to the place you want to go, we see them as having agreed to pay.[15] In a situation like that, Husak and Thomas say it's completely reasonable for the taxi driver to expect payment because it's in line with convention, offering the definition that 'a social convention is a societal "norm which there is some presumption that one ought to conform to"'.[16] The taxi example is fine, as far as it goes. But if we're thinking about sexual consent, then the fact that their examples are all transactions becomes problematic.

In the first place, it implies that sex is also a transaction. This takes away from the understanding of sex as something mutual, an act which both (or all) parties participate in together. It gets really difficult to talk about consent if you are already unconsciously categorising the sex act as being specifically for one party, and provided by the other. Even in a situation where sex is paid for and is part of a transaction, the fact that the transaction is happening doesn't give someone the right to do whatever they want just because they are paying money. The taxi driver can chuck you out of the cab if you start throwing up everywhere. They don't have to take you somewhere if it's not an area they want to go to. Sex workers do not have to have sex with you if it's outside of their personal boundaries.[17] It is not the *person* who is being bought, owned for an allotted period of time. It's the opportunity to have sex with this person, an interaction which will be governed by their own code of what is and is not permitted. Sex workers suffer abuses, and one part of this is because of the misconception that, having paid for the encounter, you are then at liberty to do whatever you like, regardless of the consent or willingness of the sex worker in question. Ultimately, this is not the case. No scenario that removes the capacity for free choice from a human being can be considered consensual. Paying money for the opportunity to have sex with a person does not give you the right to treat them as anything less than a complete human being.

Secondly, this framework plays into that gendered understanding of consent where women are cast as passive and accepting and men as active and initiatory – a view that is inherently reductive to both parties. One of the signs that we've moved forwards in recent years is an increased awareness that the gender identity of rapists and rape victims/survivors is more complex than a simple 'male rapist – female victim' binary. To imagine positive or affirmative consent as something only sought by males of females seems equally reductive (not to mention completely ignoring the entire LGBTQ+ community). Because Husak and Thomas are operating within a cis 'male seeker – female responder' structure, they automatically code the person who would not enjoy the sexual encounter as female. The transaction framework suggests that they are giving the sex in exchange for something. Implying (even accidentally) that an entire gender does not enjoy sex or is using it as leverage for something else is a really problematic position from which to discuss sexual consent.

Finally, by talking about sex as a point of exchange, Husak and Thomas fail to take into account the fact that it's an act that occurs across a period of time. We sometimes talk about consent as though it's something that only happens at the beginning of sex, but that's not right. Consent is not one-and-done, but something that must be maintained by everyone involved throughout. Even if someone consents at the start of sex, they can change their mind at any point. Most of their examples involve buying items in shops, which means that the moment of the exchange is very quick. The taxi is the closest parallel because the point of exchange is a journey, and so it reflects the reality that sex is an act that requires consent over a more extended period of time, but it's not an issue that Husak and Thomas really consider. If the hypothetical taxi passenger changed their mind on their way to the airport, they wouldn't necessarily be liable to pay the full fare since they hadn't gone on the full journey. But the question is focused on financial liability, on who owes what to whom. It relies on the fact that the passenger is aware they are using a business (the taxi service) which runs on direct exchange principles in a way that interpersonal relationships do not. Husak and Thomas argue that the social conventions which we operate by are equivalent to this kind of business transaction, and say that by behaving in a particular way, we can create the expectation of sex.

Problematically though, as the undertones of the taxi scenario make clear, the question really being posed is whether a person is *liable* for sex if their behaviour has generated that expectation in somebody else. Do they owe it to the person to have sex with them as a result? To be clear, this isn't what Husak and Thomas are specifically trying to argue – their focus is on whether it's reasonable to believe someone consented to sex by behaving in a way that society generally sees as leading to sex. But it's an inevitable extrapolation from the fact that all of the examples and scenarios they use to illustrate their point are transactions. And because Husak and Thomas are talking about women as the consent responders, it's specifically women's behaviour which is being represented as creating this social contract. This kind of thinking isn't limited to legal theorists. Whether it's the pervasive idea that a woman owes a man sex if he buys her dinner, or the view that women don't or shouldn't enjoy sex, this view of sex as something that gets owed to men is still widespread. It's just that Husak and Thomas's examples help make clear some of the assumptions and thought processes behind it.

It also highlights something important when it comes to reading and thinking about eighteenth-century courtship: courtship as a process had a series of behaviours which had to be seen to be performed regardless of the nature of the courtship in question. I say 'seen to be performed' deliberately, because their society had a significant tendency to maintain two distinct awarenesses: one for things that were publicly acknowledged within the social circle; the other to include those things that might be common knowledge, but that weren't 'officially' known.[18] (A bit like how your friend-group might know that a couple are dating, but you pretend not to until they tell you themselves. Or, on the darker side, how it might be an open secret that a particular colleague should be avoided at work events, but the company isn't officially aware of any issue until a complaint is made.) Whether a marriage was for love or for money, Georgian courtship had clearly defined social performances which were important for general acceptance. There was of course also a lot of focus on appropriate female behaviour in general, with particular emphasis on behaviours like modesty, chastity, and obedience, as well as generally being charming and polite. Young women were expected to show a chaste lack of interest in their suitors (they were to wait until they had family approval before starting to fancy them), feel gratitude for their interest (gratitude often comes twinned with obligation), and be obedient to them (as long as that didn't contradict being obedient to their family). On the flipside, there were certain things you did not do unless you *were* courting – for example, young men and women weren't supposed to write directly to each other unless they were related or engaged. Dancing too often with the same person at a ball signposts that you've got a particular interest in them. You really shouldn't be publicly unchaperoned. These behaviour patterns were well understood, but could easily be manipulated to create difficulties.

Many of the novels in this book take issue with the dangers of behavioural requirements. In *Cecilia*, one guardian's plan to marry Cecilia off hinges on making her go through all the public signs of an engagement, in the hope that this will create enough social pressure and expectation that she'll feel unable to do anything else. Her guardian can use his power to invite people to his house to force Cecilia to keep meeting a particular man. Because she's receiving him and going walking with him (and, though she avoids this, going away with him), she's seen as acting in a way that suggests an engagement. Her guardian is trying to create that social contract where she's pushed into marrying this specific man by the actions she's forced to take, because if society believes in the engagement, getting out of it is likely to be damaging to her reputation. In *The Conclusion of the Memoir of Miss Sidney Bidulph* (1767) by Frances Sheridan, Dorothea Arnold is abducted by a man who keeps her in his house alone for several days. He gives her the choice of marrying him or living with the shame of people thinking that she's lost her virginity; even though she has not had sex with him, the social circle would believe she had because she had spent time in his house.[19] He offers her the choice of being forced to have sex with him (the marriage option), or convincing everyone else that she had been seduced by him. Even though she didn't choose to go into the house, she's going to be affected by the social expectations created by her being there.

Husak and Thomas go on to pose a thought-experiment to explore what the downsides of affirmative or actively vocalised consent might be. In their scenario, a woman wants to have sex with a man, but doesn't want to say so explicitly:

> Her failure has not been a significant problem in the past; she has not been raped, and has been able to have sex without undue difficulty whenever she desires, without having to express her consent directly and explicitly. Suppose, however, that this woman has the misfortune to desire sex with a man who is persuaded by Schulhoefer's recommendations. Not wanting to be guilty of rape, he abstains from sex with this woman because he has not yet received her unambiguous expression of consent. He too feels awkward and uncomfortable about explicitly asking for sex [...] The result is that this woman is less successful in getting what she wants unless she changes her behaviour. A proposal designed to make it more difficult for men to get away with rape might have the unanticipated effect of making it harder for some women to get what they want.[20]

To address the essentials first: if the trade-off for making a traumatic and violent crime less common is to make it slightly more difficult to have sex, then it sounds like an eminently reasonable one. To equate rape with shyness or awkwardness in this way is disingenuous, and there is no sense here of the life-altering effects of rape. However, if we move on from this and look at the point Husak and Thomas are making, it's clear that what we are supposed to take away from this scenario is that people who are shy or sexually awkward would be disadvantaged or made uncomfortable by a policy that required explicit confirmation of both sexual interest and sexual consent. Husak and Thomas argue that while some 'might protest that neither adult should feel uncomfortable', that 'the point is that they do feel this way, and might resent having someone tell them how they should feel'.[21]

Here, the idea that either party would have to change their behaviour is presented as a bad thing. But the act of rape is a form of behaviour, and therefore any reduction in rape must involve some level of behavioural change. Here, two forms of behaviour are being treated in a worryingly similar ideological fashion; on the one hand, a change in behaviours from introverted parties towards a more public expression of wants – potentially awkward, embarrassing, and unwelcome; on the other, an act of violation which is intrusive, dangerous, and can cause a broad range of physical and mental trauma. The representation of this trauma as broadly female, and simultaneously as somehow equivalent to not being able to have sex when you choose to, highlights the habit it is easy to fall into when talking about acts like this in an intellectual setting. And we do intellectualise it, particularly when we start talking about it in general terms. Whether it's analysing books in class, or breaking down actions to make and interpret laws, or creating behaviour policies in schools and workplaces, we often think or talk about sexual violence in abstract and generalised ways. And that can mean that we retreat into the academic debate without always considering or acknowledging the real and significant human cost. There is a visceral nature to rape which it is essential not to sanitise by taking sole refuge in a mode of thinking which often rejects the emotional and the compassionate. Emotion is not the antithesis of logic – for things like rape, to leave out emotion is to fundamentally misunderstand how its violence operates. As Sohaila Abdulali writes, 'Sometimes people intellectually understand […] but have trouble comprehending the pain and indignity involved.'[22]

Ultimately, this thought-experiment is flawed. It relies on the idea of affirmative consent being embarrassing, suggesting a theoretical time period when the recommendation of explicit consent discussions is established enough to be known but new enough not to have become convention. Individual people can find things embarrassing all the time, but the degree to which something is generally embarrassing is often inversely proportional to how normal or familiar a certain behaviour is. A change in behavioural conventions can in itself effect a change in individual behaviours. This particular example shows its age, as affirmative consent has become more widely talked about and practised since the article was published. But people still ask whether this means they need to sign a contract to have sex or suggest that seeking consent kills the mood and removes the opportunity for spontaneity.[23] The more normalised seeking enthusiastic consent becomes, the safer sex is for everyone – and while its being more common won't remove the embarrassment of discussing sex and consent for every person, it's absolutely worth the discomfort. The fact remains that being embarrassed is not the same as being raped.

These essays transition from the purely theoretical to something more practical when they talk about incomplete rejection strategies. And just as it's useful to remember to keep the real world in mind when thinking theoretically, it can also be useful to break down the realities we're used to. Keeping the two in conversation helps highlight patterns in our actions that we might be unconscious of, and can make it easier to spot when biases are affecting our thinking. Incomplete rejection strategies are a really tangible example of how different groups can read and react to situations. The term 'rejection strategies' refers broadly to tactics used by one person or group to close down the advances or propositions of another person or group: basically, it's the things you do to perform a rejection. 'Incomplete rejection strategies' are a specific subsection of this, where the person or group wants to perform the rejection without terminating or ending the relationship with the proposer. You want to say no, but you don't want to do it in a way that creates a problem. In practice, this can look like lots of different things, from refusing an invitation to hang out from a family member while not offending them, to turning down the romantic proposition of a work colleague in a way that tries to minimise future office awkwardness. Husak and Thomas are thinking about the incomplete rejection strategy as it relates to romantic and/or sexual relationships, and they draw on data from a social experiment for their analysis. Their paper notes that the incomplete rejection strategies in the study weren't always successful, as the men in the study (which focused on cis heterosexual relationships) struggled to differentiate these indirect rejection strategies from 'seduction' behaviours.[24] Husak and Thomas write that

> If the man misunderstands the significance of the incomplete rejection strategy, he may continue to make advances. But surely common sense suggests that under normal circumstances a woman who is faced with imminent intercourse against her will should have no difficulty delivering an explicit, unambiguous 'no'.[25]

This point about common sense is dangerously wrong. In the first place, much work has been done in documenting the fact that humans have four primary responses to danger: fight, flight, freeze, and fawn. Fight and flight are the best known, but the freeze reaction refers to a kind of paralysis, like a deer in the headlights. Rape Crisis England and Wales talk about how

> it's really common for people who experience rape, sexual assault, sexual abuse or other types of sexual violence to find they can't move or speak. This is one of our bodies' automatic responses to fear and is designed to keep us safe.[26]

The fawn reaction is essentially an appeasement strategy – you attempt to minimise the danger to you by appearing compliant.[27] Thanks to the wealth of information sharing occasioned by the internet, be that through initiatives like the Everyday Sexism Project, the sharing of phone video clips, or of dating-site conversations, it is easier than ever to show the ways in which women regularly experience an extreme escalation in threat when they perform any kind of rejection strategy.[28] To give a simple example: catcalling frequently moves from supposed compliments to aggressive verbal abuse when the targeted person simply *does not respond* to the initial catcall. Years before his killing spree, Elliot Rodger was documenting incidents such as throwing his coffee over two girls who didn't smile back at him. 'Those girls deserved to be dumped in boiling water for the crime of not giving me the attention and adoration I so rightfully deserve!' he said.[29] It can escalate further than that, and there are multiple cases where women have been killed as a result of ignoring catcalling.[30]

Rejection – even indirect rejection – is risky. Husak and Thomas's 'common sense' doesn't take into account the reality of how people respond to danger. In the case of the freeze response, the question is irrelevant – no action can be taken.[31] It also fails to understand the significant risk-management decision making that can occur in the moment when an incomplete rejection strategy has been ignored. Because, in that moment, there is a question as to whether conveying a rejection will lead to an escalation of violence. All rape is inherently violent, but if you believe that rape is inevitable or is a significant risk, then your response will often shift from harm prevention to harm mitigation. How can I make this hurt as little as possible? What can I do to make this person less angry? How can I appease them?

What this thought-experiment shows most clearly is the biases that affect what we think is reasonable when we think about consent. When Husak and Thomas imagine that the woman in their thought-experiment should give an 'explicit, unambiguous no' after her indirect rejection strategy has been misread, they miss something crucial. The man in their scenario doesn't intend to hurt the woman (though the premise of the article acknowledges the possibility of harm without intent), but the writers aren't thinking about the scenario from the perspective of the woman involved. While they and the hypothetical man may know that no harm is intended, the woman does not – and she exists in a world where rape and sexual violence are common. If we allow that an unambiguous 'no' would be possible, passing over the potential for that 'no' to be misunderstood or ignored (and so also passing over their earlier less intentional arguments about owing sex if specific behaviours are performed), then we are still left with a key issue. I've said that the scenario only considers the situation from the point of view of the hypothetical man. Consider the scene using the knowledge that the hypothetical woman has: she has tried to put the man off, but he has failed to respond to this. Maybe he just hasn't understood, maybe he has and is ignoring it. They are moving towards what Husak and Thomas refer to as 'imminent intercourse', so things are escalating even as she attempts to perform these incomplete rejection strategies, and she exists in a world where outright rejection carries a notable risk of triggering violence. In such a situation, a moment arises when the woman must make a decision as to whether delivering an 'unambiguous no' is more likely to result in the man stopping or in his becoming violent. In the one outcome, the outright 'no' is a tool of safety, and this is the view that Husak and Thomas recognise – one where an unambiguous 'no' results in the sexual activity stopping. In the other, rape was already an inevitability; the unambiguous 'no' has the potential to increase the violence level, but not to provide safety. While Husak and Thomas have imagined a scenario where their hypothetical man is going to stop after he receives an unambiguous 'no', that's not information that their hypothetical woman has, and it's not a safe assumption to make.

In their follow-up paper, 'Rape Without Rapists: Consent and Reasonable Mistakes', which they wrote in order to address the responses to the first, Husak and Thomas come back to this idea of the indirect rejection strategy. In that article, they talk about something crucial – the role that confirmation bias plays in the kinds of scenarios they were exploring:

> A man who believes that his partner wants to have sex – or wants to want to have sex, or is willing to have sex whether she wants to or not – would be likely to think that his perception is at least partially confirmed if the woman delivers her rejection in a soft or equivocal manner.[32]

They recognise that a 'soft or equivocal manner' is 'likely' to be read as a *maybe* rather than a *no*. Both essays, which discuss the role of social convention in establishing whether a woman can be reasonably understood to have consented to a man through her behaviour, fail to take the time to examine how social convention affects the woman in the scenario. Quite apart from the fact that social convention actively encourages women to be 'soft and equivocal' generally, if a soft 'no' is a maybe, and a hard 'no' is an incitement to violence, then there is ultimately no real way to refuse.[33]

Husak and Thomas also discuss the idea of 'token resistance', where the woman makes a show of resistance that is more performance than meaningful refusal.[34] The idea of token resistance once again plays on social conventions, as a core part of the performance is the suggestion that the woman isn't 'easy' – she might be open to a sexual encounter with this particular man, but she's not available to every man, and she doesn't want to seem too keen. Though modesty and chastity are less common terms in the twenty-first century than they were in the eighteenth, we still talk about body-counts, we slut-shame, we measure whether women appear desperate – and we assign value to a woman based on how she conforms. In some communities that might be the used toothbrush rule, which says that sex should be reserved solely for a marriage partner because once you use a toothbrush, no one else wants to use it; in others, men are happy for women to have had other sexual partners – as long as the number of partners is below their personal threshold.

Like the eighteenth century, women are often encouraged not to appear too sexually interested; the idea of the straight man as seducer or hunter is still very much alive. It's the eroticisation of conquest which informs the perceived 'masculinity' of 'winning' a difficult prize. You'll see an increased labelling online of potential partners as high- or low-status. 'High-status females' are desirable, possible 'wife material', where 'low-status females' are characterised as use-objects. In the case of men, status often links to their income, falling back into a view that rates them by their potential as a provider. (Where low-status women are talked about as bodies to be used and moved on from, low-status men are not represented in this way – and are more typically described this way by other men than by women.) Part of that sense of winning or conquering comes from persistence in the face of refusal – you need difficulties to overcome for the prize to have value – but also the idea that refusals are fine to ignore. As the rape myths say, 'she said no but she meant yes'.[35]

When you combine confirmation bias, token resistance, and the eroticisation of the role of the conqueror, the result is the following conclusion:

> When asked whether the use of force would be justified to overcome the woman's refusal in various hypothetical dating situations, men were more than twice as likely as women to reply that force was justifiable [...] Indeed, over one-third of the males in the study, and a surprising one-eighth of the women, approved of force to achieve intercourse 'when a partner has a change of mind concerning intercourse'.[36]

Here, the thought-experiments move away from whether or not the person is understood as refusing. It is not just that social conventions might lead a man to believe that a woman has consented. Making it clear that you've changed your mind can be enough to make some people believe they then have the right to rape you. That any female behaviour that could indicate sexual interest – and thanks to confirmation bias, behaviour is more likely to be read this way if someone *wants* you to be interested – is sufficient justification for a violent attack. This perception of force as justifiable in the face of what is essentially Husak and Thomas's 'unambiguous no' is in many ways its own argument against delivering it.

What this reminds us of is a point made again and again by our eighteenth-century novelists – that social codes often force women to act in ways that they don't want to or don't mean to. By writing from the viewpoint of their central characters, the authors can let their readers know both what that character understands to be happening in any given situation, and also what they intend by their actions. We can see the chain of misunderstandings this generates, which in turn means that we are hyper-aware of how those misunderstandings come about. This insight allows for a debate which moves beyond making assumptions as to the woman's motivation, something both the eighteenth and the twenty-first centuries tend to get hung up on. The fact that it's a novel allows for a greater degree of assurance of intention and motivation than real life can offer, since we can see inside the heads of characters in a way we just can't with real people. This in turn gives the authors greater freedom to explore the issues around how female behaviour is read – and whether there are any meaningful options which allow them to show their lack of interest effectively. But what is essential to keep in mind while reading is that all of this is only possible because the authors are living in and writing about a world where sexual threats are real and are common. A world that had a lot of competing claims on how women were supposed to behave, that didn't necessarily let them showcase how they were feeling – and that put real women in real danger. A world that required specific kinds of resistances in order to have a sexual attack classified as rape – a fact that was repeatedly used to imply that real rape victims wanted the attacks made on them. As we go on to talk in more detail about the flaws in these required resistance behaviours, we must carry with us the awareness that both the people reading and the people writing these books were navigating these issues in their real lives.

PART II

INNOCENCE

4
Ophelia, or Resisting the Unknown

> Have you found a way to […] not think about being the girl whose heart was broken under […] the realization that there was no shelter in the ones we were supposed to be able to trust?'
>
> – Angel Props[1]

> I could not imagine how she could suspect him of an Action that deserved such Imputations; I thought it impossible he should be guilty of any bad Thing […] But how could I, ignorant of the Force of an unruly Passion, suspect it!
>
> – Sarah Fielding, *Ophelia*[2]

Innocence is one of those complicated concepts that feels very familiar until you start trying to explain it, and then the more you try to unpick it, the knottier it gets. Part of that is because it's a word we use for multiple things. We use it in the legal system to say that someone is innocent until proven guilty (although, as I'll go on to talk about later, we never prove people innocent). We use it in terms of sexuality to describe virginity and a lack of sexual knowledge. And we also use it for a lack of knowledge more broadly, when someone has been kept apart from knowing or seeing things which might change them, or change how they see the world.

We can think of innocence as safe; pure, unsullied, at peace. But it has some darker undertones. For one thing, the perfect victim is innocent. And as we've already established, the perfect victim does not exist. Those two things are linked, in that when people are seeking a perfect victim, they tend to seek an irreproachable level of innocence – one that is impossible to obtain. But it is also dangerous in a different way. Eighteenth-century author Sarah Fielding wrote an entire novel examining how a woman who is perfectly – completely, impossibly, ludicrously – innocent can end up falling victim to that same lack of knowledge. She asks, if a woman has absolutely no knowledge of sex, how can she tell that a threat is sexual? And if she cannot tell that a threat is sexual, how can she know that she needs to show resistance to that threat? Meet Ophelia.

Ophelia is the heroine of Fielding's 1760 novel *The History of Ophelia*, and she knows nothing at all about men, sex, or society. She's been raised by her aunt in rural Wales, and has never met any other human being until the story begins. The set-up is deliberately nonsensical: not only has Ophelia met only one other human in her entire adult life, but she and her aunt somehow manage to subsist by running a farm together. With minimal manual labour, and an awful lot of religious philosophy, Ophelia has lived the kind of idealised pure and simple country life that the eighteenth century would have called pastoral. (It's honestly very similar to the Instagram aesthetic of the simple farm life, and about as close to reality.) The extremes here are the point – it's funny and impossible, but within the world of the novel it's allowed to be true, and it means that Ophelia can view the problems of society from the outside. Her aunt was

> desirous not to lessen my Innocence and Simplicity while she dispelled my Ignorance, she gave me no account of the Manners and Customs of a People with whom she hoped I should never have any Intercourse. The Books she brought into *Wales* were chiefly Books of Divinity, and such Histories as served to enlarge and instruct the Mind of the Reader, without informing him of the existence of Vices, which a pure Imagination cannot represent to itself.[3]

Crucial things to take away: Ophelia is educated; she's very moral; but she categorically knows absolutely nothing about anything connected to vice or sin. She is that perfect innocent, and it's about to get her into trouble.

Cue Lord Dorchester, a wealthy stranger (and a *man*) arriving on their doorstep. Ophelia is impressed by him. A whole other person! And he seems handsome and well read and polite. She's delighted. However, her aunt takes one look at Dorchester – and at the way he is looking at Ophelia – and is immediately suspicious of him. She has a lot more knowledge about the world and the people in it, so she is able to recognise a threat that her niece does not. Rather than explain what she's scared of, the aunt gives Dorchester the cold shoulder and gets him to leave. And Dorchester does leave … only to come back in the middle of the night and abduct 16-year-old Ophelia.

This might sound similar to *Clarissa* – a young moral woman being kidnapped by a man who's sexually interested in her. That's deliberate on Fielding's part. Fielding was writing after Samuel Richardson had published *Pamela* and *Clarissa*, and *Ophelia* feels like a deliberate response to both. *Pamela* (though it was unbelievably popular) struggles because it plays everything straight. Richardson invites his audience to believe that Pamela really is a model for how to behave, and having his heroine get raped despite doing all the right things would undermine the idea that this book teaches proper conduct, which results in some rather contrived escapes. Pamela's good behaviour needs to appear to protect her, but the result is a novel which, though popular, was also heavily parodied. Henry Fielding, Sarah's brother, is believed to have written one of the best-known of these skits, known generally as *Shamela*, in which a horny maid manipulates her slow-witted employer into marrying her.[4] Sarah Fielding is also playing against the Pamela heroine type in *Ophelia*, though she does it in a subtler way (a great many things are subtler than *Shamela*). She's making fun of the narrative excesses generated by this kind of model heroine, and instead of trying to make a stock virtue-figure believable and realistic, she leans into the extremes and impossibilities. After all, it is only with those impossibilities that she can create a character who is innocent enough to escape blame – anything more realistic and nuanced would see her character's personal responsibility questioned.

This is where the way the book is structured does something really clever. *The History of Ophelia* is an epistolary novel, so it's told as an extended letter from a now grown-up Ophelia to another lady. Ophelia is able to explain exactly what she thought and felt, but with the benefit of many years' more life-experience. So she can hint at what Dorchester is intending to do (you will be shocked to learn he really wants to have sex with Ophelia) using her later-life wisdom, while also explaining the perspective she had in the moment. This double perspective is important in creating the impression Fielding is looking for, making it clear what the risks are from Dorchester, while avoiding any suggestion that Ophelia was aware of them at the time.

Why is this important? Well, in the eighteenth century 'knowledge' was often conflated with 'sexual knowledge' and what the courts called 'carnal knowledge', and so to create a scenario where Ophelia is completely excused from any potential complicity in her own abduction, Fielding needs to show that she doesn't understand anything. Or at least, not anything sexual. In the quote from the novel I used earlier, Ophelia talks about how a truly virtuous mind cannot imagine vice without being exposed to it. For her to understand what's happening, she would have to know something about vice, and that might in turn suggest that she had an interest in it. Again, Fielding is deliberately going to extremes with this book, but by making Ophelia's innocence so over-the-top there is no way to read her as sexually aware. It's also what makes the novel funny. Fielding uses her innocence and social isolation to create scenarios where Ophelia makes social faux pas because she only knows the right way to do things, not the fashionable way. We get her comments on society as an external observing party, even as she doesn't understand the ways she is participating in it. We know, from the fact that she's the one writing the letter and from the way she sets up the tale, that Ophelia is fine in the present, so we're not facing a *Clarissa* situation where our heroine dies – and this in turn also tells us in eighteenth-century shorthand that she doesn't get raped, as rape victims in novels do not generally live long. We are therefore able to find the humour in Fielding's prose and snippy society observations, even as the actual events of the plot are abduction, coercion, and manipulation. And because it's funny, and deliberately farcical, we're able to accept it at face value, where novels that try for similar levels of innocence but play the sentiment straight (like *Pamela*) get their heroines critiqued for actually being scheming minxes trying to trick their way into marriage.

Later in the novel, Lord Dorchester kisses Ophelia's hand, and she blushes. She says that 'Because he was pleased I was ashamed, I know no other Reason for my Blushes, for before it appeared to me, too insignificant to make any.'[5] Blushing is supposed to indicate a level of shame, embarrassment, or general consciousness of impropriety. Dorchester kissing Ophelia's hand is not proper, and is not something she is supposed to welcome as a virginal young woman, though of course she doesn't understand this. We can see here one of the problems with behavioural consent – blushing shows an awareness of having something to be ashamed of, so not blushing is the behaviour of an innocent. However, not blushing also indicates shamelessness, and therefore the flipside of that argument is that the innocent action is to blush. Behavioural consent can explain Ophelia as sexually interested whether she blushes or not. This alternative is the best of both worlds, as Fielding can show Ophelia's inherent modesty – she blushes even without really understanding why – while maintaining her entire ignorance of what is going on. And by jumping through all of those hoops, she can also make fun of the social codes that govern how young women are supposed to behave.

I talked in Chapter 1 about how Clarissa's humanity, and her inability to act perfectly in impossible situations, means that her behaviour is a really big focus for discussions of that novel. Critic

Sandra Macpherson describes Richardson's 'indictment' and disapproval of

> the culture that makes Lovelace possible – that enables Anna Howe, James Harlowe, and even William Warner, to raise questions about Clarissa's character and motives as if those questions *mattered*, as if moral turpitude could make a victim less a victim, as if harm could be deserved or consented to.[6]

Macpherson's work looks at how Richardson and other writers show that imperfect victims still experience harm. It's one tool for trying to shift the conversation on from simply blaming the character for their actions, saying okay, and so what? This thing is still wrong, let's talk about that. The other way to shift that focus is to create a very different character.

Ophelia is a kind of opposite to Clarissa – she *is* perfect. Because of that, she's completely unrealistic, and that makes it very hard to get into conversations about her personal responsibility. Instead, we're given these dangerous situations played for comedy, so that Fielding can highlight the problems with the way that the eighteenth century thinks about educating (or not educating) women. We're invited to move beyond an analysis of the heroine, and instead to consider the actions of her male counterpart. If we remember the way in which real-world cases of sexual violence, both in the eighteenth century and today, effectively place the victim on trial before they do the defendant, this clever use of humour to spotlight the actions of the male bad actor becomes significant. In books written more than twenty years apart, barrister (and baroness) Helena Kennedy talks about how common it is in today's era for a victim in court to be considered guilty unless they can prove otherwise.[7] To put it bluntly, to get people to ask questions about Dorchester, Fielding needed to get people to stop asking questions about Ophelia. Constructing her as a kind of caricature, rather than an individual with foibles and wants and flaws, means that blame can't be easily attached to her. By acknowledging the hyperbole in her characterisation, Fielding also manages to avoid a *Shamela* situation where a character's extreme innocence is played straight and therefore ends up read as knowingness in disguise.

If we go back to the initial abduction, Ophelia explains that

> At first my Terror rendered me almost senseless; I was frightened without knowing what I feared […] My Life had injured no one, nor could my Death be of any Benefit to them; therefore I could not apprehend being murdered; but my Ignorance of the Nature of the Dangers which threatened me, gave no Ease to my Mind.[8]

Here, Ophelia – and therefore Fielding – is very specific about what the danger is that Ophelia is in without ever explicitly mentioning it (the eighteenth century really loves Not Mentioning Things). The first thing we learn here is that Ophelia is afraid, which shows that she's virtuous because she doesn't want to leave her aunt or the safety of her home. She's not interested in being abducted. Where Clarissa, back in Chapter 1, was screaming 'no, no, no' and understanding exactly why being dragged into a waiting carriage was not going to be good for her, Ophelia has no clue. She does not know what it is she is afraid of, but we know reading this that what she should be afraid of is the threat of rape by the man who has carried her off.[9] We can't see Ophelia as falling for a seduction plot because she is totally unaware of even the possibility of sex in this scenario. Nonetheless, the sexual threat is clearly implied; future Ophelia recognises 'the Nature of the Dangers' and expects her readers to do so as well. Why on earth has this man carried this young and beautiful woman off on his horse, what could he possibly want with her? She doesn't have any enemies, so it's not revenge. No one's going to inherit anything when she dies, so it's not for money either. She's pretty confident, given the lack of revenge or money-based motives, that they aren't planning to murder her. Her fear without understanding shows the same kind of innate morality as her blushing did, in that she knows that something is wrong even if she does not understand it.

Ophelia is thinking things through here – she is rationally able to determine (while 'almost senseless' and thrown onto a horse in the dark by the first man she has ever encountered) that she is unlikely to be a target for the violent crime of murder, *and yet* cannot fathom what it is that this man might want with her. She cannot imagine a type of threat that she has had no exposure to. Fielding almost shepherds us into position, leaving no room for Ophelia to be afraid of anything but sexual violation, no way to view Ophelia as anything other than innocent and unaware. Unfortunately for Ophelia, this is not enough on its own to protect her.

The description of the abduction ends with Ophelia drawing attention to the fact that the main reason she has no idea what is happening to her is because she has been kept in a state of 'Ignorance'. Innocence and ignorance are twin ideas in this book, and where Ophelia doesn't know what's happening, she's vulnerable to the schemes of others. In a very real way, Ophelia's at risk precisely because she's innocent. It's all very well to be perfectly innocent and ignorant of bad actors if you're hiding out in the pastoral wilderness with a person who isn't going to hurt you. It's a completely different proposition trying to live with that perfect ignorance in a world where people will use it against you. After Ophelia is abducted by Dorchester, he is able to convince her that he is doing everything for her own good, that he is her protector and moral compass around the *ton* (or fashionable Georgian society). In fact, he is setting her up to look like his kept mistress. Fielding repeats this pattern throughout the novel: if Ophelia cannot recognise or understand the threat, then she cannot know how to avoid it. And if she cannot know how to avoid it, then the actions she takes can get her into worse trouble.

To give one final example of this, there's a moment when Ophelia is hugged by a strange man. A young rake is waiting for the lady he plans to elope with, thinks Ophelia is her, and wraps her up in a hug. To make it really clear that this young man is a cad, we also learn that he's not planning on actually marrying the woman he's eloping with – he's lying to her so that he can sleep with her. He's actually already married. This hug is not a gesture of love, it's a gesture of lust. It's not just an improper thing for him to do, it's the result an improper impulse. Because this bit of the plot involves lots of people being confused about identities, Ophelia initially thinks the man hugging her is Lord Dorchester, and that he is simply pleased to have found her again. She doesn't realise that she is actually being hugged by a hormonal stranger. Nevertheless, she reacts to the gesture as an inappropriate one even before she fully understands:

> The Rapidity with which he flew to me, and the Eagerness of his Embrace, astonished and startled me: I had never seen any Degree of such Familiarity before. I was not sensible of any Impropriety in the Expressions of Affection; but without knowing a Reason for it, I was disturbed with this Address. I could not think such Violence the necessary Consequence of Love; I was as much rejoiced, I imagined, as he could be, and yet such Behaviour did not appear natural to me.[10]

Even though she doesn't know why it should be wrong, it all seems a bit much to her. The behaviour 'disturbed' her, 'astonished and startled' her, and 'did not appear natural' – in spite of the fact that she did not know there was 'any Impropriety'. She is able to react naturally against behaviours which society does not approve of, because she has that innocence and innate moral sense. It is essential for the character that Fielding is creating that we see Ophelia's ignorance as only relating to the one area – vice. Otherwise, she's bright and educated and discerning. She knows what the right things to do are, she just doesn't understand why the wrong things are wrong. She's unable to recognise them, understand their motivations, or guard against them. Because she cannot recognise a lie, she is vulnerable to deception, and when she does do the wrong thing, it's because she's been tricked into thinking it's right. Her character is constantly being judged by society because of the way they see her acting, but she's only acting that way because she's too pure to know she's being manipulated.

It's her innocence that makes her so appealing to Dorchester as a prize, and that allows him to manoeuvre her into living under his control. He deliberately keeps her ignorant so as to keep the charade going. After the hug incident, when the character of the caddish young man comes to light, we see Dorchester controlling the narrative Ophelia gets told so that she will not suspect he is manipulating her. Rather than tell her the truth about the 'eloping' couple – that the man was married, that he was lying to the woman to trick her into sex, that living under the same roof while unchaperoned and unmarried was socially frowned upon – he lies. And since Ophelia would make a terrible poker player, she is prevented from recognising the parallels with her own situation, from asking why it's okay for her to live with Dorchester when living with a man could ruin this young woman.

> As I had no Notion a man could be guilty of so bad an Action, I simply believed the Story, as my Lord related it, who, chusing rather to take Advantage of my Ignorance, than to place his Hopes in corrupting the Innocence of my Mind, thought proper to conceal Circumstances, which must lead me into Reflections, that could not fail to alarm me on Account of my own Situation.[11]

'Innocence' and 'Ignorance' are working in tandem again here, hammering home Fielding's central point: that jokes aside, a strong sense of morality is ultimately not enough protection from being harmed. The novel is comedic, but the message is clear – being innocent will not keep you safe, especially if the person you think you can trust is lying to you.

Dorchester does not intend to marry Ophelia. He isn't planning to marry anyone at all, as he's not a big fan of the idea of matrimony. But that doesn't mean that he doesn't have plans for her – he wants to have her as his mistress. He sets her up in a house where he can control who visits her, making sure that she never comes to suspect him or to learn that she's flouting social conventions. (The joke is on Dorchester by the end, because he does actually fall in love with Ophelia and marries her at the close of the book – in part because he is won over by her goodness and her innocence.) To sell the set-up to Ophelia, he represents himself as her guardian, and therefore as someone it is proper for her to spend time alone with (actually, to spend all her time with). She has no awareness that such a practice is uncommon, or that Dorchester is ruining her chances of marrying anyone else, until one of Dorchester's cronies tells her in a bid to get her to go off with him instead. Future Ophelia explains her behaviour, saying that

> I could not suspect him of any ill Design against my Innocence; of all such Views I was totally ignorant. I knew not what they meant [...] perhaps, he [Dorchester] was fortunate in having none to observe him, but one so blinded by Ignorance, that she could not easily suspect him of ill [...] A Woman sensible of the Dangers attending her Situation, might, perhaps, have taken Alarm frequently, when I saw no Cause for Fear; thus far my Ignorance was convenient to his Design.[12]

Here again is the emphasis that it is her ignorance of vice which makes her vulnerable to Dorchester's schemes. In fact, his plan is only possible *because* she is so 'blinded' – her ignorance is not a passive factor but an enabling one. In this section, we also see that term 'innocence' being used deliberately to signal multiple meanings. It is not only a moral or religious state, it is not only an unknowingness of the world – it is also the state of virginity. I began this chapter talking about how 'innocence' as a term is flexible, sometimes moving nebulously across morality, unknowingness, and virginity, and sometimes being used in one firm sense. In *Ophelia*, Fielding is primarily addressing the paradox that, in order to maintain a state of innocence (loosely all three forms), one firm form will be compromised. The tragic ending would be if Ophelia's virginity were the element lost. For comedy, it must be that 'unknowingness of the world' that is removed. One must know in order to know how to avoid; innocence itself is what puts you in greater danger.

I spoke earlier about how the novel's being funny, being deliberately extreme in Ophelia's ignorance, is what lets us accept her as being so innocent, but it goes further than that. Ophelia isn't a realistic character. She's an over-the-top pattern of behaviour, a collection of extremes. Yes, this makes the novel funny, and without it there wouldn't really be any plot happening, but it also has the unusual function of making Ophelia invisible. If we think about the way conversations about consent and responsibility (culpability, blamability) happen, we know that the victim's behaviour is the first thing to be analysed and dissected. Ophelia has to be performatively naïve in order for her behaviour to pass without criticism. There isn't really anything to dissect, and it's much easier – and more interesting – to move on to Dorchester, whose behaviour is pretty abysmal. And when Ophelia finally does understand Dorchester's plan for her, and tries to explain it to her correspondent, what comes out is not a defence of her own innocence so much as an acute commentary on men taking advantage of women:

> I did not suspect anyone of inclining to a Vice, of whose Existence I was totally Ignorant; and if I had been in that Particular better informed, I should have thought nothing so great a Security as being under a Man's peculiar Care and Protection. Some knowledge of the World was necessary to make me believe any one could wish to injure another, long Experience only convinced me that a Man could think of injuring one, whom he was bound by every tye [*sic*] of real Honour and Humanity to defend; nor could less have taught me that Men who act with the strictest Integrity to their own Sex, should imagine themselves less obliged to do so by ours, when they acknowledge that Nature by giving us greater gentleness of Mind, and more delicacy of Body, makes us dependent on them; which Custom has through Policy not only confirmed but increased.[13]

Here, Ophelia states that even if she had been 'better informed' of sexual threats, she would have thought that being under the care of a man would be the best method of protection. By making the statement about young women generally, rather than just Ophelia herself, Fielding highlights the real-world issue. The epistolary format of the novel allows future Ophelia to explain that even after being exposed to 'Some knowledge of the World', it took 'long Experience' before she could believe that men harm the very women they are supposed to protect. The virtuous nature of her character is shown by the fact that she doesn't automatically believe the worst of people – but the flipside of this is that she clearly has now seen enough examples of this to confidently assert it. Her 'long Experience' is not just of being in the world – it is an experience of men harming women. Coming like this, from the voice of the wisdom and experience that innocent Ophelia has grown up to acquire, tells us that this is an idea Fielding is expecting her readers to agree with and to recognise. She doesn't present it as a shocking conclusion – it's just the ugly truth. Being ignorant of a danger makes you vulnerable to it, and you cannot trust people to protect you, even if they are the exact people you think are supposed to.

If we look at the end of this passage, there's something clever going on. Fielding gets Ophelia to say one thing, which ends up emphasising something else entirely. Ophelia seems to agree with the idea that women are 'dependent' on men – by their very 'Nature' they should be submissive and subordinate. I can't say that's an idea I am personally on board with, but she then goes on to emphasise that this dependence is manufactured into something more significant by 'Custom' – specifically by 'Policy' – meaning that any difference between the sexes is less significant than the way in which society has acted upon the notion of that difference. This passage appears to speak in passive tones about the idea that women require male protection, and are naturally more delicate than men. In practice, it highlights how common it is for men to harm women, and how a change in social practices – like better education for women, or more autonomy – would reduce the dependency they have on men. Underneath this book's humour, and its sniping at the hypocrisies of polite society, runs the awareness and observation of a central threat. It's what makes the plot work in the first place – Ophelia's coming of age as she comes to understand 'how much our Sex had to fear from the other'.[14]

If we pull back from Ophelia to the real world, it's worth thinking about what the novel could offer to the young women who may have read it. Reading the novel, we are aware of what the threat is – we are expected to be aware, because the person grown-up Ophelia is writing to is also aware. She's not writing to a young girl raised in total isolation. But even if we didn't really understand what was happening at the beginning, we as readers are given all the benefits of Ophelia's hindsight. We get the details of Dorchester's schemes, we get her commentary on how she didn't understand why something was improper – which in its own way highlights that it is behaviour to be careful of. By the end, we get her thoughts on how people often abuse the people they are supposed to protect. Reading *Ophelia* isn't going to teach someone how to stay safe – particularly as that's not something that's in their control – but it can help to overcome some of the ignorance that makes the character of Ophelia more vulnerable. It's something that I think a lot of these books are doing – having conversations and making arguments publicly to help give young women information and change how the broader society thinks.

This function of storytelling as information sharing is really key when it comes to storytelling around sexual violence. Thinking about this power of storytelling, and about Ophelia's vulnerability to abuse carried out by someone she believed she could trust, I find myself thinking about USA Gymnastics and the Larry Nassar case. Nassar worked with USAG for nearly thirty years as a physiotherapist, and he was a trusted member of staff. In the documentary *Athlete A* (a brilliantly handled piece of television covering Nassar's abuse and the process of breaking the story on it), the gymnasts discuss how at elite training camps held at the Karolyi ranch, Nassar was the only adult who was kind to them, who would sneak them food when they were hungry, would make them feel safe. However, during the medical treatments that Nassar would perform on these gymnasts over the years – many of them children – he would sexually assault them. He told them it was a normal part of the treatment. Olympian Jamie Danvers told the press that she was abused from the age of 12 or 13 until she was around 18, and that she 'didn't report the alleged abuse at the time because she didn't know it was wrong [...] "It felt like a privilege to be seen by him," she said. "I trusted him."'[15] Maggie Nichols said 'he violated our innocence'.[16]

Rachel Denhollander was the first woman to be publicly named in relation to Nassar's abuse:

> 'I was terrified,' she recalled. 'I was ashamed. I was very embarrassed. And I was very confused, trying to reconcile what was happening with the person he was supposed to be. He's this famous doctor. He's trusted by my friends. He's trusted by these other gymnasts. How could he reach this position in the medical profession, how could he reach this kind of prominence and stature if this is who he is?'
>
> She said she figured the problem must be with her.[17]

Danvers's lawsuit showed a similar belief in the normality of the abuse, saying that she was 'under the impression that this inappropriate contact was part of treatment'.[18]

In the end, after more than 150 women came forward, Nassar was convicted of multiple crimes, including seven counts of first degree criminal assault in addition to child pornography charges. He is now in the process of serving multiple life sentences in prison.[19] But if we look at the steps which occurred on the way to that conviction, you can see how important storytelling is for information sharing. Athlete A, now identified as Maggie Nichols, reported Nassar's treatment of her before any articles were written. Both her parents and USA Gymnastics were made aware of the issue, but the Nichols family were told that because there was an investigation into Nassar as a result of their report, they could not talk about what had happened without risking it jeopardising the case. Gina Nichols has commented on how her daughter's ability to tell her story and communicate information was effectively shut down by USAG, saying that 'she just did what she was told to do, and she was told to keep quiet'. (USA Gymnastics says that these claims of silencing are 'entirely baseless' and that it was simply following the directives of the FBI, which they turned the case over to.)[20]

Separately, the *Indianapolis Star* (known as the *Indy Star*) newspaper was reporting on sexual abuses in USA Gymnastics for their Out of Balance series. Rachel Denhollander, who had been abused by Nassar when she was younger, saw the article and contacted the *Indy Star*, telling them about her experiences and encouraging them to look into Nassar, launching the investigation which ultimately ended in his conviction. One thing that stood out to me in the *Athlete A* documentary was the way in which Nassar's invulnerability unravelled because of people talking. When the initial story broke in the *Indy Star*, featuring Rachel Denhollander and an anonymised Jamie Danvers (who was nonetheless identifiable to the small elite gymnastics community), it graphically detailed the kinds of abuses Nassar was perpetuating.[21] Their account of their treatment was familiar to many of Nassar's victims. By publicly acknowledging what the behaviour was which was problematic, it allowed other victims to see the similarities in their own 'treatment', inviting the question: if it was wrong for him to do this to her, wasn't it also wrong to do it to me? Consciousness raising has long been a part of feminist practice; we might not call it the same thing, but its presence is still clear.

Moreover, the account in the article was followed by this statement: 'Nassar's attorney said his client never used a procedure that involved penetration.'[22] Over the years, Nassar had performed these treatments on hundreds of gymnasts, and each time the narrative had been that the treatments were entirely normal and were necessary for the health of the athletes. They were aware they had been penetrated, but they had been told it was a necessary medical procedure. Suddenly, the fact that it had happened at all was being denied – indicating that it had never been a legitimate procedure in the first place. After this story broke, '36 people filed sexual assault complaints with Michigan State University police at addresses where the doctor worked.'[23] By the time the case came to court, 156 women had testified against Nassar.[24] In this instance, the act of storytelling enabled the sharing of crucial information, both in terms of reaching those women who had lived for years being told that their abuse was acceptable, and by their testimonies evidencing and corroborating the crimes which had taken place.

There is one more element of storytelling in this case which never fails to move me. During the trial, as a condition of the plea bargain Nassar entered into, all 156 of those women were given the opportunity to make a victim impact statement, either speaking themselves or having a statement read on their behalf. Nassar was required to be present in court for the presentation of the impact statements and, unusually, was required to sit in the witness box while the statements were delivered, so that the victims could face him.[25] (Ordinarily, the statements would be made with the defence and prosecution sitting side by side parallel to each other. Chanel Miller, whom I discussed in this book's introduction, describes her frustration at not being able to face or directly address her attacker while delivering her statement on the harm he had caused her.)[26] This was an active redefinition of the power dynamic in the relationship between the gymnasts and their abuser, and in offering them the opportunity to speak, it also offered them the opportunity to heal. *Athlete A* highlights the power of this moment, showing footage from the courtroom as the survivors and their families were finally allowed to reclaim some sense of control and power.

Certainly, what happened to those women is far more serious than any novel, far more serious than *Ophelia*. But I think it's important to talk about the similarities between our times, and the novels are a tool to do that. The message of the novel – that people (particularly men) who are in positions of authority are not necessarily trustworthy and actually represent a sexual threat – is there for a reason. You do not warn people about something that you do not believe exists. Fielding was using the medium available to her, and she was using humour and comedy to make the book entertaining rather than tragic or moralising, but she's warning her readers about abusive men in positions of authority, and she's warning them about how innocence is an easy target for predators, and she's helping them recognise what those threats look like. In both centuries, it is the innocence of the victims that makes them vulnerable. It's the trust placed in people who are supposed to be trustworthy. For the women involved in the Nassar case, there was a specific abuser they were reporting, there was a legal process, and there was the very real and traumatic harm they suffered. The two are clearly not the same. But through the telling of their stories, through the articles, the court testimonies, the victim impact statements, and the documentaries, these women also used stories as tools of solidarity, healing, and warning. They came to understand what had been done to them by the sharing of their stories, and they made sure to say loudly and publicly that this kind of behaviour is dangerous and wrong. That they deserved to have been safe. They deserved to have their innocence protected by the people they trusted, the people whose role it was to take care of them. It is impossible to recognise a threat if you don't know what it looks like – and you need people to speak up so as to find out.

5

Camilla and Eugenia, or What You Don't Know Can Hurt You

> Many of the students I've spoken to have been shocked to learn just what they have the right to be protected from. When I speak at universities and colleges, and describe the UK's legal definition of sexual assault, I'm often approached afterwards. 'This can't be sexual assault,' they tell me, 'because it's normal…'
>
> – Laura Bates[1]

> That process can start with what you notice. You might notice how you are noticeable. And in noticing how you become noticeable, how you stand out, you come to see what you otherwise would not if you participated in something, or what you could not see from the vantage point you previously enjoyed. This is why I think of noticing as political labour. In noticing the world, we hammer away at it.
>
> – Sara Ahmed[2]

> 'Those women,' said she, calmly, 'are not to blame; they have been untutored, but not false; and they have only uttered such truths as I ought to have learned from my cradle. My own blindness has been infatuated; but it sprung from inattention and ignorance. – It is now removed!'
>
> – Frances Burney, *Camilla*[3]

You may be intelligent, educated, and moral, but you can still be in danger if your smarts don't extend into the right areas. Frances Burney, the same author who wrote *Cecilia*, also wrote our next book. This one is called *Camilla, or A Picture of Youth* (1796), and it looks at what happens when clever characters are made vulnerable because people assume that they know everything already. In this book Camilla comes from a large, happy family. She grows up with both her parents, one brother, two sisters, several cousins, and an uncle – an unusual situation for one of Burney's heroines. Because this is another doorstopper book with a lot of interweaving characters and plot threads, we're going to be concentrating on Camilla and her younger sister Eugenia. Though they're both well educated (Eugenia is actually a classical scholar), they both end up getting caught out by bits of the world their family didn't think they needed to know about. In a much more practical and realistic way than the last chapter's *Ophelia*, Burney highlights the dangers of behavioural consent, and the way that innocence can simply be a synonym for ignorance – something that puts at risk more than it protects.

Camilla is in many ways the most morally flawed of her sisters, though also (unsurprisingly for a heroine) the most lovely. These flaws are minor – she tends to act without thinking things through, but she's always motivated by a desire to help others and do the right thing. She falls in love with wealthy childhood friend Edgar Mandelbert, and she falls in love with him before she knows if he likes her. This is not the way you're supposed to do things, and so Camilla struggles a lot with the fact that she isn't supposed to acknowledge these feelings (let alone have them) until after Edgar tells her that he's interested. Burney is writing against the idea that female desire gets created in response to male desire – Camilla is supposed to have no sexual or romantic urges at all until a suitable and family-endorsed man pops up and tells her he wants to marry her. Then she should immediately have all the appropriate feelings. It's worth noting, then, that Camilla's struggles are with the fact that she feels it's a bit presumptuous of her to fancy Edgar before he's given her permission, but there's no suggestion that she's less moral for having those feelings. She simply knows that she is not socially permitted to acknowledge or act on them. This emphasis on performing the 'correct' feelings is central to Edgar and Camilla's romance, as Burney puts the miscommunication trope through the wringer to demonstrate the gulf between intention and reception when it comes to behaviour. Both Edgar and Camilla spend a significant amount of time analysing each other's behaviour, rather than just telling each other what's going on. In Camilla's case, we even see her crafting her own behaviour to try to convey specific ideas or messages to Edgar (spoiler: this does not work). The pair consistently manage to misread each other, in what becomes an exercise in why you should actually talk to people and not rely wholly on behavioural analysis.

Here's an example. Very conveniently for all concerned, Edgar is also in love with Camilla. However, he has a misogynistic mentor with a bad experience of marriage, and he convinces Edgar to put Camilla to the test to make sure she's good enough for him. What could possibly go wrong? To make sure that she isn't too flighty, and prove she's not after his money, Edgar convinces her that he doesn't love her and waits to see how she reacts. Camilla doesn't realise that this is a manipulative test, and so is extremely upset that the man she is in love with doesn't love her back. However, she is also determined to respect his decision and rejection, and to show him that she has heard and understood him. With impeccable timing, they have a conversation about this just before they go on a group boat trip, so Camilla has to try to work out what to do while surrounded by other people. She really doesn't want to look like she's despairing because that would be heavily frowned upon, partly because despair was seen as a kind of criticism of God, and partly because she's not supposed to be into Edgar in the first place so she shouldn't be completely cut up about this. Because she respects his rejection, she wants him to see her doing the work of moving on from the heartbreak she's feeling, and so she seeks out company on the boat rather than staying by herself. She chooses to socialise with Lord Valhurst, an older gentleman, rather than the younger men, because his age makes her see him as a chaperone figure. Therefore, in her own mind, her behaviour demonstrates her moral character by showing that she isn't pining, but also isn't flirting with anyone else.

What Camilla has failed to realise is that Lord Valhurst does not think he's too old for her. He's convinced that because she's paying him attention, she's flirting with him. (He's also jealous of the fact that a lot of the older men on the boat have young wives, and thinks this seems like a great thing to get in on.) He proposes, which is something of a shock to Camilla, and with perfect narrative timing, Edgar walks past while she's politely turning the old man down.

> O! happy moment! thought she; he must have heard enough of what was passed to know me, at least, to be disinterested! he must see, now, that it was himself, not his situation in life, I was so prompt in accepting – and if again he manifests the same preference, I may receive it with more frankness than ever, for he will see my whole heart, sincerely, singly, inviolably his own![4]

Camilla is overjoyed, as she believes that Edgar will see that she is not simply interested in money. After all, if she was then she would have no reason to refuse Valhurst, since he's also rich. She concludes that Edgar must understand that she wanted to marry him because she loved him, and feels overjoyed at the fact that she's proved this. Even if he doesn't love her, at least he knows that her feelings all come from a genuine place. She spends the rest of the excursion 'with a renovation of animal spirits, so high, so lively, and so buoyant'.[5] As far as Camilla is concerned, everything is going as well as it could.

Edgar, however, reads the situation entirely differently. He saw her choosing the company of a wealthy older man over the other poorer young people present, and also assumes that her paying Valhurst attention (read: chatting) is a form of flirting. Had Camilla accepted Valhurst, he would have been unhappy because he'd have his evidence that she was only in it for the money, but because he thought she was inviting the proposal by her supposed flirting, he manages to also be unhappy with her refusal:

> Is this, thought he, Camilla? Has she wilfully fascinated this old man seriously to win him, and has she won him but to triumph in the vanity of her conquest? How is her delicacy perverted! what is become of her sensibility? Is this the artless Camilla? modest as she was gay, docile as she was spirited, gentle as she was intelligent? O how altered! how gone![6]

Edgar is disgusted, assuming that Camilla is playing with Valhurst to stroke her own ego.[7] This scenario is typical of the novel's misunderstandings; Camilla attempts to behave in a way that shows her morality, and Edgar reads it as proof that she's immoral. Burney shows us – repeatedly – a big problem with constructing consent through interpreting behaviour: people often misread or misinterpret it, particularly when they have their own agendas. Burney describes the same kind of confirmation bias that Husak and Thomas did back in Chapter 3 when she writes that 'the fairest observers misconstrue all motives to action, where any received prepossession has found an hypothesis'.[8] Whatever Edgar's mentor thinks, Camilla isn't after money. She's well-off enough that she's never really had to think about it, but she's also not desperate to get more. She doesn't work, she doesn't go without, and she doesn't look for more than what she's given. She is not greedy, mercenary, or luxurious. This is a good thing in eighteenth-century terms, but ironically, it's also this that gets her into trouble. Though not raised in the same kind of farcical isolation as Ophelia in Fielding's novel, she has nonetheless been brought up in a bit of a bubble, and this ignorance causes her to get tangled up in difficulties which a more practical education would have avoided.

When Camilla leaves her uncle's home of Cleves to go into town with society lady Mrs Arlbery, her parents give her money for her expenses. To Camilla, this seems a vast amount. She can't imagine how she could possibly spend that much. But luckily, her opportunistic brother Lionel, who has more debts than he should, is ready and willing to take most of it off her hands before she leaves. Though Camilla tells him off for his spending – and his habit of leeching money off their uncle – she freely gives up her own personal resources. This is very generous, and also a mistake. What Camilla fails to appreciate is that she is going to need to *spend* money when she gets to town, in a way that she has never had to when living with her family. Now instead of a significant lump sum, all she has is the money in her purse. Not only that, but she doesn't understand what things actually cost, so she ends up spending her money much faster than she should. Mrs Arlbery, who is looking after her, likes to show off to the *ton* by overpaying for things. She pledges large sums of money everywhere she goes, because it makes her look rich and generous, and because other society people will see it. Unworldly Camilla, on the other hand, doesn't understand the society subtext – she thinks that's just the amount you pay. Though she's had lots of practice at saving money, she doesn't understand how to spend it. She finds herself burning through her limited resources, getting herself into the kind of trouble that would have been completely avoidable had she had better information.

Mistakes pile on to misunderstandings, and ultimately Camilla ends up in debt. It's not just because of Lionel and her copying of Mrs Arlbery – she also meets a Mrs Mittin, who takes it upon herself to spend a lot of money Camilla doesn't have because she believes Camilla is an heiress. And Camilla makes her own mistakes. At one point she decides to go to a ball because she thinks she'll see Edgar there, and it's vital that she speak to him. But to go to the ball means she needs a dress. Still, it's justified because she must see Edgar – she will just have the dress made as cheaply and economically as possible. She realises later that this was a bad idea, that even a cheap dress is a waste of money that she did not have. It's exactly the kind of impetuous decision Edgar would disapprove of. But the dress, which was procured by Mrs Mittin, ends up costing Camilla far more than she expected.[9] This is because, in multiple ways, Camilla does not know what things cost. It's not just a lack of awareness of the standard price of fabric. She quite literally doesn't know the prices she's paying for things, because Mrs Mittin is buying them on her behalf and won't tell her the actual costs. She just keeps assuring her that the items are extremely cheap.

Here we see again the dangers of misreading, as Camilla's idea of low-cost and Mrs Mittin's idea of what an heiress should consider low-cost are fundamentally different. Mrs Mittin sees Camilla behaving like Mrs Arlbery, putting down lots of money for things, and hears the rumours that she's her uncle's heiress. She judges from Camilla's behaviour that Camilla has a fortune – so she doesn't realise she's spending money that Camilla doesn't have, and Camilla is unaware of how much debt she is being drawn into. She believes people when they tell her that expensive items are bargains, or that these costs are what everyone pays. She has no idea what's expensive and what's cheap. When Mrs Mittin tells her that she can get a dress made for next to nothing, she thinks that legitimately means it's only going to cost a small amount, and she doesn't realise that that was never going to be the case. If she understood the costs of fabric and labour better, not only would she be able to estimate the cost of having a dress made, but she'd know that the one Mrs Mittin was buying for her was actually expensive. She'd be in a position to speak up. Camilla's not mercenary or worldly (as Edgar fears) – but because she has no idea how to spend money, she's financially illiterate. She finds herself getting embroiled further and further into the coils of debt and obligation as the novel progresses.

Getting into debt is different for Camilla than it is for her brother. While several of the young men in the novel look on accumulating debts almost as a signifier of masculinity, Camilla feels guilty and ashamed of her expenses.[10] Lionel, on the other hand, owes increasingly vast sums of money to the wealthy Sir Sedley Clarindel – far more than Camilla's comparatively minor debts – but rather than try to pay him back himself, he hatches a different plan. He brokers a marriage between Camilla and Sir Sedley without Camilla's knowledge. Much like Mr Harrel in *Cecilia*, he's effectively selling her to the baronet. This will make his current debts go away and will, he thinks, give him a wealthy bankroller for the rest of his life. He sees running up debts as something a gentleman does; he makes fun of the young men who budget, and happily gives his word that he's good for money he doesn't have on the assumption that other people will cover the debts for him. It's more ungentlemanly in his book not to spend than it is to scrounge money from his relatives. When she finds out what's actually going on, Camilla feels like she has no choice but to accept the baronet's hand in marriage. The amount of money he gave Lionel was so large that she cannot hope to pay it back herself, and she believes it was contingent on their wedding. By accepting the money, Lionel has as good as given her word of honour that she'll marry Sir Sedley, and although Camilla greatly resents her brother for effectively selling her, she still intends to follow through on the agreement. Her sense of honour is demonstrably greater than his.

It's clear from this plot sequence that Camilla understands the repercussions of debt, even if she doesn't know enough to keep herself out of it. This consciousness of consequence is what prevents her from telling her family about her debts early on – she is so very aware of how those debts are going to impact them, and she feels extremely guilty as a result. Each time she plans to tell them, something happens which makes it seem like an impossible time to add her own transgressions to the score. Each time she decides she can't add to their troubles. Unfortunately, this doesn't mean the debts go away. With no way to pay them off, Camilla signs an illegal and high-interest deal with a moneylender, which of course does not help matters.[11] This deal is something of a last resort; she can't earn anything, so she has no personal income, and though she confides in her sisters, they are unable to help either. None of the sisters have the means to generate money for themselves, demonstrating their paralysing dependence on male figures.[12] In the unmarried Lavinia's case, it's because she doesn't own anything valuable enough to sell. Eugenia, on the other hand, *does* have valuable items – but her husband blocks her ability to sell them or to access the money that was her inheritance. Indeed, the difficulty she has in getting a few pieces of jewellery to Camilla demonstrates just how much control it was possible for a husband to have over his wife's finances and personal life. Though the girls each theoretically get an allowance from their parents, Camilla spends most of the novel unable to access hers while she's in town. Once Lionel's enormous debts come to light, the family have to stop the allowances altogether. Lionel, in a very real way, spends his sisters' money before it can get to them, with the whole family paying for his lifestyle.

Careless Lionel, who racks up substantially more debt than his sister, is able to borrow on credit. Camilla, who has a far stronger notion of honouring contracts, must rely on the selling of material possessions. Here, much like *Cecilia*, we see Burney highlighting how the concept of a word of honour can be extended to male characters who don't deserve it, while the female characters are (at least most of the time) the ones with a stronger sense of honour, and the ones unable to make financial use of it.[13] But even though Camilla is honourable, she still finds herself in debt. Her parents know that she's moral, and they know that she's not extravagant, but by failing to educate her on what things cost and how to spend, they send her out into the world vulnerable. And that debt is more dangerous for her than for Lionel. Burney emphasises how restrictive and dangerous the financial situation was for women. Unable to generate an income, unable to control or access family accounts, they are limited to what they can physically put their hands on – unless given access or permission by a male relative. That lack of control is binding, whether it's because they don't understand how to manage their money in the first place, or because they're so dependent on others that they can't afford to run away.

This brings me back to Eugenia. There's a real sadness to her storyline, as Eugenia – the brightest and most moral of the sisters – gets trapped in a horrible situation by her honour and her ignorance of the world. She's taken advantage of by a deeply unpleasant man, and through her plotline Burney explores the idea that honour isn't compromised by breaking a promise when it has been manipulated or extorted from you. She also drives home the point we've been discussing above about the vulnerability that's created by a lack of knowledge. Specifically, by a lack of worldly knowledge – what we might call street smarts.

Injured as a child by a combination of smallpox and a see-saw accident, Eugenia is smaller than average, walks with a limp, and has significant scarring. Her uncle Sir Hugh feels responsible for this, and decides to make amends to Eugenia by making her his heir. His original plan was that Camilla, his favourite niece, would inherit the estate, but he's starkly aware that he has impacted Eugenia's life and damaged her future prospects. He figures that it's the least he can do. He also decides that she should marry his nephew and ward Clermont Lynmere. Because he believes that Clermont will be a great scholar, Sir Hugh arranges for Eugenia to be educated outside of the standard female curriculum so that she'll be a good companion for Clermont. Eugenia loves it. She is clever, well educated, and has a strong sense of morality. She's the one her sisters come to when they have a quandary. And while she turns out to be an excellent classicist, she never loses her footing in the real world – quite unlike her esteemed academic tutor. As a result, she is highly respected by the characters the novel is sympathetic to. She doesn't seem ignorant. Eugenia, however, has been deliberately raised to be completely unaware of the fact that fashionable Georgian society would find her looks and her disability ugly and shocking.

When Eugenia first goes out in public, she is completely unprepared for the way that people react to her. Her ignorance was supposed to be for her own good, but it doesn't protect Eugenia from painful knowledge half as much as it protects Sir Hugh from painful guilt.[14] To be treated as a spectacle – as a kind of monster – is deeply distressing and horrible, and Burney is absolutely highlighting the ableism in society here. But Eugenia's larger grievance is with the family who failed to prepare her for what she would experience, who misrepresented her situation to her, and who sent her out into that ableist world with no warning. Eugenia rebukes them for

> representing to me, that thousands resembled me! of assuring me I had nothing peculiar to myself, though I was so unlike all my family – of deluding me into utter ignorance of my unhappy defects, and then casting me, all unconscious and unprepared, into the wide world to hear them![15]

She tells her father off, mourns for the fact that she was robbed of the chance to compose herself beforehand. She accepts the awfulness of society, but is at her most vocal in criticising others when she tells her family that they harmed her when they ensured that her initiation came from the cruelty of strangers. She's more vocal about this than anything else that happens to her in the book – including her own abduction. And the fallout from this trial by social scorn is that she becomes deeply conscious of her appearance, believing that no one will ever love her romantically.

This ignorance doesn't just hurt Eugenia by leaving her unprepared for the *ton*'s verbal abuse – it makes her uniquely vulnerable to her abductor. Alphonso Bellamy (real name Nicholas Gwigg) is secretly tipped off that Eugenia is the heir to Sir Hugh's fortune, and decides to marry her to get his hands on the money. He's one of the only people outside of the family who knows that she's Sir Hugh's heir, after one of Lionel's jokes convinces people that Camilla is actually the heiress. The upshot of this is that Bellamy is intent on getting his hands on Eugenia's fortune, and since he's the only one who knows she's getting it, he's the only one pursuing her at all. He comes to the ball determined to make her like him, and after this ball, where she is subject to public mockery, she decides that she's unlovable. She doesn't want to see people because she doesn't want to see them react to her, doesn't want to be commented on. But she's already seen Bellamy before. *He* didn't act shocked by her. Her memory that 'though new, in some measure, to herself, she was not so to this gentleman' means that she talks to him at a time when she's keen to avoid everybody else.[16] He tells her he loves her. If anything, her new awareness that she isn't considered as attractive as her siblings makes her trust him even more, because she doesn't think he knows about her inheritance. '"Ah!" thought she, "I have rendered, little as I seem worthy of such power, I have rendered this amiable man miserable, though possibly, and probably, he is the only man in existence whom I could render happy!"'[17] He is the only one, she thinks, who will ever love her. The fact that he's attractive only adds to her surprise and feeling of gratitude.

If we compare Eugenia to Ophelia from the last chapter, we can see that things are a bit more complicated here. Like Ophelia, Eugenia doesn't know she's at risk, and she also doesn't understand why someone would mean her harm. However, where Ophelia is largely unprotected and alone, Eugenia is surrounded by family. Some of them – including Camilla – are aware of the danger she's in, and even warn her about it. But Eugenia is a victim of her own cleverness – her family is so used to her being knowledgeable that they don't notice, or don't consider, the areas where she's completely ignorant. They forget that she has very little experience of the world, or of the baser motivations of people. Just like Ophelia, Eugenia generally assumes that people are telling the truth and takes them at their word – so when she's being lied to by Bellamy, she has absolutely no chance of catching it.

Eugenia meets with Bellamy a second time. He has already proposed to her, and she has already rejected him, but her rejection letter was so polite and so full of gratitude that he takes it as a sign of encouragement. (To be strictly fair to Bellamy, even Eugenia's mother thinks it's encouraging when she reads it.)[18] Eugenia fails to communicate her rejection because she is so conscious of her obligation to be kind – she feels as though she owes Bellamy something for making him miserable, and he says he will be miserable if he doesn't marry her. When Lionel plays another one of his jokes – pretending an angry bull has got loose – Bellamy takes advantage of the moment and tries to run off with Eugenia. His plan is foiled, but Eugenia doesn't manage to figure out the scheme. Edgar, Camilla's love interest, is able to put the narrative of Bellamy's motivations together immediately, but Eugenia struggles much more, both with her fundamental belief in Bellamy's innocence, and her sense of obligation to him. Where Edgar sees impending abduction, Eugenia sees only concern for her safety.

Edgar decides that he needs to speak to Eugenia's parents, both about Bellamy and about how Eugenia's innocence is putting her in danger. He suggests warning her 'upon the danger she had probably escaped, and of which she seemed wholly unconscious'.[19] Eugenia's mother understands what's going on, but she thinks Edgar is worrying too much. She considers the scene as 'underserving the least serious alarm […] her lofty contempt of all low arts made her conclude her well-principled Eugenia as superior to their snares as their practice'. She thinks Eugenia is too smart to fall for what is, in effect, a confidence trick. Eugenia's father decides that it's better to keep her in the dark, and 'not to raise apprehensions that might disturb her composure, nor awaken ideas of which the termination must be doubtful'.[20] He doesn't want her to be worried or to grow unreasonably suspicious. So, because she's really clever and they wouldn't want her to get paranoid, Eugenia is left vulnerable and ignorant.

To his credit, Edgar does try again. When he discovers a second attempt to abduct her, Edgar ignores the wishes of their parents and presents both Eugenia and Camilla with his evidence. Edgar's proof is largely practical: Bellamy has a coach hidden nearby, with a driver paid to be on standby. He has contrived to get Eugenia alone. As readers, Burney encourages us to see this threat as valid.[21]

Camilla is also convinced. But, though Eugenia respects Edgar, she insists that this is 'a business on which he has no information' – a response that confuses Camilla. Still, Camilla tries again to make her sister see the danger she is in.[22]

> 'My dear Eugenia, I cannot at all understand you; but it seems clear to me that the arrival of Edgar has saved you from some dreadful violence.'
>
> 'You hurt me, Camilla, by this prejudice. From whom should I dread violence? from a man who – but too fatally for his peace – values me more than his life?'
>
> 'If I could be sure of his sincerity,' said Camilla, 'I should be the last to think ill of him: but reflect a little, at least, upon the risk that you have run; my dear Eugenia! there was a post-chaise in waiting, not twenty yards from where I stopt you!'
>
> 'Ah, you little know Bellamy! that chaise was only to convey him away; to convey him, Camilla, to an eternal banishment!'
>
> 'But why, then, had he prevailed with you to quit the park?'
>
> 'You will call me vain if I tell you.'
>
> 'No, I shall only think you kind and confidential.'
>
> 'Do me then the justice,' said Eugenia, blushing, 'to believe me as much surprised as yourself at his most unmerited passion: but he told me, that if I only cast my eyes upon the vehicle which was to part him from me for ever, it would not only make it less abhorrent to him, but probably prevent the loss of his senses.'
>
> 'My dear Eugenia,' said Camilla, half smiling, 'this is a violent passion, indeed, for so short an acquaintance!'
>
> 'I knew you would say that,' answered she, disconcerted; 'and it was just what I observed to him myself: but he satisfied me that the reason of his feelings being so impetuous was, that this was the first and only time he had ever been in love. – So handsome as he is! – what a choice for him to make!'[23]

There's a real sadness here. Burney is mixing the trope of the intelligent-but-unworldly girl who believes sentimental extremes (popular in books like Charlotte Lennox's hilarious earlier novel *The Female Quixote*) with the awkward fact that there are characters in this book who do genuinely act so extremely – but only towards the more conventionally attractive characters. Indiana Lynmere,

Camilla and Eugenia's cousin, is so beautiful that when her suitors make speeches about how overwhelming their love is, no one bats an eyelid.[24] (The real surprise comes when one suitor is so deeply in love that he also calls Indiana intelligent…) But in this conversation with Camilla, the elephant in the room is that Eugenia is the only one who believes that Bellamy could really feel this way about her. Camilla thinks it's far more likely that this man is scamming her sister than that he is madly in love with her – but that's also not something she can say out loud. It's worse, because now that Eugenia's aware that most of the *ton* society will find her unattractive, she sees this as a love she doesn't deserve and won't find again. The more unlikely the scenario, the more Eugenia sees it as proof of Bellamy's sincerity. And the fact that he's very handsome only serves to make her more grateful, and her sister more suspicious.

Eugenia is clearly attracted to Bellamy, and doesn't recognise the way her biases are affecting her judgement here. She wants Bellamy to be in love with her; a handsome and kind man who chooses her when he doesn't have to, even as the rest of the world turns away from her. She believes that this is the only love she will ever inspire, and so she finds it cruel of her sister to insist that it's faked. Camilla's warnings don't make Eugenia doubt Bellamy – the speech act fails to function. Because Eugenia believes Bellamy is telling the truth about being in love with her, she instead interprets warnings about him as a commentary on how she isn't worthy of inspiring his feelings. The attempts to warn her end up isolating her further from her family because they echo her own fear that he is too good for her.

In the end, Bellamy succeeds in abducting Eugenia. And he lies to her so successfully that she gets into his coach willingly, because she thinks he's going to take her to safety. Until, that is, it's too late:

> She had not the most remote suspicion of his design […] and then, in one quick and decided moment, she comprehended her situation, and made an attempt for her own deliverance – but he prevented her from being heard. – And the scenes that followed she declined

> relating. Yet, what she would not recount, she could not, to the questions of her Father, deny, that force, from that moment, was used, to repel all her efforts for obtaining help and to remove her into a chaise.[25]

I find the lack of detail here really moving. Eugenia 'declined relating' the specifics of what happened, which tells us a lot about the effect they had on her, and speaks to the way trauma victims often find it painful and difficult to describe or explain what has been done to them. It shows that this has had a lasting impact on her, since she's relating these events some time after they happened but still struggles to speak about them. It also means that the validity of her struggle is not up for debate. You can't question whether she resisted this enough, or whether any of her behaviour could be seen as inviting it. By restricting details, Burney invites the reader to fill in the blanks with whatever they would characterise as sufficient force, sufficient violence. The discussion is moved beyond the question of female behaviour. But this blankness also refuses to excuse Bellamy from any kind or level of force, making Eugenia's continued attachment to him even more horrible: 'She theh briefly narrated, that though violence was used to silence her at every place where she sought to be rescued, every interval was employed, by Bellamy, in the humblest supplications for her pardon, and most passionate protestations of regard.'[26]

It's clear just how much this kind of manipulation affects a character as principled and as innocent as Eugenia. Throughout all of this, she believes that Bellamy is doing it because he's so in love with her – not because he wants to steal her money. Because she believes in his passion, she believes that she is causing him pain. As readers, we know that Bellamy's lying to her, and that only makes it worse. We can see Eugenia desperately trying to do right by this man, feeling guilty about making him feel bad, while he lies to her and hurts her and manipulates her morality to make his abduction of her easier. She feels guilty, and as though she has an obligation to heal the pain her rejection is causing – the pain she sees herself as responsible for – and this stops her from being able to take action to try to safeguard herself, even after the fact. Bellamy needs to marry Eugenia in order legally to take control of her fortune. He understands Eugenia really well, and so he tells her he'll kill himself, knowing that she will agree to marry him in order to prevent this. He knows that once she gives her word, she sticks to it – sees herself as bound to it – and so he can use any promise he extracts from her like a snare:

> Instantly he lifted up his pistol, and calling out; 'Forgive then, O hard-hearted Eugenia, my uncontrollable passion, and shed a tear over the corpse I am going to prostrate at your feet!' was pointing it to his temple, when, overcome with horror, she caught his arm, exclaiming; 'Ah! stop! I consent to what you please!' It was in vain she strove afterwards to retract; one scene followed another, till he had bound her by all she herself held sacred, to rescue him from suicide, by consenting to the union. He found a person who performed the marriage ceremony on the minute of her quitting the chaise. She uttered not one word; she was passive, scared, and scarce alive; but resisted not the eventful ring […]
>
> When Mr Tyrold had heard her history, abhorrence of such barbarous force, and detestation of such foul play upon the ingenuous credulity of her nature, made him insist, yet more strongly, upon taking legal measures for procuring an immediate separation, and subsequent punishment; but the reiterated vows with which, since the ceremony, he had bound her to himself, so forcibly awed the strict conscientiousness of her principles, that no representations could absolve her opinion of what she now held her duty; and while she confessed her unhappiness at a connection formed by such cruel means, she conjured him not to encrease [*sic*] it, by rendering her, in her own estimation, perjured.[27]

The power and tension of this storyline is that Eugenia is so moral, and so intelligent, and yet falls victim to this scheme – and refuses to free herself, even though she has a perfect right to.[28] Even though she's smart and educated, she ends up trapped. We can see here that she verbalised both consent and refusal before the ceremony, but that her expressions of consent are clearly forced.

They are not recognised as binding by Camilla, by Edgar, by her parents, or even by the novel's depiction of the law. Eugenia does not actually speak at the wedding itself ('she uttered not one word'), which was a legal requirement at the time the novel was written, but Eugenia appears to be operating on an earlier understanding of marriage where just expressing the intention to marry is binding in and of itself.[29] Eugenia's insistence on sticking to her word, despite the fact that she was coerced, demonstrates perhaps more clearly than an essay on her rights just how important it is to recognise when consent is forced. Burney positions us with Camilla; wanting Eugenia, with all her brains and cleverness, to understand that she does not need to stay with Bellamy, that she would not be betraying her morality if she were to dissolve the marriage, that she is not to blame for her situation.[30] In doing this, Burney also positions her readers on the side of meaningful consent. She emphasises clearly that there is no value or validity to consent obtained at gunpoint. And in making those readers so frustrated with Eugenia's viewpoint, she encourages them to apply that awareness and that thinking to their own lives.

6
Evelina, or The Value of Virginity

> [T]he spectacle of imminent and outrageous female suffering may not be the unthinkable crime which chivalric sentimentality forestalls, but rather the one-thing-needful to solicit male tears and the virtues that supposedly flow with them.
>
> – Claudia Johnson[1]

> In her day, a woman's safety from humiliation depended not on her own worth but on the solvency and status of her parents, her ingenuity in preventing herself from being compromised or jilted, and her success in disclaiming strength of intellect and emotion.
>
> – Rebecca West[2]

> I walked from place to place, without knowing which way to turn, or whither I went. Every other moment, I was spoken to by some bold and unfeeling man, to whom my distress, which, I think must be very apparent, only furnished a pretence for impertinent witticisms or free gallantry.
>
> – Frances Burney, *Evelina*[3]

Across these novels there is a spectre of sexual violence, so prevalent that it frequently goes unsaid. Reading them centuries later, it's something that can go under the radar, especially if we're more used to seeing the period through the lens of a beautiful glossy costume drama. I think we're more aware of danger with books from our own time, where we recognise the cues to what is threatening and know when things are out of the ordinary. There are places, though, where that sexual threat becomes visible, and in those moments we also get a sense of how constant it actually is in these novels. This threat is bound up with the idea of virginity.

'Innocence', 'virginity', and 'virtue' were often used synonymously in the eighteenth century. Virginity, under the headings of chastity and modesty, is characterised as an intrinsic virtue for women; a part of themselves that they must maintain in order to have value. But if this were the entirety of the case then spinsters, who successfully preserve their 'virtue' for their entire lives, ought to be regarded as models of virtue or innocence. Instead, unmarried women are the subject of social scorn (the very term 'spinster' is in itself not a particularly flattering nickname), which tells us that what is considered important is not the preservation of innocence in the abstract, but the preservation of innocence from a threat. Innocence is fundamentally conceptualised as a thing designed to be lost; it is of great importance to the young woman, but must be surrendered or given to her husband in order to avoid it becoming a burden. This innocence is a substance or concept lost in the transference – it neither becomes a part of the husband, nor exists after sexual consummation. The same transfer technically occurs outside marriage, but then the innocence is actively imagined as lost or taken, rather than given or transferred. It's not something that is thought about as a mutual exchange, because male virginity isn't seen in the same way. You don't get endless conduct manuals telling young eighteenth-century men to preserve their virtue for their wives…

This creates a state where innocence-as-virginity is an intrinsic virtue for women, but exists for men only as a contextual virtue. Virginity derives much of its social importance from its practical benefits; the implication that a husband can be sure that any children his wife has are his.[4] It's seen as a valuable state before marriage, but becomes the subject of scorn once the woman stops being seen as marriageable. Therefore, virginity – innocence – is a desirable quality only when the woman herself is seen as desirable. There is a twofold fallout to this: innocence is only socially relevant when it relates to potential wives; and as a result, innocence becomes a marker of privilege which indicates social status.

If the only innocence that is relevant is that which relates to a potential wife, then the innocence of lower-class women is irrelevant to the gentlemen class who are focused on in these courtship novels.[5] Because those women (generally) cannot aspire to be the wives of gentlemen, their innocence does not have any practical purpose or benefit to those gentlemen, and can be dismissed by middle- or upper-class men who want sex without 'ruining' women of their own class (though, of course, this also happened).[6] By extension, this means that a woman who has preserved her innocence can be seen as protected, either by her class, her family, her friends, or similar; she is one whom people have chosen not to violate. Marrying a woman of this type carries some assurance of social approbation. An appropriate wife is one whom society has allowed to maintain her virginity. This is where the spinster caveat comes into play – the woman must be seen as desirable for the innocence to convey this message. In other words, whether she's beautiful, well connected, or rich, the woman must be someone who men are interested – or seen as interested – in. As soon as society decides that men aren't interested in a woman, her innocence becomes a marker of the fact that she was not considered desirable enough.

So this where we come to: innocence requires a threat to itself in order to exist as a socially valuable quality. Virginity is desirable when it's under threat, but not afterwards. I'm not saying that there are no other values to it – both people and characters would have argued for its importance on religious grounds – but the men in these books (and the real men raping their servants) don't take that into consideration in their actions. In thinking about ideas relating to behavioural consent, we've talked about having to consider social codes of behaviour – what particular actions are understood to mean, or how they are viewed. The question here therefore is not 'How did the eighteenth century understand innocence?', and nor is it a matter of understanding the religious justification for virginity as a moral requirement in unmarried women. Instead, we need to consider the social coding of these actions, which include justifications for the rape of lower-class women on the basis of their not having anything to lose. Their virginity is viewed as ideologically meaningless by the dominant groups in these novels. They will not be involved in breeding the next generation of heirs. They represent a lesser financial opportunity. This view of the value of virginity intersects with the way rape was thought about for many years: as a property crime or burglary, rather than a violent or sexual crime. The harm caused by the violent act was represented as the damage done to a good, and when that good has less financial value, there is understood to be less harm.[7] Because a virgin bride was seen as important, a raped virgin was understood to have lost something more than a raped woman with sexual experience – not just the abstract state of virginity, but the practical reduction of her marriage prospects.

Even when it is not explicitly stated, the heroines of these courtship novels move through the world in the constant shadow of sexual threat (even when, like Ophelia, they don't realise it). Let's take a scene from Frances Burney's best-known novel, *Evelina, or the History of a Young Lady's Entrance into the World* (1778). The important things to know for this example are that Evelina is an orphan who is illegitimate, which means that her social standing is shakier than that of many of our other heroines. She's travelling in a carriage with her grandmother, Madame Duval, who is not a very likeable character (most of the characters in *Evelina* are deliberately unlikeable). Some of the men in the novel *also* don't find Madame Duval particularly likeable, and they have decided to play a hilarious trick on her by pretending to be highwaymen and holding up the carriage. Evelina gets advance warning from them that she will be in no danger, but Madame Duval, as the object of the scheme, receives no such reassurance. Evelina is initially too anxious about the potential consequences to tell her grandmother that the whole situation has been set up to scare her – though 'it was with the utmost difficulty I forbore to acquaint her that she was imposed upon; but the mutual fear of the Captain's resentment to me, and of her own to him, neither of which would have any moderation, deterred me'.[8] Evelina's fear of dealing with the 'resentment' of Captain Mirvan – something of a nemesis to Madame Duval – is enough to prevent her from giving relief to her grandmother – but crucially here, this is impacted by the fact that she does not believe that her grandmother is in danger.

Though Evelina wants to reassure her grandmother and tell her that she is safe, it is precisely *because* she believes that she is safe that she is able to keep quiet. When the 'robbers' appear, Evelina decides to break her silence, but she's too late:

> Here the chariot was stopped, by two men in masks, who, at each side, put in their hands, as if for our purses. Madame Duval sunk to the bottom of the chariot and implored their mercy. I shrieked involuntarily, although prepared for the attack: one of them held me fast, while the other tore Madam Duval out of the carriage, in spite of her cries, threats, and resistance.[9]

But what would warning her grandmother have done? The only difference between this attack and a 'real' one is that Evelina knows it's going to happen, and has been told that she'll be safe. The actual events are the same, and even with the promise she has been given (which does not, in reality, guarantee her safety), Evelina is still shocked and is still 'really frightened and trembled exceedingly'.[10] Burney highlights that the difference between the gentlemen and actual robbers is notional at best, as we watch Evelina jump through hoops in her own head to explain them as distinct ideas even when their actions entirely overlap. Evelina is not prepared to question what it would mean if gentlemen could be 'real' robbers; she clings to a belief that nobility is a personal quality as well as a rank. Burney allows the hollowness of this view to shine through.

The two robbers (who are actually Evelina's unwelcome suitor Sir Clement Willoughby and his friend) eventually flee, and Evelina is able to go to her grandmother. Over the course of the not-a-real-robbery, Madame Duval has been dragged from the carriage, beaten, shaken, thrown into a ditch, tied to a tree by her feet, and had her cap dragged off and her wig destroyed. Evelina 'could not forgive myself for having passively suffered the deception',[11] but though she clearly feels pity for Madame Duval, she also finds humour in the situation. Her grandmother looks ridiculous, and as she knows the whole thing was a joke, Evelina goes so far as to think that her grandmother is over-reacting. On the other hand, when Sir Clement took time out of the robbery and ditch-throwing to sit in the carriage and flirt with Evelina, she felt anxious and uncomfortable, and didn't find it remotely funny.

Evelina persists in making the distinction between the men who attacked them and 'real robbers', despite the fact that Madame Duval suffers real harm. Her primary concerns after the event are not for her grandmother, but with propriety:

> Her dress was in such disorder, that I was quite sorry to have her figure exposed to the servants, who all of them, in imitation of their master, hold her in derision: however, the disgrace was unavoidable [...] her face was really horrible, for the pomatum and powder from her head, and the dust from the road, were quite *pasted* on her skin by her tears, which, with her *rouge*, made so frightful a mixture, that she hardly looked human.[12]

The word 'figure' here carries the double meaning of both the overall person of Madame Duval, and of her semi-naked body specifically, given the state of disarray Evelina goes on to describe. There is a great deal of violence in this episode, though it is figured as comic – *Evelina* as a novel is full of moments of comedy which rely heavily on violent components.[13] But Evelina's desire to get her grandmother into the carriage does not stem from anxiety about her injuries or her state, but the disgrace of her being seen by the servants. When she has had the full story related to her, 'this narrative almost compelled me to laugh, yet I was really irritated with the Captain, for carrying his love of tormenting, – *sport*, he calls it, – to such barbarous and unjustifiable extremes'.[14] Her unsympathetic description of Madame Duval makes special reference to the state of her grandmother's *rouge*, drawing an unspoken contrast with the fact that as a young and beautiful (and modest) woman, Evelina herself does not wear any.[15] The *rouge* signifies Madame Duval's age and sexual experience, and highlights her Frenchness (with all its attendant stereotypes) in contrast to Evelina's Englishness (Evelina, we know from earlier in the novel, does not wear rouge, and is apparently more attractive because of it).

The key point in this encounter is that Evelina does not perceive her grandmother to be in danger. That is what allows her to view the circumstance as a practical joke – albeit one that has gone too far. But if we consider what has actually occurred, the ridiculous Madame Duval has been exposed to violence. She has suffered humiliation, injury, and damage to property. Though she has not had her purse stolen, she has suffered a significant financial loss since her entire wardrobe, including her wig, is damaged – this will take significant money and time to replace. So, this incident raises the question: what would it have taken for the attack to have constituted actual danger? I believe it is the very thing that makes Evelina scared for herself, even though she has been expecting the men on the road: the fear of a sexual threat. Evelina sees Madame Duval as being too old to be at risk of sexual assault, and therefore thinks she has nothing to fear (Madame Duval would not agree with her assessment). Evelina knows that the supposed 'joke' will not result in Madame Duval's death, and so sees the violence as being in the spirit of '*sport*' rather than attack. Through the treatment of Madame Duval we see the contrast to Evelina's own position, where the threat to her innocence is read as a constant.

Having said that the novel usually treats violence with comedy, it takes moments of sexual threat seriously. Take Evelina's experiences in the long alleys of Vauxhall Gardens (for *Bridgerton* fans, these are the Dark Walks that Daphne runs into trouble in during Season 1). This scene also includes laughter, but where the carriage scene made Evelina laugh, here the laughter is a threat. The joke is at

Evelina's expense – it is *sport* in multiple senses of the word this time – where her fear and perception of being hunted add to the male narrative of conquest and entertainment. Evelina has been brought to Vauxhall Gardens by the Branghton family. They're not her favourite people to spend time with, and Evelina's generally the smartest and most moral one in the room when she's with them. She finds herself walking through the long alleys at the instigation of the two Branghton daughters. Evelina follows them 'quite by compulsion', signposting to the reader that she does not share any personal blame for what happens next.[16] They encounter 'a large party of gentlemen, apparently very riotous', who proceed to encircle and surround them, stopping them from moving away.[17] The women scream, which makes the men laugh; in this instance, with the presence of a sexual threat, we are not on the side of the joke and are not sharing in the laughter. Both Evelina's fear and the dangers to her are clear.

One of the men, 'rudely, seizing hold of' Evelina, calls her a 'pretty little creature' and makes her feel 'terrified to death'. She ultimately struggles enough to break free of him and manages to run away.[18] However, as she attempts to escape, 'I was met by another party of men', and Evelina finds herself caught in the walkway between the two groups. One of the men in this second group 'placed himself so directly in my way, calling out, "Whither so fast, my love?" – that I could only have proceeded by running into his arms'. Evelina is now trapped.

> In a moment, both my hands, by different persons, were caught hold of; and one of them, in a most familiar manner, desired to accompany me in a race, when I ran next; while the rest of the party stood still and laughed.[19]

This incident has far less physical violence than the scene with Madame Duval and the carriage, but Burney is working here to create a sense of threat and panic rather than of humour. The pace is less measured, and Evelina herself finds with less and less space to describe the scene in between reporting the speech of the men. That there are multiple men touching her, leering, and laughing at her in this way is terrifying to her. It cannot even be viewed as being the actions of one specific group of individuals, since this is the second group to accost her, and even while she is being held, yet another man walks past 'and desired to be of the party'.[20] The danger, Burney makes clear, comes from men generally rather than any particular man.

When Evelina finally finds her voice and protests, she discovers that instead of freeing her, her voice renders her more desirable:

> 'Heaven and earth! What voice is that? – '
> 'The voice of the prettiest little actress I have seen this age,' answered one of my persecutors
> 'No, – no, – no, –' I *panted* out, 'I am no actress, – pray let me go, – pray let me pass –'[21]

This exchange is crucial – not only does Evelina find that her voice is the complete opposite of a deterrent, but it makes it clear why she finds herself in this predicament: Evelina is a young, unaccompanied woman walking in the long alleys of Vauxhall Gardens. Because of this, she is mistaken for an 'actress' or prostitute. This assumption of her station is based entirely on her behaviour (that is, being female and being in that location without an escort), and as the men feel that they have the right to treat particular classes of women in this way, they take no issue with harassing her. Once she has asked for help and is removed from these men, one of them actually threatens a duel – he 'vowed he would not give me up, for he had first right to me'.[22] The objectification here is clear – it's not just that this man feels that he has a right to her, but that he has right to first usage from that group. If order of use is in question, then the perception is clearly that the entire group has a right to her, simply as a result of her being where she is and who they think she is. Also telling is that Evelina buys into this class view; as a character with liminal social status, she cannot afford to risk people making this mistake about her, and it is more important for her to declare that she is not an actress than to argue that they should let her go (leaving the implication that this is appropriate treatment of lower-class women unchallenged).

Evelina is then recognised by the man who called her an actress, who turns out to be everybody's favourite fake robber Sir Clement. Evelina turns to him for help, and in theory is now safe, since she has been recognised and she's with a man who she knows. But the danger is not over when Evelina stops being seen as of a lower class than she is – her presence in the alleys is enough to signal consent to Sir Clement:

> And then I saw, what the perturbation of my mind had preventing my sooner noticing, that he had led me, though I know not how, into another of the dark alleys, instead of the place whither I meant to go.
>
> 'Good God!' I cried, 'where am I? – What way are you going? –'
>
> 'Where,' answered he, 'we shall be least observed.'
>
> Astonished at this speech, I stopped short, and declared I would go no further.
>
> 'And why not, my angel?' again endeavouring to take my hand.
>
> My heart beat with resentment; I pushed him away from me with all my strength, and demanded how he dared treat me with such insolence?
>
> 'Insolence!' repeated he.
>
> 'Yes, Sir Clement, *insolence*; from you, who know me, I had a claim for protection, – not to such treatment as this.'
>
> 'By Heaven,' cried he with warmth, 'you distract me, – why, tell me, – why do I see you here? – Is this the place for Miss Anville? – these dark walks! – no party! – no companion! – by all that's good, I can scarce believe my senses!'[23]

Here we are given another reminder that Evelina is not to blame for her location (just in case we were going to hold that against her). We have a situation where Sir Clement is assuming behavioural consent from actions that Evelina did not choose to take.[24]

Although Burney doesn't explicitly spell out what Sir Clement is meaning to do, the sexual intention is clear from the fact that he is seeking a place where they cannot be observed. They are already alone in the dark, already in close proximity, already without a chaperone. There is no reason to seek a more secluded place unless he wants to increase the familiarity of his behaviour and minimise the chances of interruption while doing it. How far he intends to go is delicately uncertain – and while this is typical of eighteenth-century euphemistic politeness, it also allows the reader to understand his intention without being given specifics of degree to factor in to a potential defence of his actions. (If we know he was only intending to kiss her, would that change how scared we think Evelina should be? The point is the threat, not the precise specifics of what that would look like.) He also clearly believes that Evelina is up for this until she calls him '*insolent*', as he doesn't hide what he is trying to do. Evelina's defence of herself is more effective here than it was against the group, and I would argue that is in large part due to the fact that she is no longer being perceived as an actress, but as 'herself'.[25] Here, when she rebukes Sir Clement, she does not tell him off for behaving in this way to a woman, or to a lady (a title which Evelina might shy away from claiming, given her liminal status). Instead, she complains that as they know each other, she is deserving of his protection – both because he knows her as an individual and therefore should treat her well, and because he knows that she mixes in a society that would not be happy about her being used in this way. She is asserting that she has protection – she is potential wife material, and therefore her innocence is valuable.

Sir Clement's response is perhaps the most interesting aspect of this scene. He collects himself, but instead of apologising (which he does later, sort of), he launches into a series of questions about what Evelina is doing in the long alleys by herself in the first place. Instead of acknowledging his behaviour at once, he interrogates her for having created his misunderstanding – she is not the sort of person who ought to be in this situation, he says, almost asking to be excused on the grounds that he is just treating her as he would treat any other woman in this situation. A woman in this location, he assumes, must be seeking an encounter. For Sir Clement, a man we are not supposed to agree with, location is consent. He is not the only one. Look at the response of the Branghton brother when Evelina gets back and he hears that his sisters are still in the walks: 'pray, what had you to do in the long alleys? why, to be sure, you must all of you have had a mind to be affronted.'[26] Why were you there if you did not want it to happen?

Both here and in their tête-à-tête during the carriage robbery, Evelina is worried about a sexual threat. In the long alleys the threat is more explicit. It comes from men generally – strangers whom she never identifies, as well as the man she recognises. Every man in that location saw her presence there as invitation enough. To walk around in a body that can be seen as on offer depending on where you happen to be is to walk around perpetually under threat. Especially if you don't always have control over where you go. In the carriage Evelina knew that she wasn't going to be robbed, wasn't going to be beaten, wasn't going to be tied up and thrown in a ditch. She knew it with enough confidence that she could laugh at it happening to her grandmother. But she was still scared of Sir Clement when he sat and flirted with her. As with Ophelia's abduction earlier in this book, we can see exactly what Evelina is afraid of, and Burney makes it clear by pointedly not saying it. These are two instances where the sexual nature of the threat breaks through, but Evelina's desirability and vulnerability are clear – and remain throughout the novel.

Eventually, Sir Clement remembers himself enough to launch into a series of extravagant apologies. However, he nonetheless keeps demanding an explanation from Evelina for how and why she found herself in the position to be harassed. Once he has taken her back to her party, and realises that it's the vulgar Branghton family and not the refined Mirvans who typically accompany her, 'he seems disposed to think that the alteration in my companions authorises an alteration in his manners'.[27] Sir Clement is a character whose view of female bodily autonomy and right to self-interest is directly proportional to the class and financial value of the woman in question; it is equally clear that Burney does not intend us to see this view favourably. The emphasis here is that Evelina does not deserve the treatment she receives, and neither her location, her social status, nor the desirability of her innocence are forms of consent to it.

Innocence is a complicated term, bleeding between the different meanings attached to it: innocence as virginity; as a moral state defined by your actions or your intentions; as a state without knowledge of the world (or at least its baser parts). But 'too innocent' has another meaning, one which highlights the final and perhaps most significant issue with behavioural consent raised by these authors. Being 'too innocent' can imply that you're fabricating that innocence, because no real person is that moral, that naïve, or that unknowing. Innocence gets turned into a performative quality, something adopted to display desirable feminine characteristics. If you are performing something to seem desirable, then the thing you're performing becomes part of what you could call a seduction strategy. But if the innocent response to sexualised advances is to reject them (assuming you've recognised them in the first place), then what gets socially coded as a seduction strategy is the rejection itself. Which leads you into a place where someone saying no is playing hard to get, so as not to look easy. Refusal itself is a mark of acceptance.

This idea of people being 'too innocent' crops up across the courtship genre. Maria Edgeworth, one of the most highly regarded novelists of the day (and the author Jane Austen references next to Frances Burney when she lists great novels in *Northanger Abbey*), makes a real focus of this in her novel *Belinda* (1801). The novel is very funny, and a part of that humour comes from the fact that the heroine Belinda – a very innocent girl – has an aunt known for matchmaking and husband hunting. Because that's all that society really knows about Belinda, they assume she'll be exactly the same as her scheming aunt (spoiler: she is not). As a result of her aunt's reputation, their social circle interprets everything Belinda does as deliberately designed to catch a man – no one thinks that she's acting demurely because she's an innocent, they think it must be a kind of flirtation. Whatever she does is interpreted as making a play for the male characters, so there's no behaviour available to her which isn't read as invitational behaviour. They see everything she does through the lens of it being designed to attract men. To go back to Burney's words from *Camilla*, 'the fairest observers misconstrue all motives to action, where any received prepossession has found an hypothesis'.[28] In this kind of scenario, behavioural consent becomes very dangerous, because if someone's working hypothesis is that you want them, willingness can be assumed from any action up to and including refusal. So not only is there is no action that gets your refusal recognised, but that very refusal can be used as evidence that you are actually inviting the interaction that you are trying to stop.[29] To be female in this social context *is* to have your behaviour read as consent.[30]

It wasn't just in novels that people showed the obvious dangers of this. Writing in *A Vindication of the Rights of Woman* in 1792, Mary Wollstonecraft raised concerns about the way she saw innocent behaviour getting coded as sexual. Academic Jenny Davidson describes how Wollstonecraft 'is even more disgusted by the consensus that sexual modesty is one of the arts of seduction', drawing attention to the ways in which this type of behaviour is given a sexual subtext, and taking issue with the (generally male) writers who promoted this.[31] Wollstonecraft's engagement with texts that acted like conduct manuals – those guides to feminine behaviour – actually emphasises the way in which female behaviour is written about as designed – specifically designed – to appeal to men, even when the desirable behaviour is supposed to appear 'natural'. Wollstonecraft quotes philosopher Jean-Jacques Rousseau in the *Vindication*, highlighting his description of his idealised woman Sophia:

> 'Her dress is extremely modest in appearance, and yet very coquettish in fact: she does not make a display of her charms, she conceals them; but in concealing them, she knows how to affect your imagination. Everyone who sees her will say, There is a modest and discreet girl; but while you are near her, your eyes and affections wander all over her person, so that you cannot withdraw them; and you would conclude, that every part of her dress, simple as it seems, was only put in its proper place in order to be taken to pieces by the imagination.'[32]

Here, we see non-sexual dress being sexualised precisely because (as with innocence requiring a threat to itself to be valuable) the act of concealment becomes read as an invitation to reveal. If dressing in a manner that is 'simple' and 'modest in appearance' invites being 'taken to pieces' in Rousseau's mind, the alternative is to reveal, to 'make a display of her charms' – achieving the same ends with less use of the imagination. It's not just the physicality of a woman's body which is being described as appealing here – a big part of the sexual appeal is the need to overcome obstacles in order to access that body.

This becomes more apparent in Wollstonecraft's discussion of Fordyce's *Sermons* (1766), another well-known text which was intended to provide moral instruction to young ladies. (Mr Collins reads it to the Bennet sisters in *Pride and Prejudice*. The fact that it's the reading choice of such an obnoxious man tells you everything you need to know about it.) She takes issue with a particular paragraph which emphasises the idea that women's appeal comes from their vulnerability to men:

> 'He [God] makes Nature address man. "Behold these smiling innocents, whom I have graced with my fairest gifts, and committed to your protection; behold them with love and respect; treat them with tenderness and honour. They are timid and want to be defended. They are frail; oh, do not take advantage of their weakness!

> Let their fears and blushes endear them. Let their confidence in you never be abused. But is it possible, that any of you can be such barbarians, so supremely wicked, as to abuse it? Can you find it in your hearts to despoil the gentle, trusting creatures of their treasure, or do anything to strip them of their native robe of virtue?'''[33]

One thing to notice in this (very sentimental) passage is that it shows rape as entirely within male control. There is no suggestion that the women are able to employ any strategy to defend themselves, other than seeming weak enough to inspire pity and care. But the language here is problematically erotic – returning again to what Laurie Penny would describe more than a century later as 'the erotics of "no"'.[34] It is the 'fears' of women that make them beloved, the 'blushes' – an action supposed to come as a result of shame – that are endearing. Putting fear and blushing next to each other like this also encourages the reader to relate them, implying both that there's an element of danger to the scenario generating the blush, and that there's something sexual going on.[35] The women of this passage are 'smiling innocents' and 'gentle, trusting creatures', neither description indicative of much – if any – capacity for thought, placing them into the role not just of children, but of pets.

Even the final lines here, which figure virginity as a 'treasure' (and treasure is always to be sought, hunted, and won), use the loaded metaphor of stripping a woman naked ('strip them of their native robe of virtue'), which not only brings the idea of literally stripping women to mind, but further locates female virtue within the domain of the sexualised body. As Wollstonecraft says, 'It would almost provoke a smile of contempt if the vain absurdities of man did not strike us on all sides, to observe how eager men are to degrade the sex from whom they pretend to receive the chief pleasure of life.'[36] Wollstonecraft critiques the figuring of chastity as a specifically female virtue, and goes on to highlight the way in which male treatment of women as objects demonstrates a lack of respect for women as people. She argues that unless women are educated properly – including encouraging virtues that are general, and not based on gendered identity – society will keep them in a form of ideological and political bondage. As Wollstonecraft puts it, 'all women are to be levelled, by meekness and docility, into one character of yielding softness and gentle compliance'.[37]

I opened this book by reflecting on how I came to write it. These last years have been loud in relation to sexual assault, but it has also become increasingly obvious that a backlash is developing against this. Newspaper headlines ask whether #MeToo has gone too far. Most dangerously, the internet, always under-understood, has become a tool of radicalisation.[38] Victims of sexual violence are more vocal about what we have suffered, but as we demand greater accountability, there are those pushing back. As the ever-wonderful Sara Ahmed puts it, 'to expose a problem is to pose a problem'.[39] Our speaking out is posing a problem.

In her book *Men Who Hate Women*, Laura Bates talks at length about the groups that make up what is colloquially known as the 'alt-right' – incels, Pick Up Artists (or PUAs), Men Going Their Own Way (also known as MGTOW – a group that supports male separatism to free them from the oppression of what they see as a female-centric society), to name a few.[40] One thing she notes is how quickly a perceived threat from a woman today results in threats of specifically sexual violence. These perceived threats include women holding higher-paying jobs than men, or wanting to work, or expressing an opinion publicly as an expert. And one reason why the resultant vitriol centres around the area of sexual violence is that if you view women as bodies designed and designated to fulfil your sexual needs, then the norm that is being violated is inherently a sexual one. A woman working becomes perceived as a threat to male sexuality or virility, making the mental gymnastics of jumping from 'a woman getting a promotion' to 'a woman deserving to be raped' marginally easier to follow (though no easier to agree with).[41] More than that, a woman refusing a man who believes that she owes him sex becomes a woman disrupting the 'natural order of things'.

And while this may sound hyperbolic, I refer you to the killings at Santa Barbara University, when Elliot Rodger took a gun to a sorority because the women in it did not provide him with the sex that he felt he was owed. Elliot Rodger, known in online circles as 'The Supreme Gentleman', and an aspirational figure.

I refer you to the fact that Chanel Miller, who we talked about earlier, had to make her recommendations about what should happen to her rapist in the wake of this shooting. A shooting that occurred at her university while her case was going through the courts. She writes that she was terrified that if Turner did not feel that he had a way out, there was a risk that he might also pick up a gun.[42] Not because she knew him personally – she didn't – but because she had hidden in her room waiting for an all-clear to sound while Rodger shot her fellow students. She couldn't know that Turner wouldn't do this. She felt she had to make recommendations that made it clear to him that he had another option.

I refer you to Anita Sarkeesian, whose video essay series on female representation in video games upset men online so much that they doxed her (leaking her home address, among other things), made an online game to beat her up, and threatened her with rape, with bombs.[43] I could very easily go on.

The level of sexual violence in our world today is terrifying. And perhaps it seems that it has no place in a book on eighteenth-century novels. But I hope I have shown that this is not the case. The overwhelming threat made to women who exist loudly and publicly is one of rape. The more marginalised that woman is – be she disabled, a person of colour, trans, working-class, or any combination – the greater the threat to her. And this in turn is part of an ideology which sees women as beings who lack the capacity to think as well as cishet men, to do jobs as well as cishet men, or indeed to do anything as well as cishet men, other than be soft and receptive. This ideology is grafted on to a mythic idea of The Past – Rodger's title of Supreme *Gentleman* is a reminder of exactly what kind of past is being imagined here. The eighteenth century, with its *femme couvert* and its consent at the point of marriage and its limitations on female labour, is one of the pasts being appropriated by these groups as a state of existence to return to.[44] When Men Were Men and Women Were Women (and when queer people, black people, disabled people, can be imagined out of existence; one consequence of the erasure and suppression of their narratives and voices). It's an imaginary past, but one that is used to justify real violence.

PART III

VIOLENCE

7
Anon., or The Context of the Courtroom

> Then I looked at crime statistics and found that on average more than 2 women are killed every week by a current or former partner, that there is a call to the police every minute about domestic violence, and that a woman is raped every 6 minutes – adding up to more than 85,000 rapes and more than 400,000 sexual assaults per year. That 1 in 5 women is the victim of a sexual offence and 1 in 4 will experience domestic violence.
>
> – Laura Bates[1]

> to avoid so miserable and lasting Reproach I am of the Opinion That many honest virtuous women have suffered in this Manner and kept it Secret for fear of making their lives miserable
>
> – Anon.[2]

Most of this book thinks about rape and sexual violence as actions rather than as crimes, but in this chapter we're going to take a look at what was going on in eighteenth-century courtrooms. Much of what we'll talk about here is going to look very different from the novels. That's because the kinds of sexual assaults that made it to the courts are very limited and very specific. I will say up front that there is some content here that might be distressing: across this chapter, I will be talking about child abuse, describing physical violence, and quoting directly from the victims' testimonies. It's not easy reading, but I think it's worth talking about. This is the reality that our authors and their readers were living in, and these cases make clear why the courts would not have been a realistic option for most of them if they experienced rape. The records give us an idea of how extreme an attack had to be for it to be worth taking through the legal system, as well as the kinds of evidence that were needed. I invite you to keep in mind as we go through these cases that these names and numbers were all very real people. And as we respect their trauma, to note also how few of them there are, and how many absences there are where other victims are not.

The Old Bailey was one of the main courts in London where rape cases were tried, so I looked at the records of every rape case tried there over a fifty-year period (1752–1802). I wanted to get a snapshot of what kinds of things were happening in the courts – who was using them, how they talked about consent, whether there were any common factors between the cases which got Guilty verdicts – and I used a fantastic resource called the Old Bailey Proceedings to do it.[3] It's important to say that the Old Bailey Proceedings are not full transcripts of the trials: while everything in them was said at the trials, not everything that was said at the trials is in them. This is partly because the information was being published in newspapers, and people were worried that criminals would learn how to escape prosecution by reading about successful Not Guilty defences. Because they were for regular people to read, the proceedings also skip a lot of the detailed legal content, concentrating on the testimonies of those involved rather than the arguments made by their lawyers. They are regarded as 'probably the best accounts we shall ever have of what transpired in ordinary English criminal courts before the later eighteenth century'.[4] I'm going to spend the rest of this chapter talking about what I found in these cases, but you'll also find some visual representations of the data in the appendix.

The first thing you notice looking at this data is just how few people were actually using the legal system to bring sexual crimes to court. In our fifty-year window, only 135 defendants were tried for rape – an average of less than three a year. Of those 135, only

24 were found Guilty.[5] To put that into context against another serious crime, 404 defendants were tried for murder in the same period, with 284 found Guilty.[6] Almost exactly three times as many people were up on murder charges as were up on rape charges. Nearly twice as many people were convicted of murder as stood trial for rape. If we compare the convictions directly, the difference is even more stark: more than ten times as many people were convicted of murder as were convicted of rape. This means that while murder had an average conviction rate of 70%, rape's average conviction rate was only 18%. It is completely unrealistic to believe that the act of rape happened a total of 24 times over a fifty-year period within the bounds of the Old Bailey's jurisdiction in the densely populated capital city. The number of Guilty-verdict cases represents an unfeasibly low estimate of the number of rapes committed in this area at this time. Murder is not ten times as common an occurrence as rape.

If we look at what happened when capital punishment stopped being applied to rape cases in 1841, we can see further evidence that rape was under-reported. While the death penalty was in place, conviction rates for rape were as low as 5% in some decades; after 1840 they sit at around 50%.[7] If we compare our fifty-year window with the fifty years after capital punishment was removed, we can see a stark difference in both the conviction rates and the number of cases being brought to trial.[8] We go from 135 rape cases in 1752–1802 to 1,060 cases in 1841–91. That's almost an 800% increase.[9] If we look at murder cases again to see if this increase is comparable, we find that while the number of cases has increased, it's only by around 60%, and the conviction rate remains reasonably stable.[10] Rape is a crime that is known to be under-reported in every time period, resulting in something that scholars call the 'dark figure' – a term that represents the number of rapes actually happening in any particular period, rather than those that make it to court.[11] We cannot know what the dark figure is for our fifty-year window, but we can get an idea by looking at the numbers for other serious violent crimes, and the way that the number of cases increased once the death penalty was removed.

We can still see trends in the cases the Old Bailey does report. It's just important that we remember that they aren't definitive across rape at this time – trends in age, class, or anything else can only be seen as trends in *reported* rapes. Firstly, we can see that, just like today, you were more likely to be attacked by someone you knew than by a stranger.[12] Anna Clark, who made a study of Old Bailey rape cases in an overlapping period (1770–1845), found that in 73% of cases the assailant was known to the victim.[13] She also noted that 20% of cases (9 of 45) specifically fell into the category of servants prosecuting their masters, or their masters' relatives. Laurie Edelstein, who investigates and debunks the idea that malicious rape prosecutions were common in the eighteenth century, reminds us that the degree to which someone is 'known' varies and is hard to quantify.[14] Nonetheless, the dominant narrative from the courtroom is not of being attacked by a stranger in a public place but of being hurt by someone familiar. When I looked at these Old Bailey cases, I also could find very few where the defendant was a complete stranger to the victim. I did find two cases where people were charged with aiding and abetting a rape, where the person accused of actually carrying it out was an unknown person. One potential difficulty with prosecuting a stranger is that it's harder to ascertain their identity, and so there are logistical difficulties with bringing a case against them.

Prosecuting acquaintance rape comes with its own complications, and my instinct is that these played a key role in why case numbers increased after the death penalty was removed. Prosecuting a person from within a limited social circle has big repercussions at the best of times, but when the result of a guilty verdict might be death, these can only be exacerbated. If you're prosecuting someone you know, it could be a family member, or a relative or partner of a friend. It could be someone who employs you and people you're close to – people who depend on that employment for their income.

Maybe you know the children who would be affected by the conviction of the prosecuted. Where a person is known, there must be more complex feelings of guilt and attachment than when it is a stranger, giving the victim (and witnesses) greater pause for thought about whether they are willing to speak up. Not just that, but pursuing a legal verdict also carries the risk of fracturing or fragmenting a community, since the likelihood is that the community will know both the victim and defendant. The death penalty means that while there is one question that asks whether the accused committed the crime, the other question that runs alongside it is whether the harm done to the victim was bad enough to be worth the defendant's life. It puts the victim in the position of having to say that what was done to them not only meets the standard for conviction, but should also result in the death of another person – even though they aren't the ones who set that as the appropriate outcome. It is easy to see how they – or their community – might construe this as the victim choosing to kill another person. Something which they might get blamed for, and something which is a heavy burden to carry even without blame.

If we consider who *was* bringing cases to trial, we can see that most of the people come from the servant classes. Of the 92 Not Guilty cases which give information about the status of the participants, in nine cases the victim was the servant of the accused, with a tenth who was interviewing for a position; another three involve a defendant who was employed by the plaintiff's family.[15] Eighteen further plaintiffs were servants, meaning that a full third of the cases that we have information for involve servants. This number would be higher if we included the occupations of the parents of children too young to have their own professions. The picture is similar with Guilty-verdict cases – the majority of the victims were servants or children too young to have a profession. What we can see from this is that the legal system was being used by those with enough money to pay the fees, but not those who had a significant income or fortune of their own. I did find one higher-ranked man in this period – a Daniel Lackey, Esq. – who was acquitted following character references from a number of other high-ranked men, including an Earl.[16] In cases such as this, with a defendant from the upper classes and a plaintiff from the lower, the defendant could pay off the plaintiff, outspend them in terms of counsel and witnesses (as the prosecution was required to pay trial costs, and calling witnesses incurred charges), or just present the victim as fabricating the whole thing in order to raise money. Anthony Simpson, who has written extensively on the courts in this period, has also highlighted that in cases involving masters and servants, it was not unusual for masters to bring a counter allegation against the servant (typically for theft) in order to damage their character and therefore weaken their case.[17] The closest I came to finding an unmarried woman from the upper classes in these court records was Ann Boss – she was simply a lodger who could afford her own maid – but to assume that no women of the upper classes were raped would be foolish. It would be extremely important for the families of such women to protect their sexual reputations, since there would be financial repercussions if their marriage prospects were damaged.

The other big trend I found was – perhaps unsurprisingly – that cases with a lower burden of proof had a better chance of being successful. Guilty verdicts were most common when there was some kind of venereal disease, which could show that sex had taken place, and/or when the victim was young, below the age of consent or above it but a virgin. As I've talked about earlier, the conviction rate was only 18%, so the numbers are still low even with this consideration. But one third of Guilty-verdict cases involved venereal disease, and at least 45% of the Guilty-verdict cases had a victim aged 11 (the age of consent) or under during this fifty-year period. The oldest known age of a victim in a Guilty-verdict case is 19. (Even in the Not Guilty cases there are only two ages given that are past the teens – one is 20 and the other 32.)

Simpson finds across England generally that 'almost half [of rape victims] were under the age of *ten*'. He categorises 'the typical rape victim' as being 'very young', and finds that it's 'not possible to tabulate the age of victims' over 10.[18] It is crucial when reading this not to conflate the rapes that went to trial with all the rapes that happened in reality. We know that a great many instances of rape went unreported. Just as there is a dark figure for rape, there are what we might call 'dark averages' for the ages, professions, and circumstances of those involved. We only have the information that was taken down in court, so we need to remember that our data is limited to those cases that went to court – and by extension those cases that were thought to have a good chance of being successful. We can't assume that society is a microcosm of the trends in this court data. Both the ages of victims and the presence of venereal disease are factors that can cause a skewing in which cases are brought to trial.

Simpson suggests that one reason why venereal disease was so common in the court cases of this period was the popular 'folk belief that sex with an innocent provided a cure for venereal disease'.[19] In the cases I looked at, judges actively asked the medical professionals in court about this, with the clear purpose of giving them a platform to tell people that this kind of 'cure' does not work.[20] This belief represents a link between venereal disease and the age of the victim, and increases the likelihood that when a case involved one, it would involve the other as well. Both of these factors individually reduced the burden of proof, and when combined they reduced it further still. When a rape victim is below the age of consent, you only have to prove that sex took place. When the victim is considered an adult, you also have to prove that they did not consent, and so in the eighteenth century you had to prove a degree of resistance. However, being below the age of consent also meant being too young to be under oath. If the victim was legally a child, they needed an adult who would speak for them in order to formally identify the perpetrator. There were five cases in my sample where the only evidence was the word of an underage child – because they didn't have an adult to speak for them, the defendant could not be convicted.[21] While the courts were convinced that the victims had been raped, none of these victims could swear under oath who the specific person was who had hurt them. If the child did have an adult who could tie the case to the defendant, then the presence of venereal disease was usually enough to prove that sex had taken place, giving a stronger chance of a Guilty verdict.

But this was not always enough. One key element that the eighteenth-century courts relied on was medical evidence testifying to the state of the victim's vagina. Doctors would look for lacerations or tearing to prove that force had been used.[22] The absence of laceration could be taken to mean that penetration hadn't happened, and penetration had different requirements in law at this time. It wasn't a binary question of whether the penis had entered the body or not, but whether it had entered far enough. One surgeon went so far as to argue that the vagina is present only beyond the hymen, and so claimed that the defendant couldn't have committed a rape in the legal sense. While they had inserted themselves, the doctor said, they could not have inserted into the specific area of the female sexual organ which would qualify the act as a rape.[23] In the cases of John Birmingham (1753) and William Allam (1768), even though both victims were under the age of consent and both cases involved venereal disease, the court felt that there wasn't enough laceration to prove that the rapes had happened. The men were prosecuted for the lesser charge of assault with intent to rape instead. In John Birmingham's trial, the surgeon explained that it was impossible for the disease that Elizabeth Wheeler had been given to 'be committed without a contract [*sic*]', meaning that she could not have caught the disease without making physical contact with the defendant; but when asked whether he thought she had been penetrated, he said 'I believe she had not.'[24] Across multiple cases, we see venereal disease described as being spread by contact, rather than necessarily by penetration. What 'contact' actually means in these cases also varies, from insertion into the body (up to but not past the hymen), to simply sharing a toilet seat. The medical examinations therefore also put a lot of focus on whether the hymen was still intact.

These medical examinations were another factor in why cases involving children had a better chance in court. Children, with their smaller bodies, were more likely to sustain the kinds of physical damage that the courts were looking for. In contrast, women who were older, and in particular those who were married, were not expected to suffer the same type of harm. In the trial of Luston Vaughan, we see an example of how the woman being sexually active impacted her questioning:

> How so, as to connections, you might be sure they would not kill you, that you had tried before often, how came you to think of this rape?
>
> *Because he took me against my will.*
>
> [...]
>
> He took you by the hand?
>
> *No, he took me round the middle, and dragged me.*
>
> Did not he tumble your clothes?
>
> *My bonnet was doubled.*
>
> That would have happened you know if you had lain down of your own accord?
>
> *You would not have him kill me.*
>
> No, no, I would not have him hurt you?
>
> *Then you think a woman is not hurt, unless she is quite killed.*
>
> What injury you might receive in those parts would not hurt you know, you had tried that before;[25]

The lawyer here argues that because Mary Hunt, though unmarried, had been living '[a]s man and wife' with her partner for several years, she wouldn't be hurt by any kind of sex – even the forced kind. The simultaneous requirement for laceration and the expectation that there wouldn't be any in older or sexually active women might be a reason why fewer of these cases went to trial or had Guilty verdicts returned.

The medical requirements could also work against children. One surgeon testified that there couldn't have been a rape because he was barely able to insert his finger into the child (a reminder of just how unpleasant and re-traumatising these examinations were). Another case involved this exchange: 'Q. Are you clear from these circumstances, that she never could have been entered by a man? – *It was impossible; the orifice was not larger than the size of a large quill.*'[26] The lack of understanding around the way that female sexual organs work means that there is no awareness shown that vaginas undergo changes, and can constrict as a result of physical trauma. The idea of a child being too small to be penetrated resulted in some cases where lacerations were attributed to the man's fingers, because the authorities believed anything else would have been impossible. The medical examinations were traumatic and were interpreted subjectively. If you wanted to bring a case, you not only needed to have specific kinds of injuries, but you had to be prepared to undergo an examination that required a man you probably didn't know to put his hands into you, and then have the results debated in a public court.

The other thing that the Old Bailey Proceedings make clear is less to do with the crimes themselves and more with the way that people talked about them. It's clear – unsurprisingly – that it was uncomfortable to talk explicitly about rape, and about sexual acts more broadly. The Proceedings are written accounts of verbal testimonies given in a court of law – both a very public and a predominantly male environment. When delivering the testimony, you'd be confronted with challenges to your word and critiques of your behaviour. You'd have to respond to these in the moment, and in front of a responsive audience. That audience would most likely include the person who had hurt you, which only made the process more traumatising. Speaking about trauma is a difficult and painful task at the best of times; testifying was not made easier by the fact that it wasn't considered proper for women or children to talk about sexual things openly. Nor was it helped by the fact that they made themselves socially vulnerable by admitting that they'd had sex outside marriage. And while the Proceedings record shortened versions of what was said in court, they don't report how many people were in the public gallery, whether they heckled, or how they behaved.[27] It's also worth remembering that the Proceedings were published, meaning that all those testifying could be sure that their words were going to be made public for strangers to pick over. You had to be prepared for the publicity – and potential notoriety – that came with making a case.

Thomas Homewood, the father of one of the victims, was questioned about why he had brought the case to court on behalf of his daughter. In that questioning, he makes it clear that he had originally held back from going to court because 'I thought it would make an alarm in the neighbourhood, and disgrace the child's character; I thought he [the defendant, Scott] would go off to Scotland.' He goes on to say that 'if he had gone out of the way, so that it was not to be known, I would have put up with the misfortune' – the ideal was clearly for this to be kept quiet. When asked why he had decided to prosecute Scott after all, Homewood replied that it was 'Because I found he did not go out of the way; and as my wife had made it known to Mrs Green, I thought we could but be disgraced.'[28] Going to court became necessary once he felt that the family's reputation was going to be damaged.

This same case has a great example of the kind of polite euphemism that the eighteenth century preferred for talking about anything connected to sex. The opening speech of Mr Knapp, the lawyer for the prosecution, begins:

> Gentlemen, what followed, I will not state from the regard I have to decency, and that I would not anticipate a witness of this sort will prove more satisfactorily; but that after having so laid her down, the fact attributed to the prisoner was committed, and committed in such a sort of way, if you believe the evidence, as no question of law can be raised upon it, for the ingredients of the offence are every one to be found in this case.[29]

Here, he uses 'the fact attributed to the prisoner' as a polite way of saying 'raped'. This is not unusual. Across these cases even the indictments can avoid the word rape; multiple cases have variations on 'for feloniously and carnally knowing and abusing' instead.[30] In the trial of Hugh M'kave, the dominant phrase is 'ill used' or 'used ill', while the trial of Edward Brophy tends to say 'meddled with'.[31] You see many cases describing the attacks by saying 'he lay with me', or that they had been 'served so', or talking about the defendant 'having connection with' or being 'concerned' with the victim. When the victims had to describe penetration – which they had to prove as part of proving the crime – the language is similarly vague. 'The part' was the most common term I saw for describing female genitalia, and though there were more explicit references to men's anatomy than women's, Mary Brickinshaw's declaration that 'he put his thing into me' was not unusual.[32] If people had to talk about whether the man had ejaculated, it was phrased as 'feeling something come from [him]'. One witness politely described the victim as having 'a great deal of human nature upon her'.[33] In 1789 we get an account which says '[Here the witness proceeded in a narration too indelicate for publication, which, however, did not amount to legal proof of the crime charged against the prisoner in the indictment.]' Even though there wasn't enough legal proof for a conviction in this case, it was still remarked on as 'the most indecent behaviour a man could be guilty of to a young girl of her age'.[34]

From 1798 the Proceedings stopped publishing the testimony from rape trials entirely. There was a growing sense of what it was decent to publish, and even cases like theft were censored if they featured sex workers or had taken place in brothels. Discussing sex, even in print, was increasingly seen as vulgar, if not downright taboo. This is worth commenting on, because testifying in court during a rape trial is the one place where it *is* proper to be explicit. Cases rely on conveying specific information, and the victims are asked to describe things clearly. The fact that euphemisms are so commonly used, even in this scenario, tells us that euphemism was an integral part of how the eighteenth century talked about sex and sexual violence. And the fact that cases relating to sex stopped being published makes it clear that there were limits to what you could put in print. From this we can see that a silence or a gap in explicit conversation does not mean that these crimes did not exist, nor even that they were uncommon. If anything, what these cases from the Old Bailey Proceedings demonstrate is a series of absences – absences of certain ages, classes, and even language – which highlight how likely it is that these discussions and experiences are present elsewhere, euphemistically coded.

The most notable thing that these cases show are gaps. I believe that conversations about some of these gaps are happening in the period's courtship novels. The vast majority of sexual threats against the heroine in eighteenth-century novels come from characters of roughly her own class (though there are notable exceptions, like Richardson's *Pamela*). More specifically, they come from the upper-middle and aristocratic classes – one of the large social groups who did not use the courts.[35] They too focus on acquaintance rape, rather than the potential threat of random strangers. As we saw in *Evelina*, the heroine encounters a party of men in Vauxhall Gardens who frighten her, but it is the man she knows who poses the most serious threat. When her coach is beset by highwaymen, again they are people she knows. Sarah Fielding's Ophelia is carried off three times; twice by people she knows, and once in a case of mistaken identity by people who know the woman they are trying to kidnap. Cecilia experiences violent scenes in public places frequently: none are perpetrated by strangers. Eugenia's abductor is the man she believes is in love with her. The sexually dangerous characters in Jane Austen's novels all know the women they ruin.

Consider this quote from Austen's Anne Elliot in *Persuasion*:

> We never can expect to prove any thing upon such a point. It is a difference of opinion which does not admit of proof. We each begin, probably, with a little bias towards our own sex; and upon that bias build every circumstance in favour of it which has occurred within our own circle; many of which circumstances (perhaps those very cases which strike us the most) may be precisely such as cannot be brought forward without betraying a confidence, or in some respect saying what should not be said.[36]

Anne is talking to her friend Captain Harville, debating the differences between the way men and women love. Captain Harville challenges her, saying that history is on his side, that there are endless songs and books about how women are fickle and inconstant, how they fall out of love with their partners. Anne says that's because men have been better able to tell their side of the story, because they have been the ones writing the books. The above quote is part of Anne's counter-argument. She's talking here about circumstances within her own circle where men have stopped loving the women they cared about. Unhappy relationships, unhappy marriages. It implies that she may know of instances of abuse, but can't use them to support her argument because they're confidential. They are things she is not supposed to say, the subtext being that certain topics are socially off-limits.

What Anne's trying to emphasise here is that men's monopoly on writing history has shaped the cultural narrative. But by combining these points, Austen reminds us that much of what is viewed as 'evidence' of women's poor behaviour has been written by men, while women were generally prevented from making problematic male behaviour known. She places the capacity to influence societal perceptions in the shaping and sharing of narratives. More than that, for us to get this suggestion from Anne – the idea that she has a range of examples of problematic behaviour that she could draw upon if only she were allowed to talk about them, that this is a standard thing to have – means that we have to think about where this idea came from. The likelihood is that this is something which rings true for Austen as well. She's aligning us here with the idea that knowing unspeakable things is normal.

8
Mary, or Violating Convention

> To report a rape can mean being further victimized not just by the victim-blaming system but also by the support structures we thought we had in place, like friends and families and school social circles. It can mean losing a job along with a reputation. It can mean being called a liar, and it can mean being accused of ruining young men's lives.
>
> – Marianne Kirby[1]

> Who will credit the tale you tell? What testimony or witness can you produce that will not make against you? What are your resources to sustain the vexations and delay of a suit of law, which you wildly threaten? Who would support you against my wealth and influence? How would your delicacy shrink from the idea of becoming, in open court, the sport of ribaldry, the theme of obscene jests? [...] Simple girl! how impotent, then, is your rage!
>
> – Mary Hays, *The Victim of Prejudice*[2]

The incidents of sexual violence that appear in these novels aren't ones that would play well in the eighteenth-century courtroom. They would be problematic to prosecute from the descriptions given; the books don't go into the kind of detail you'd need for a case, either to prove how much you resisted or how much force was used against you, and the attacks don't have witnesses. This isn't surprising – novels aren't generally required to replicate legal standards of proof, and as we've said, even in court the descriptions were euphemistic. There's a freedom that comes with that though, and an opportunity. By operating under the protective umbrella of fiction, the authors are able to move the focus of their discussions beyond an analysis of the attack and the victim's behaviour, and towards an analysis of both the perpetrator and the society that enables them. They open out the conversation about the kinds of harm sexual violence does far beyond the limited factors that the legal system was able to deal with.

Although rape is a common spectre haunting these novels, it is never erotic or titillating. The women suffer personal harm, but any sense of ruin is primarily social – though they feel injury, though they may also die before the end of the novel, they do not stop having value as a person. They mourn what has been done to and taken from them, not what they have lost as though they were the ones culpable. Their options are narrowed, their futures are compromised, they may become pregnant, or ill, or be cast out by family members. But they do not cease to value themselves. We are with them as readers, the bird dying, not the one mourning the loss of bright feathers. As a result, we have narratives which are more invested in the emotions, feelings, and fallout of scenarios – particularly those which an eighteenth-century law court would regard as grey areas. Yet because the form of the novel allows readers insight into the minds and intentions of the characters, readers are aligned with the victims of these acts and able to *know* with certainty that this was not something that the character wanted. It is much harder to construct consent when you are a party to the distress being felt.

This in turn results in a genre of novels which, though they have an educative function, do not attempt to teach women 'how to avoid rape'. The acts of rape, and the overt threats of it, occur because of the actions of men, of society, and of impossible circumstances – not as the result of an unforced error or a lapse in judgement. They are not presented as preventable for the women in question; there are no warning signs to recognise and avoid, no specifically dangerous locations or somehow inappropriate dress decisions, no way of putting off the relevant men. They do not give credibility to the rape myth that women can consent by their dress, location, or even simple attractiveness to the rapist.[3] The role of the abused women is not to provide a cautionary tale of what happens if women behave improperly, but to demonstrate that it is possible to take every precaution and still get hurt. As a result, these novels do not fit into a 'fall as negative example' paradigm, because the texts do not suggest that it is possible for the women involved to escape from or materially alter the circumstances which lead to them being subjected to sexual violence. And generally, while those acts of sexual violence are important parts of the narrative, they are by no means the only part – just as the novels are interested in more than simply a discussion of whether the act took place, they are also interested in more than simply describing a form of violation.

If we compare these novels to something like Matthew Lewis's *The Monk* (1796), the shocking novel that the young women in Austen's *Northanger Abbey* whisper about, we see the differentiation clearly.[4] Lewis's text – a gothic horror rather than a courtship novel – uses sexual violence as a voyeuristic form of entertainment; both rape and its shadow are present for the sensation they provide, the eroticised stacking of taboo on top of taboo. When the virtuous Antonia is finally raped by the eponymous monk, it is as part of *his* story, not hers. The violence is the culmination of his forbidden sexual desires, and once he is done defiling her, he is disgusted by both her and himself. I say 'defiling' with good reason – the emphasis in this novel is on rape as an act of degradation which reduces and ruins something pure. Antonia is made less to him as a result of his violation. A key part of the reason he wants Antonia is because she does not want him. It is not merely sex that is desired, it is rape; to take, to dominate, to enact punishment on another for the feelings they apparently engender in you. Antonia is an object, a quintessential example of philosopher Edmund Burke's beauty in distress, where what is narratively important is that she is desirable and then destroyed. *The Monk* revels in the rape fantasy, eroticising unwillingness and non-consent.

The Monk offers a stark difference to something like Mary Hays's 1799 novel *The Victim of Prejudice*. Hays, a contemporary, friend, and fan of Mary Wollstonecraft, was often too open in her writing for Georgian society. She was nationally ridiculed after writer Elizabeth Hamilton caricatured her as being obsessed with men and sex in *Memoirs of Modern Philosophers* (1800) – one result of Hays using some of her own love letters in *The Memoirs of Emma Courtney* (1796), her best-known novel. In many ways, *The Victim of Prejudice* isn't a particularly good novel – it feels a lot like a political rant thinly veiled as a novel. But it is a really good political rant, one that digs into the lasting harm that rape creates and the structures that enable it to happen. (Brace yourselves – from here on in, pretty much every single woman is called Mary.) The novel's protagonist, Mary, is raised and educated well. She falls in love with her young sweetheart William Pelham, and the two are planning to get married up until Mary's foster-father tells her that she's actually the illegitimate daughter of a disgraced woman. Her mother, she learns, ran away from home with her seducer, and ultimately became a prostitute. There's no way that Mary can marry William now – she's too far below him socially, and she can't bear the idea of dragging him down to her level. Once her foster-father dies, she travels to the city to start a new job, but she falls victim to a lecherous nobleman. Sir Peter Osborne, a neighbour of Mary's, has spent the early part of the book making sexual advances towards her, all of which Mary has rebuffed. He resorts to abducting her when she's on her way to the city, and so Mary finds herself not at her new job, but in Osborne's house and under his power. He holds her in his house, and ultimately he rapes her. Though Mary gets away, and tries to get on with her life, the novel shows just how difficult this is, as it follows her struggles to find work and avoid being revictimised, up until her eventual death.

Mary has many confrontations with Osborne, and Hays always makes a point of detailing how she resists him – and how she isn't able to. What this allows us to see as readers is the problem with the legal requirements that women resist in a particular way. Near the beginning of the novel, Mary encounters Osborne in a garden. She says that he 'seized me, and, clasping me in his arms, kissed me with an odious violence. I shrieked, struggled, and fought, with all my strength.'[5] Here, we can quite clearly see that Mary is enacting resistance 'properly'; she resists verbally by 'shriek[ing]' – a word which suggests both volume and vehemence – and resists physically, and both these forms of resistance are crucially performed 'with all my strength'. Osborne's actions are also emphasised – he seizes, clasps, and kisses, three verbs in a short sentence casting him firmly as the active party – and all this is capped off at the end with the reminder that not only was this done violently, but that both the violence and the actions themselves were 'odious'. The actions run together, giving a sense of both suddenness and speed. These events happened fast.

In contrast, this is the section where Mary describes her rape by Osborne:

> Deaf to my remonstrances, to my supplication, regardless of my tears, my rage, my despair, – his callous heart, his furious and uncontrollable vehemence, – Oh! that I could for ever blot from my remembrance, – oh! that I could conceal from myself, – […] I suffered a brutal violation.[6]

This is a stark difference. There is almost a dearth of verbs, and those that are present are either passive or represent impossibilities. We are presented with the inverse of Osborne's power and energy through Mary's impotency and utter inability to *do*. Even as she runs through a litany of actions she took and strategies she tried, her actions are all presented as nouns, robbed of any sense of active power.

Crucially, the sense of speed is also lacking. Mary's description of her responses acts to form a timeline, moving from 'remonstrances', through pleading, weeping, anger, and finally the evocative 'despair'. With the possible exception of 'rage', these terms do not carry explicit suggestions of volume – which would have been a relevant factor in a courtroom in determining whether she had sought to attract help from others in the house. What they do suggest, however, is that this struggle with Osborne occurred over a significant length of time; certainly long enough to move through all of these stages. While it may be possible to 'shriek' and resist with all of one's strength in a brief struggle, Hays subtly highlights here the exhaustion of spirit that can occur when an attack is ongoing, and therefore one of the problems with the resistance level required by the law.

More importantly, the focus here is on Osborne's responses to Mary's resistance; as the sentence opens, we already know that any attempts she made were futile, the word 'deaf' setting up the failure of any vocal response she might make. The relevant fact is that Osborne was 'deaf' to them, not how loud or how wholehearted her struggling was, precisely because whatever Mary does in this situation *will* fail. 'Successful resistance' is not a thing that can be enacted by the victim. Rather, the decision to take or not take the action to rape lies with the perpetrator, and therefore all Mary can do in this instance is attempt to convince him to take an alternative course. If he refuses to hear her, she is powerless.[7] But also, therefore, she is not to blame for failing to resist correctly.

In the first example, the role of her shrieking is to attempt to attract attention from other people, as well as being a response to a shock.[8] In the second, the only one listening is Osborne, and because they're in his house, he is the only person in the building with the authority to rescue her. Mary's vocal responses therefore cannot function as an alarm, and must instead function as a persuasive device – the privacy of the location means that their role must be different. The value of a disapproving male onlooker is made clear in an encounter which takes place between these two scenes, when Mary is rescued by Osborne and his companions on their boat. In this instance, Mary tells him clearly that she expects him to let go of her ('I insist upon being released this moment'), but while he 'seemed struck with awe at my resolute and spirited manner', action is not taken until the following sentence. Though there we are told that 'he was persuaded', it is not before the crucially important qualification with which the sentence begins: '[h]is companions interfering [...] he was persuaded'. Hays's grammatical separation makes clear that, whatever effect Mary's resistance may have had on Osborne, it is his companions who cause him to stop.

Resistance, then, the central requirement for showing that consent was refused, is highlighted as a complex construct. We see the reality of what 'with all her strength' looks like when that strength runs out – and your strength must run out for you to have used all of it. We get to see how the function of resistance when you can't get away varies depending on where the attack takes place. In public, resistance can attract attention, potentially bringing a third party in to help convince your attacker to let you go. In private, in isolation, no one is there who can help. But there's still a chance your resistance will persuade the person to stop. Resisting becomes something to show non-consent, rather than an escape strategy. In emphasising this, Hays draws attention to a flaw in the way the crime of rape was set out: if we understand that there is a persuasive component to resistance when in private, then we also understand that the victim is already adopting a harm-minimisation strategy. Hays doesn't go so far as to show Mary capitulating so as to try to minimise the violence done to her (her heroine doing that would distract from the overall message of the novel), but she puts elements of this into Mary's mother's storyline. By emphasising the futility of resistance as a purely preventative action, Hays challenges the uneasy eighteenth-century attempt to categorise rape and seduction, laying the groundwork for her readers to understand that adopting a harm-prevention strategy is not the same as freely given consent.

But the thing I found most striking about the way Hays writes about rape is the emphasis she gives to its psychological effects. After the rape, Mary tells us that the 'Three weeks that followed were a blank in my existence; yet I had intervals of reflection, dark and dreadful. Imaginary terrors, broken recollections, strange phantoms, wild and wandering thoughts, harassed and persecuted me.'[9] The after-effects of the rape are not simply physical. The three-week 'blank' Mary experiences shows that she continues to suffer from the attack after the act itself is finished. We now know that this happens to a lot of people after experiencing sexual violence. RAINN (the Rape, Abuse, and Incest National Network) lists common side-effects such as flashbacks, depression, dissociation, panic attacks, and post-traumatic stress disorder – all things that have elements in common with the description above.[10] Compare the mental effects Hays specifies, the 'broken recollections', the 'wild and wandering thoughts', the 'imaginary terrors', with the NHS website's description of the symptoms of PTSD: 'flashbacks', 'nightmares', 'insomnia', and '[trying to] push memories of the event from their mind'.[11] Though this condition wasn't diagnosed or named in the eighteenth century, evidence of a condition always comes before that condition is named. PTSD existed long before we had a definition for it. The fact that Hays's description of the symptoms that follow Mary's rape closely matches the symptoms of responses we now know to be common for victims of rape, but which weren't medically recognised at the time, suggests that Hays was familiar with the way that people reacted to sexual violence.[12] There's a realism to Mary's response which makes it feel observed – especially given the fact that there was no official medical link between these things in the eighteenth century.

I'm not suggesting that Hays was the first person to make this connection, but if we look at the history of how we began to officially recognise that rape results in psychological trauma, we can see that she's talking openly about it a long way ahead of the diagnosis. In her seminal text *Trauma and Recovery: The Aftermath of Violence – From Domestic Abuse to Political Terror*, Judith Herman describes a breakthrough moment in recognising the links between PTSD and rape:

> In 1972, Ann Burgess, a psychiatric nurse, and Lynda Holstrom, a sociologist, embarked on a study of the psychological effects of rape […] They observed a pattern of psychological reactions which they called 'rape trauma syndrome' […] They remarked that in the aftermath of rape, victims complained of insomnia, nausea, startle responses, and nightmares, as well as dissociative or numbing symptoms. And they commented that some of the victims' symptoms resembled those previously described in combat veterans.[13]

Herman charts a history of the understanding of psychological trauma which she begins with early investigations into hysteria, moving through the effects of war on combat veterans, to this appreciation that domestic violence and rape can occasion these kinds of trauma responses too. Looking at her discussion of hysteria, the investigation of which peaked in the late nineteenth century – a hundred years after *The Victim of Prejudice* – I am struck by the similarity of her treatment and Hays's. Both describe 'nightmares' and flashbacks, in addition to the 'blank' and 'dissociative and numbing' periods.

Herman names French neurologist Jean-Martin Charcot as the person who legitimised the study of hysterics, and who was succeeded by three avid followers: Pierre Janet, William James, and Sigmund Freud. Although there was an 'ancient clinical tradition' which made links between hysteria and sexuality, this group rejected the premise, up until Freud became involved in the cases which would lead to the publication of his 1896 paper *The Aetiology of Hysteria*.[14] This was the paper in which he famously 'put forward the thesis that at the bottom of every case of hysteria there are *one or more occurrences of premature sexual experience*'.[15] But these initial cases were drawn from what Herman describes as the 'proletariat of Paris' – a class group Freud was willing to believe could have significant rates of child abuse, incest, and other forms of sexual trauma. The bias that says that working-class people are natural criminals was very much alive and well. When he found the same results replicated in the higher classes, Freud could not accept his own findings. It did not match with his perceptions of what that class-group was like, and he effectively disowned both his theory and his patients on the basis of wilful blindness. What struck me here was Herman's subsequent observation:

> Out of the ruins of the traumatic theory of hysteria, Freud created psychoanalysis. The dominant psychological theory of the next century was founded in the denial of women's reality. Sexuality remained the central focus of inquiry. But the exploitative social context in which sexual relations actually occur becomes utterly invisible.[16]

The idea that it took more time to identify that sexual violence was a cause of trauma because the theorists were unwilling to accept the volume of incidents, and the fact that their peers were perpetrators, makes me deeply angry. Looking at Hays's description of how Mary feels after she's raped is like recognising your own face in an ancestral family photo. It's too familiar to look away from.

After her attack, Mary manages to get away from Osborne, but both he and the shadow of rape follow her wherever she goes. It continues to affect her, and to affect how she reacts to sexual threats. When faced with the advances of a lecherous shopkeeper, she is '[o]vercome by recollections which crowded upon my mind' and finds herself 'unable to reply'.[17] Where earlier in the novel she regularly spoke up for herself, now she is plunged back into an immobilising trauma. As the novel goes on, she ends up getting arrested for debt. The sheriff's officer presents her with a choice: go to prison or accept Osborne's help. She is seized by a 'frenzy of terror' at the thought of him; when he enters the room she's being held in, she describes how 'uttering a fearful shriek, I fell in convulsions at his feet'.[18] After her 'long' unconsciousness, she comes around, only to once again see Osborne. He kisses her hand.

> Springing from his touch, and rushing past the officer, I once more endeavoured to gain the door, but discovered it, with inexpressible anguish, to be locked. Staggering towards a chair, and supporting myself on the back, an agony resembling the pangs of death shook my frame.[19]

Mary is not simply swooning here, or fainting delicately. This isn't ladylike or modest. She is shaking and fitting, and perhaps most importantly, she is initially speechless. When she is first arrested she is able to speak with 'assumed firmness', and to reproach the officer for his rude comments.[20] When it is Osborne confronting her though, she 'attended in speechless anguish'.[21] She is limited in her ability to verbally resist Osborne as a direct result of the harm that he has done her. Her capacity to perform 'proper resistance' has been compromised by the trauma she has already suffered.

The next time Mary meets Osborne (he crops up repeatedly, refusing to leave her alone), it's unexpected. Six months after their previous encounter, sitting on a grassy bank near where she grew up, Mary is horrified to see Osborne appear with a party of huntsmen.

> I shrieked involuntarily, staggered backward, and was sinking to the ground when, catching me in his arms, he prevented my fall. A convulsive trembling shook my limbs; while, petrified with horror, and unable to speak, I continued to gaze wildly on this terrible apparition, my strength utterly failing me, and my senses wholly bewildered.[22]

Again she cannot speak. Again she is disordered. Again she cannot stop herself from shaking. Her shriek here is different to the one we broke down earlier. Although this shriek also indicates volume and vehemence, it is 'involuntary', and therefore unlike the earlier example cannot be understood as an intentional refusal of consent. It highlights that she is not taking this action as a deliberate sign of her resistance. She's not doing anything deliberately. Here, she shrieks from alarm as a direct result of seeing Osborne. After the attack, whenever Mary sees Osborne, she exhibits symptoms similar to those of a panic attack. He holds a terror for her which he did not do before. While he has physically violated her, harassed her, damaged her prospects, and insulted her, the stress that Hays places on the mental anguish that Mary suffers is such that we cannot overlook its significance. Mary is scared when she sees Osborne, something which emphasises the traumatic nature of the rape. Mary is fearful of Osborne as a person who has harmed her and who could harm her again. This in turn tells us that rape is being conceptualised here as violence in and of itself, not simply because it is an act which carries a specific social cost. Hays shows us that rape harms, regardless of whether virginity has already been lost, whether rape has already been experienced. Mary carries the effects with her: 'the tone of my mind was destroyed [...] broken spirits and a shattered constitution sunk me to the weakness of infancy, imaginary terrors haunted my mind, and a complication of nameless depressing pangs racked my frame'.[23] Her rape has damaged her – not as a commodity, in the sense of damaged goods, but as a person who has been fundamentally harmed by an act of violence perpetrated against her.

Hays's ascription of responsibility for the rape is greater than a court's could be. Had this rape occurred in real life, it's clear it would have struggled to gain a legal conviction, even as it's also clear that it ought to be able to succeed. Hays is very direct about the fact that the legal system does not support women who want to take their attackers to court. Though Mary theoretically has the ability to challenge Osborne for his actions, the reality is that the disparity in their resources is too great. Mary's lack of money equates to a lack of protection, which not only makes her more vulnerable to the attack in the first place, but also prohibits her from pursuing any legal form of justice. In the novel, Mary has faith in the protection provided by the law, declaring to Osborne that she will take him to court for what he has done to her. But Hays explains exactly how futile that is, using Osborne as a mouthpiece to highlight how that would be both painful and ineffectual.

> Who will credit the tale you tell? What testimony or witness can you produce that will not make against you? What are your resources to sustain the vexations and delay of a suit of law, which you wildly threaten? Who would support you against my wealth and influence? How would your delicacy shrink from the idea of becoming, in open court, the sport of ribaldry, the theme of obscene jests? […] Simple girl! how impotent, then, is your rage![24]

Reduced to its fundamentals, this speech is a summary of the problems facing women wishing to make a case. A lack of credibility, a lack of witnesses, a lack of resources. The tendency of society to fall in with the wishes of those with greater power and resource. The emotional toll, obscured when we encounter cases as documents, of having to actively speak of trauma in a courtroom full of people, and have that trauma both dissected and ridiculed. The continued erosion of dignity and privacy. Osborne sums up the situation here: no one will believe you, you can't afford it, and it will be personally horrible for you. That these difficulties are emphasised in the novel in this way, when the reader is completely confident that the victim is speaking the truth, allows these flaws to be raised without the distraction of questioning the particulars of an individual involved in a real-life case. The reader knows and can feel the injustice of Mary's inability to seek reparation.

Perhaps most telling is that final line, when Osborne exclaims 'how impotent, then, is your rage!' Author and feminist activist Soraya Chemaly writes that

> Gender-role expectations […] dictate the degree to which we can use anger effectively in personal contexts and to participate in civic and political life […] A society that does not respect women's anger is one that does not respect women – not as human beings, thinkers, knowers, active participants, or citizens.[25]

One thing we can see clearly from Osborne's speech is that it's not just Mary-the-character who is angry – it is Mary Hays too, an anger that is presented here as a response both to the oppressive and violent treatment of women, and their inability to challenge it. If we think back to the description of the attack, the character Mary attempts to use 'my rage' as a tool to stop Osborne. Her rage fails. Here, afterwards, when she confronts him, we see that her rage is 'impotent'. Osborne implies that she should have known it could hold no power. Osborne's anger, on the other hand – and, by implication, the anger of men generally and powerful men in particular – is dangerous. Mary's is insubstantial. It's not that her anger is weak, it's that while it's strong in feeling it is simultaneously *impotent* and cannot create the effects that she wishes. And, as Chemaly points out, this impotency of anger signifies society's lack of respect for women. If Mary's anger does nothing, then angering Mary has no consequences. And this in turn makes Hays angry.

It's not simply a failure of the courts to offer redress to specific women for crimes committed against them – it is their share in the responsibility for the gendered violence which is directed against the sex as a whole. By rendering their process prohibitive, the courts act in a way that silences women. Mary's mother, who experiences abuse herself in her early life, leaves a letter behind in which she denotes the way in which she wishes her daughter to be raised, and the events that led ultimately to her death. In that letter, she writes that '*Law* completes the triumph of injustice', declaring that 'a legal process, assuming the arm of omnipotence, annihilates the being'.[26] But even more than her arguments about the role the court plays in the revictimisation of those who suffer sexual violence, Mary senior states that, first and foremost, women are deliberately made vulnerable by the kind of education they are given. Women, she says, are trained to defer and question the validity of their own views by the social requirement that they submit to the judgement of others, and so their convictions and principles are weakened. They are taught to value vanity rather than how to investigate and challenge ideas, and this creates easy prey for unscrupulous men. The inability to discern the threat intrinsically increases the threat. Because she wants her daughter to grow up safe, she asks Mary's foster-father to take specific steps in raising her. She asks him to

> cultivate her reason, make her feel her nature's worth, strengthen her faculties, inure her to suffer hardships, rouse her to independence, inspire her with fortitude, with energy, with self-respect, and teach her to contemn [*sic*] the tyranny that would impose fetters of sex upon her mind.[27]

She describes these qualities – independence, worth, fortitude, energy – as things women are perfectly capable of possessing. It is not some kind of gender-based incapacity, but that they are limited by the reductive educational practices that were common at the time.

Hester Chapone, one of the most famous eighteenth-century writers of conduct books for young women, talks about this in her *Letters on the Improvement of the Mind* (1773), specifically addressing that problematic tension between innocence and ignorance. She says that 'Young women know so little of the world, especially of the other sex, and such pains are usually taken to deceive them, that they are every way unqualified to choose for themselves, upon their own judgement.'[28] The problem here is multifaceted. Young women do not know enough of the world in general, and of men in particular, and are frequently the victim of a deceptive presentation of such things – all of which reduces their capacity to make meaningful choices, because they lack the information. Their judgement isn't impaired by nature; it's impaired by practice. Even the eighteenth-century moralist Hannah More, whose view on what she would have girls grow up to be is wildly different from that of Hays, puts forward the same opinion of the damaging potential of the education system, calling the standard female education 'defective', and labelling it a 'singular injustice to train them in such a manner as shall lay them open to the most dangerous faults, and then censure them for not proving faultless'.[29] Now, More doesn't want the same kind of education that Hays's characters are looking for. Hays was a big fan of philosopher Mary Wollstonecraft and her teachings, while Hannah More thought that Wollstonecraft herself was a big part of the threat to young women. Hays is worried about girls being vulnerable to sexual predators because they don't get to practise making their own decisions; More is worried about people coming up with justifications for living with a partner without being married. Even so, the fact that two such politically disparate figures are both dissatisfied with the support provided to young women by their education reinforces the fact that women were expected to use something very limited to govern a significant amount of their lives.

Interestingly, when her foster-father tells Mary what his aims were in raising her, they don't quite match up to the ones her mother asked for. Although her mother urged him to 'rouse' her daughter to 'independence', Mr Raymond tells Mary that he would have failed to have done his duty in rearing her 'If I have not secured your happiness and rendered you useful to society; if I have not taught you to subdue yourself, to subject your feelings.'[30] Learning to subdue herself and her feelings feels more like putting the 'fetters of sex' on her mind than helping her stand up for herself. It feels more in the Hannah More school of morality – just compare Mr Raymond's parental plan with More's definitive work on women's learning, *Strictures on the Modern System of Female Education* (1799):

> Girls should be led to distrust their own judgement; they should learn not to murmur at expostulation; they should be accustomed to expect and endure opposition. It is a lesson with which the world will not fail to furnish them [...] It is of the last importance to their happiness, even in this life, that they should early acquire a submissive temper and a forbearing spirit.[31]

What More, captures here (though less critically than we would maybe like) is a significant part of why it was considered important for girls to be raised to 'subdue' themselves. They 'should be accustomed to expect and endure opposition' because they will inevitably be faced with it if they try to stand by their own will. The subsequent 'distrust' this embeds in their own judgement is precisely what Mary's mother in Hays's novel complains about. While More is not arguing that this should be changed, as Hays is, it reinforces the point that the expectation was that independence in women would be met with opposition – a fact that the narratives of these courtship novels testify to.[32] In a particularly ironic moment, Hays has the closest thing to the novel's primary love interest, Mary's first sweetheart William Pelham, use the rhetoric of independence to try to manipulate Mary into doing what he wants. In a scene where she is refusing to behave the way he wants, he declares that 'you are a victim to control, you have tamely submitted to a tyranny that your heart disavows; your wonted spirit and firmness are subdued'.[33] Though independence is the quality he's presenting as desirable, across Hays's novel it's only endorsed by the male characters when it involves Mary following their desired course of action. It's Cecilia making decisions about her money all over again. The principles behind Mary's independent judgement are seen as less valuable than her submission to the male character's will.

Even though Mary does get a robust education (subduing her feelings notwithstanding), she still finds herself caught in the same cycle of abuse that her mother was trapped in. Hays makes it clear that education is the first link in a chain of disempowerment, not the sole thing that needs to be fixed. We see that Mary's mother, as a young girl, is taken from her home by her 'triumphant seducer', leaving the family willingly, but without properly understanding why what she's doing is wrong.[34] When she is thrown over by that seducer, she gets help from a friend of his, who also turns out to be 'a practiced deceiver'. She finds herself once again being 'betrayed'.[35] Mary's mother trusts men who let her down, and she ends up trading on her sexuality for her safety – only to find that the promises made to her don't get honoured. Mary, on the other hand, is never taken in by Osborne. Her 'fall' to Osborne is the result of imprisonment and being physically overpowered – neither of which are things her education could help her avoid. Even though she's better educated and more moral, she still ends up being the victim of sexual violence. And after the attack she finds herself in a similar position to her mother, needing either to stay with the man responsible for her situation and engage in transactional sexual relations, or attempt to find a way to live respectably in a society that doesn't like to rehabilitate rape victims. What Hays shows us clearly is that, regardless of the manner by which the woman finds herself in such a position, the opportunity for living some form of respectable lifestyle is not allowed.

What this reminds us of is that Hays (among other eighteenth-century authors) is actively arguing for the fair treatment of and rights of rape victims. That Mary consistently takes the morally correct course of action is no accident – it is a deliberate choice on Hays's part, making clear to readers that it is possible to be raped without sharing culpability. Perhaps the most important line in the novel is the thought which comes to Mary when she finds herself unable to live morally and survive, when she finds herself pushed away from a society that she has taken no action as an individual to deserve her repulsion from: 'surely, *I had a right to exist*'.[36]

But Mary, like her mother, struggles to exist. After Osborne's rape, Mary finds it very hard to get work. When she does eventually manage to find a position in a shop, she has to leave very quickly after her employer starts making sexual advances. That means she leaves without a reference. Mary doesn't have the proof of good character that getting respectable work requires. She doesn't have the right markers of respectability (or the right skills) for a lot of work. When she was at Osborne's house, he criticised her for making a fuss instead of simply submitting to him, as that meant that her having had extramarital sex would be known by more people. The fact that she was raped carries little relevance for many potential employers – what's more important to them is the fact that she's had sex outside marriage. The doors to respectable employment are closed to her, in a set of circumstances where it is not difficult to see that once you've been cast as having a bad reputation, the only opportunities open to you are in those places happy to have someone with a bad reputation. Places that are liable to make that reputation worse, creating a spiral effect in which intention and willing participation are meaningless. Reputation, as distinct from character, is all about the way things seem.

Towards the end of the novel Mary settles in a village where no one knows her. She's hoping that this can be her fresh start. But when she finds herself in a difficult situation and wants to ask the villagers for help, she faces the same problems she would have had in reporting Osborne:

> for what credit has the simple asseverations of the sufferer, sole witness in his own cause, to look for against the poison of detraction, the influence of wealth and power, the bigotry of prejudice, the virulence of envy, the spleen and corruption engendered in the human mind by barbarous institutions and pernicious habits?[37]

She does not trust that telling her story will get people to help her – she has been warned by both Osborne and her own experience not to.[38] She borrows money from a neighbour who seems sympathetic, but he tries to leverage that debt for sexual favours. 'I was now daily importuned', she says, 'by our neighbour for the debt which I had incurred; while he scrupled not, with gross hints and coarse language, to suggest that an equivalent might be accepted for a loan I professed myself unable to repay.'[39] In the case of both the shopkeeper and the neighbour, it is Mary's financial need and her inability to earn money which put her at the mercy of these unscrupulous men. She borrows money from her neighbour, she can't pay it back, and she finds that her only options are debtors' prison or to have sex with that neighbour until he decides that her debt is paid off (if he ever actually does).

Mary chooses to go to prison and dies there, the result of a novel's worth of mistreatment and the damp and unhealthy conditions. Hays sets this up as a stark choice: death or prostitution – effectively, death or rape, given the coercive nature of the choices. Crucially, although Mary's decision to go to prison is the 'correct' one, the novel does not advocate it. In the parallel figures of Mary and her mother, the one who goes to prison and the other who becomes a prostitute, Hays is able to show both choices, and how both lead the characters to misery and death. It's a conclusion that speaks to a broken system. The important takeaway here is not 'which choice is the morally correct one' or 'which choice is the better one', but the message that this is a circumstance where there are no good choices. While Mary's choice is presented as the more morally upstanding, Hays's real focus is on the society which does not provide a route back in.

When Mary senior writes her long letter to her daughter – a letter which takes up a significant portion of the book and which reads an awful lot like a political polemic – she talks about the lack of options for social rehabilitation: 'I perceived myself the victim of the injustice, of the prejudice, of society, which by opposing to my return to virtue almost insuperable barriers, had plunged me into irremediable ruin.'[40] That this letter is where Hays takes the title of her novel from tells us how critical this issue is to both the book and its message. If you've had sex outside marriage, society says that the sinner can repent, but can never be restored – even in those circumstances where the sex was against their will. If society insists on educating women in a manner which Hays describes as setting them up as ideal marks, limiting them to a field of awareness where their fall is almost an expected by-product, while simultaneously closing the door on any return to respectability, then society carries responsibility for the abuses these women suffer. Essentially, she argues, it trains them to make a particular mistake and then exiles them for making it. By closing the door on the possibility of rehabilitation, Hays contends that society forces women in this position into a life of vice: prostitution, crime, violence.

If we look at what people were writing about women's education, we can see this debate echoing through those texts too. Hannah More's *Strictures* sets out the impossibility of rehabilitation clearly, though from a very different ideological perspective to Hays. More says that 'If unhappily she be your relation or friend, anxiously watch for the period when she shall be deserted by her betrayer; and see if by your Christian offices, she can be snatched from the perpetuity of vice.'[41] Here, we see what appears to be the limited endorsement of the forgiveness of friends and relations in such a situation. Mary senior, who finds herself pregnant and abandoned by the man whose child she is carrying, does what More advocates and seeks help from her parents. She turns up on their doorstep and appeals to them for aid, clearly hoping to be, as More puts it, 'snatched from the perpetuity of vice'. However, she writes that her plea to them 'drew upon me bitter reproaches: I was treated as an abandoned wretch, whom it would be criminal to receive and hopeless to attempt to reclaim'.[42] Mary senior is turned away by her parents, and as a result finds that she can only get help from men whose aid requires the transaction of sexual favours. While her parents seem to be adopting a harsher line than More here, it is not by as much as might first appear. If we look at a little more of More's argument, she writes that

> if, through the Divine blessing on your patient endeavours, she should ever be awakened to remorse be not anxious to restore the forlorn penitent to that society against whose laws she has so grievously offended; and remember that her soliciting such a restoration, furnishes but too plain a proof that she is not the penitent your partiality would believe, since penitence is more anxious to make its peace with heaven, than with the world […] To restore such a criminal to public society, is perhaps to tempt her to repeat her crime, or to deaden her repentance for having committed it.[43]

In short, though a woman might regret her actions, if she is restored to society she might cease to feel bad, and might be tempted to act in such a way again. Though More does not wish such women to continue to live in what she perceives as sin, she views the desire to return to society as proof that their penitence is lacking. Though they might be rescued from 'vice', they can never return to the way in which they used to live, their 'crime' a permanent weight around their neck. Finding the line between snatching from vice on the one hand, and not allowing social restoration on the other, is practically difficult. Mary senior's parents do not succeed at performing virtuous behaviour in the way that More endorses, but only because they prioritise one aspect to the exclusion of the other.

It is this 'hopeless[ness]' of her rehabilitation which Mary senior particularly critiques. She compares her situation to that of a desperate man, and finds that there's a gendered component to this shutting out: '*Despair* shuts not against him every avenue of repentance; *despair* drives him not from human sympathies.'[44] While men are able to move around freely despite being publicly known to have raped or 'betrayed' women, the women themselves are the ones cast in the role of social pariah. The rapist is welcomed back, while his victim is shunned. There are, she suggests, no incidents that can make a man desperate that do not leave him the hope of rehabilitation. That specific ceiling is reserved for women. Without a means to return to society, Hays suggests that women are essentially coerced into prostitution as the only trade left that they have the opportunity to earn a living from. As Mary Wollstonecraft put it in her most famous work, *A Vindication of the Rights of Woman*: 'necessity never makes prostitution the business of men's lives; though numberless are the women who are thus rendered systematically vicious'.[45] The threat of sexual violence becomes greater than any individual act: while an act of rape has impact and trauma, it also carries the risk for the victim of being pushed into a life of forced sex. The risk of future abuse is much higher. The threat therefore becomes more of a life sentence than an individual act; the control provided by the fear of rape and its subsequent difficulties is only the greater as a result of this.

This draws upon that final image in Mary senior's letter: that the limitations prescribed for women and justified on the grounds of their sex are 'fetters of sex'. Not only does the image refer to the limitation of intellect (and personality) imposed on women by the constrictions of the gendered education system, but contextually it speaks to the effective creation of social sex trafficking. The argument follows that, in the first instance, girls are educated in a manner which makes them easy prey to unscrupulous men. Once they have 'fallen' in some manner, society does not allow for their rehabilitation. They cannot return to their former station, nor are they able to work and earn a respectable independent living. They have little recourse through the legal system to protest their treatment, and are likely to suffer further abuses. The choices left for them so as to support themselves are therefore seriously narrowed – chiefly to theft and the various faces of sex work. Therefore, Hays is telling us, the manner in which women are educated, and the way in which society treats those who suffer rape, both perpetuate a situation where there will never be a shortage of sex workers, because there will constantly be women who do not have any other options. That is itself both a kind of tyranny and a form of enslavement.

It's a truism to say that sexual violence damages the life of the victim far more than that of the perpetrator. Even more so to acknowledge that the most vulnerable people in our society are often the most likely to be attacked. That damage has its psychological side – trauma that takes time, space, and safety to heal from. All of which can be luxuries that – as with Mary - victims don't have. Then there's the ripple effect. In the introduction to this book, I talked about my friends' experiences at university. About how every woman I knew had stories. And those stories had costs, costs which rippled and spread out from the event, and are still impacting on their lives today. The National Sexual Violence Resource Centre suggests that the number of women raped during their university experience in the United States is 1 in 5.[46] And I think about that, and about my own cohort, and I remember hearing two academics debating why girls seemed to under-perform in university exams. (There was a concern at that time that women were getting fewer firsts than men.) And I heard these academics wonder if it was because the exams were taking place in an imposing building, or because they preferred a coursework model, or if it was because male students were rewarded in class for the type of thinking that was likely to get you a first where female students might be treated differently. And part of me was desperate to get up and march over to their table and ask them if they had considered the fact that so many of their female students were trying to learn and cram for exams while also recovering from being assaulted.

How long does it take to process trauma? In the abstract, to suggest someone gets over it in a week or two or three is clearly ridiculous. But a few weeks can be a quarter of a university term. Maybe even a third. How much learning are those women losing out on because they're surviving something? How many of them are having to navigate going to classes or to the canteen with the person who attacked them? Women are able to be formally educated now, and for that I am earnestly and profoundly grateful. And we're not all raised to be vulnerable in the way that Mary Hays was talking about. But we do raise girls to be nice. To self-efface. To not be too loud or too angry or too much. We teach girls that when they are harmed, even when that harm becomes known, they must be the ones to accommodate for it.

Schools tell girls that the thickness of their shoulder-straps is the problem, and not the adult men who are aroused by their underage charges. Universities tell you that if your attacker is in your class, then you're the one who'll have to miss it – but you'll still have to take an exam on it. Your education is somehow both the most important thing for you, and the thing that expects you to be the one to bend. Somehow, you end up losing in every direction. If you're assaulted, you lose time, you can lose the ability to think and process clearly, you can lose your short-term memory. And if all of that means that you miss your grades, then you miss out on opportunities; on jobs, on funding, on anything that values the precise scores you come out of a degree with. In some fields that has a long, long echo. Yet even if someone is known to have committed sexual abuses, the more powerful they are, the more likely it is that the repercussions against them will be limited, that the burden of proof before something can be done will be higher. I remember a boy who assaulted me asking our case-worker how long his actions would follow him around for, because he wanted to have a career in politics, and it would be unfair to lose out on that. I could have told him then he'd be fine. It wouldn't stop him. It wouldn't stop him even if he wanted to run an entire country.

9
Theodora and Dorothea, or The Bystander Effect

> And now, Falkland, that you may not have any qualms upon you, take my most solemn oath, which I never violate to *man*, that I will not injure the fair one. Miss Arnold is not a Theodora Williams, she was not born to be the mistress of any one; but I think she will make an admirable wife.
>
> – Frances Sheridan, *The Conclusion of the Memoirs of Miss Sidney Bidulph*[1]

> Methinks you should in the midst of your passion have some regard to your reputation; for matches of this kind are rarely concluded with the consent of parents, but where there are reasons to which, for the lady's sake, her friends are obliged to yield.
>
> – Frances Sheridan, *The Conclusion of the Memoirs of Miss Sidney Bidulph*[2]

The courtship novels save their most biting condemnation for their critiques of how society excludes the victims of rape or seduction. There's a lack of any mechanism for recovery once a woman has been in some way discarded by a sexual partner (consensual or otherwise). How damaging this is depends on the social class of the woman, because the less protection you have, the more vulnerable you are to repeated abuse. Part of the reason rape was (and still is) so damaging a crime is because it comes with serious social repercussions for the victim that the perpetrator often avoids. A cycle is created – one which is propped up by the social fallout that victims of sexual violence experience. I want to talk more about that cycle, and about how class exacerbates the precariousness of a victim's situation. Because I think the minds that these authors are trying to change with their writing aren't those of potential rapists. They're the minds of the bystanders – the people who make rape a more harmful crime by isolating and excluding the victims.

In her novel *The Wrongs of Woman, or Maria* (1792), Mary Wollstonecraft addresses this idea that the abuse of vulnerable women in turn perpetuates further abuses against those same women by pushing them into prostitution. In her preface, Wollstonecraft says that her 'main object [is] the desire of exhibiting the misery and oppression, peculiar to women, that arise out of the partial laws and customs of our society'.[3] Like Hays, she believes that the legal system fails women, in that it promotes or condones their oppression. She goes on to say that it was the consideration of this view and purpose which 'restrained [her] fancy', calling the novel a 'history', and suggesting that this 'history' should 'be considered, as of woman, than of an individual'.[4] She explicitly tells us that *The Wrongs of Woman* should be understood as a representation – not of one individual's story, but of the scenarios and harms occasioned by what we would today call rape culture. In making such a declaration, Wollstonecraft authorises her readers to consider the difficulties faced by her characters as being common – both in the sense of a thing which happens often and that of something shared by a particular group. That Wollstonecraft talks about sexual abuses in this novel is a clear indication that she viewed sexual violence and the lack of protection from it as a major issue faced by a significant number of women at the time. We are also encouraged to view the events and abuses as realistic, rather than fantastical or exaggerated for narrative purposes. The abuses Wollstonecraft describes are serious both in nature and consequence, and we must not assume that every woman suffered them. But that does not mean that these kinds of abuse did not regularly occur.

It is in the character of Jemima, a former servant forced into prostitution after suffering rape and sexual abuse, that Wollstonecraft's arguments are most similar to those of Hays.[5] Jemima spends a long time relating her history to the titular character Maria, describing the circumstances and abuses which led to the two of them meeting. She begins with her early life, describing the treatment she endured as a servant while she was pre-pubescent, saying that

> Often had my mistress, for some instance of forgetfulness, thrown me against the wall, spit in my face, with various refinements on barbarity that I forbear to enumerate, though they were all acted over again by the servant, with additional insults, to which the appellation *bastard*, was commonly added, with taunts or sneers. But I will not attempt to give you an adequate idea of my situation, lest you, who have probably never been drenched with the dregs of human misery, should think I exaggerate.[6]

She is routinely abused on account of her illegitimacy and her low station, and we can see here that the abuse is not limited simply to behaviours practised by a higher-status person on a lower-status person. Rather, the behaviours of the higher-status person are then replicated (and exacerbated) by a lower-status person – the servant – who is nonetheless still a higher-status person than Jemima. The abuse of social inferiors is a mark of class behaviour, and therefore its practice becomes an enactment of station. If you want to show that you are higher up than someone, and higher-up people mistreat them, then mistreating them marks you as being higher up too. What we also see here is that the perpetuation of the abuse of women is not a universally male issue – these behaviours are being performed by the mistress of the house, who is not made a friend simply because she is female. Women, Wollstonecraft highlights, perpetuate abuse too. Wollstonecraft also draws attention to a significant challenge when discussing abusive behaviours. Once mistreatment reaches a particular threshold, in terms of both degree and prevalence, then explaining the problem becomes more challenging. The more extreme, widespread, and/or serious the problem, the greater the risk of its being perceived as a made-up narrative. There's a threshold for how bad uninvolved people will accept a problem as being before they assume that you must be exaggerating or making it up.[7]

Once Jemima reaches puberty, the mistreatment transitions into sexualised abuses. After commenting on the changes in her body, she says that her master began to catch her 'in the passage' with 'disgusting caresses', before going on to recount in extremely limited detail two occasions of penetrative sex; the first time, and the time they were caught.[8] The first instance contains the hallmarks of 'proper resistance' as the master 'compelled me to submit' by 'blows – yes; blows and menaces', suggesting that there were both threats and multiple instances of physical violence. Therefore, despite the lack of explicit information regarding penetration and emission, we might have confidence that a general eighteenth-century reader would view this as an instance of rape in the criminal sense.

Jemima goes on in the same sentence to say that 'to avoid my mistress's fury, I was obliged in future to comply, and skulk to my loft at his command, in spite of increased loathing'.[9] The subtext here is that, having once been involved in a sexual encounter with the master, any knowledge of that reaching the mistress of the house would result in 'fury', as Jemima would be blamed for it. In these subsequent interactions, we see the realities of a diminished capacity to consent. Jemima is not being physically forced to submit to sex with her master, and we do not witness her resisting. However, following the initial act of rape, her theoretical choice is not 'to have sex or not to have sex', but rather 'to have sex or be turned out of the house without a reference, limited prospects of future employment, and the probable necessity of turning to prostitution to survive'. Jemima is vulnerable, and as discussed earlier, would not find ready rehabilitation into society. We then witness this exact narrative when Jemima is finally found with the master.

Framed in this way, it becomes clear that as soon as the initial rape happens, Jemima is effectively transformed into a sex worker (in that she must comply with the sexual demands of her master in order to retain her employment and financial stability). Her choice in subsequent interactions is therefore not between maid work and sex work, but between a single client and a broader pool. That she will have to engage in sexual acts to earn a living is effectually understood, and so she describes herself as being 'obliged' to continue to fulfil her master's sexual demands. Her capacity to give meaningful consent to sex has been removed, and her choice reconfigured to choosing to be a sex worker for her current master or for the more general public. Though the requirements for 'proper' resistance are not met following the initial rape, Wollstonecraft still encourages us to view Jemima as a victim, or 'prey'.[10] She is robbed of her capacity to give consent by a continuing compulsion – meaning that the interactions cannot be consensual – despite the fact that she does not perform the behaviours that a strict adherence to the eighteenth-century legal definition of consent would require. The idea that one's capacity can be reduced to the point where the notion of consent in that situation is essentially a sham is clearly set out.

The mistress of the house does ultimately find out and expel Jemima. Without a reference or a good character, Jemima is forced into a more recognisable form of sex work. Wollstonecraft highlights here the way in which servants are particularly vulnerable to this kind of abuse, as they live in the homes of their masters, and rely on their references to enable them to find reputable work elsewhere. When they lose their work, they also lose their home; needing a new job is about needing shelter as well as employment. Abuse of such a system is both all too easy and all too common.

If we compare Jemima to *The Victim of Prejudice*'s young Mary, we can see the role that class plays in this funnelling of abused women into prostitution. Jemima is mistreated by her employers. Her word is viewed as less legitimate because of her social class, and so she is often accused of lying or stealing. It is made clear that she cannot give testimony which will be believed, regardless of the nature of the crime she is being accused of. On the other hand, Hays's Mary has an impeccable character, which makes her realisation that she would not be believed were she to attempt to prosecute Osborne an evil specific to a sexual crime. If we consider why that might be, and why Mary herself agrees that her mother's circumstances and her own illegitimacy mean that she cannot marry William, we can draw some fairly logical conclusions. Firstly, that being lower class means being perceived as less – less moral, less reliable, less valuable. Secondly, that being a (willing or unwilling) participant in a sexual act outside marriage has the same type of impact on one's status, and therefore one is also perceived as being worth less. Finally, that as prostitution was one of the only avenues of employment for sexually violated women needing to earn their living, a conflation occurs whereby known victims of sexual violence are prostitutes – therefore lower class – and so women of the lower classes are inherently viewed as prostitutes.

Author and playwright Frances Sheridan takes this question of social pressure and class and places it at the centre of one of her novels. Her best-known book, *The Memoirs of Miss Sidney Bidulph* (1761), was influenced by the work of her friend Samuel Richardson (of *Pamela* and *Clarissa* fame). This novel explores the tension created between female desire and appropriate obedience to your family, and follows Sidney through her courtship time and her unhappy marriage. It proved to be very popular, and so Sheridan went on to write a sequel – the *Conclusion of the Memoirs of Miss Sidney Bidulph* (1767), which was published posthumously. While the *Conclusion* doesn't have explicit rape scenes in the way that *The Victim of Prejudice* or *The Wrongs of Woman* does, it is explicit in its threats and focuses both on the evils of coercion and the importance of meaningful consent.

The epistolary novel follows the narrative of Sidney's two daughters, Dorothea (Dolly) and Cecilia, who fall victim to a scheme devised by their adoptive brother Falkland and his friends, the Audley siblings. Cecilia and Falkland love one another, but neither has admitted it to the other. Edward Audley, who knows of Falkland's feelings, would also like to marry one of the two sisters; he has a preference for Dolly, but he's more interested in their fortunes than their personalities. Edward decides that his best bet to marry one of them is if both girls are involved in love affairs, because this will influence their behaviours and make it more likely that their families will accept an undesirable marriage. The scheme is, in true eighteenth-century fashion, very convoluted. Audley first convinces Falkland that Dolly is in love with him (he's actually right about this), and he gets his sister to convince Dolly that Falkland loves her back. Falkland loves Cecilia, but he has no idea that she cares about him, and so he allows himself to be manipulated into proposing to Dolly. Dolly and Falkland become engaged, but Falkland quickly comes to regret this when he finds out that Cecilia did actually love him back. This is the set-up that Audley needs in order to convince Falkland to help him entrap a sister for himself. If Falkland wants to marry Cecilia, he's going to have to break his word to Dolly, and so he's motivated to believe that Audley wants to help him make things right by marrying Dolly himself. (Like I said, very convoluted.) The novel is set before the Marriage Act of 1753 – an Act which changed the requirements for marriage. Before the Act prohibited it, you could be considered married if you expressed your *intention* to get married in the present tense. The Act was trying to crack down on clandestine marriages, requiring people to have a licence to get married, as well as a ceremony in a church or chapel. As the novel is set before this Act was passed, and Falkland and Dolly have promised to marry each other, they are considered as good as married already. Falkland would have to effectively commit bigamy in order to marry Cecilia.[11]

Audley has what he thinks is a foolproof plan. He believes that if he kidnaps Dolly and keeps her in his house, it will look as though she has run away with him, damaging her reputation. He would prefer that she doesn't know she's been kidnapped – he pretends that there is a problem with the carriage that means that they need to stop for the night at the nearest house, when he has actually just driven directly to his friend's house – but he's willing to have her discover that she has been abducted if it makes her say yes to his proposal. His idea is that dutiful Dolly won't want to face the shame and social stigma of looking as though she has engaged in extramarital sex, and so will agree to marry him in order to preserve her reputation.

In the meantime, Cecilia is fighting to have her choices recognised and supported by her family. She wants to marry Falkland, and doesn't know that he's secretly got engaged to her sister. She knows the family won't approve of her marrying him, but she's hoping she can at least talk her mother around. However, as Falkland hasn't asked her to marry him, she can't openly ask them about it, since she's supposed to wait for the man to make the offer before having feelings herself. Another man, a much more suitable match, does ask her to marry him, and Cecilia finds herself alienated from her family as she keeps refusing this match which they want, and she won't explain why.

The plots here, revolving around forced marriage, the right to refusal, and the value of the female word, throw up important considerations about the role of consent in marriage – and in families. A key reason why Audley is not worried about Dolly finding out that he deliberately kidnapped her, and that Falkland was in on the scheme, is that 'when she is my wife, you know, I can command her lips, so that you will have nothing to fear from her'.[12] As her husband, he sees it as within his power to control the words that she utters and the facts she discloses. Quite apart from the fact that consent was legally considered to be present from the point of marriage, this therefore implies that from that point her word of any kind is irrelevant, and comes directly under the authority of her husband. She could not consent even if the law said she had the capacity to, because a wife's responses are her husband's to decide. Moreover, if he is going to be able to stop her from disclosing something as significant as a kidnapping, a scheme in which her adopted brother helped entrap her into a marriage she doesn't want in order to free himself to marry her sister (casually causing her to commit bigamy too), then this suggests that her communications to her nearest and dearest will be stopped as well – or that they won't matter. Audley's assumptions here highlight how difficult it was in the eighteenth century to talk about abuses that happened inside a marriage, the way in which controlling and domineering spouses were able to enact abuse without fear of reprisal.

There is another woman, called Theodora (a subtle nod from Sheridan that we are supposed to compare her and Dolly – or to use her full name, Dorothea). Theodora is not of the same class as Dolly, and she isn't someone Audley thinks of as a potential wife. Theodora is respectable enough that she's not willing to have sex outside marriage, but Audley has a scheme to counter that too. He tells Theodora that he loves her and wants to marry her, going so far as to have a sham wedding so as to get her into bed. Once he's done, she finds out that it was all a lie, and she's left to pick up the pieces. Audley is not a character we are supposed to sympathise with – we're supposed to hate him. His plans, his casual disregard of the rights and feelings of our heroines, are emphasised so as to make him distasteful. Sheridan is encouraging her readers to consider this type of behaviour as gross, as disgraceful, and as something which is to be shunned by right-thinking gentlemen. But in disapproving of this behaviour, we are not just disapproving of kidnapping. We are disapproving of coercion, of the violation of consent that misrepresentation can allow, and of the entitled idea that a wife's word is entirely her husband's to command. We are being encouraged to view the decision to marry – and to consent, since the two are tied together – as one which ought to take place without misrepresentation, since this materially affects a participant's ability to legitimately give consent.

Unlike Hays, Sheridan does not direct her energy towards the social lack of rehabilitation for Dolly once she is believed to have had sex outside marriage. Instead, she draws attention to the way in which a woman's reputation was founded on public belief, and therefore that what's important is what is publicly agreed to have occurred, rather than either what did happen or what is believed to have happened. What do I mean by this? Dolly's having spent several nights under the same roof as Edward Audley without a chaperone, having left the city in his carriage, will result in a public belief that they have had sex – which will in turn damage her social position. The public belief is therefore that she has lessened in value. However, if Dolly were to marry Audley as he intended, her reputation would not be damaged in the same way – while people might believe that she had engaged in sexual acts before marriage, the fact that they did subsequently get married would allow them to be socially acceptable people, and she would not be expected to feel shame. The problem would be corrected by the marriage. Therefore, whatever people privately believed or gossiped about regarding their relations, the public position would be that nothing had happened (or that they were simply a little too keen).

Dolly's position in the novel, where she must either choose to *be* virtuous and appear sinful, or *be* sinful (through bigamy) but appear virtuous, is a mark of Audley's cruelty and his amorality; he thinks nothing of placing her in this bind, since he himself places no value on the practice of virtue – simply on the appearance. His faithlessness is shown to be an active imposition on women, and his disregard for his word to them is frequently the subject of Sheridan's criticism. One conversation that Audley recounts to Falkland involves his making this declaration:

> Oh, but to break one's promise! One's oath! Suckling, who ever thought that an oath made to a woman was binding? The creatures themselves don't expect it. Is not the most solemn of all oaths, the matrimonial oath, violated every day? Is the husband thought the

> worse for infidelities to his wife? And would not the wife be laughed at who complained of them?[13]

Here we see the extrapolation of Dolly's situation, whereby, although her reputation will be harmed by Audley's scheme if she does not give in to it, his will not suffer. The double standard for adultery is shown as universal; Audley suggests that adultery is in itself so common that a wife ought to expect that it will occur, because any complaint about it would be 'laughed at' for being nothing out of the ordinary. Audley does allow that this type of oath breaking can be performed by women too, when he tells Falkland that *they* would not have to fear cuckoldry even if the two sisters did not come to be in love with them, 'for the poor dears, trammelled as they have always been with their notions of duty, would never once take it into their heads that there were any consolatory wanderings beyond the matrimonial pale'.[14] However, the implication remains that, even though married women have affairs, not all affairs married men have are with married women. Therefore the expectation that men will commit adultery as standard practice is indicative of a society where there are women to marry, and women to have affairs with, ones who aren't seen as being materially damaged because they did not have sufficient reputation to enable them to marry well in the first place. They are not seen as, to go back to our chapter on virginity, wife material.

It is heavily implied that the only reason Audley does not rape Dolly is because he intends to marry her. Her station, and the social potential that she represents to Audley, is what protects her from sexual violence here, rather than any inherent personal quality. The decision over whether Dolly is harmed is shown to be entirely in Audley's hands. Dolly is more valuable to him than Theodora, according to a valuation of the two women as usable objects; Sheridan does not suggest that Dolly has more value as an individual. In a letter reassuring Falkland that he does not intend to actually harm Dolly, Audley writes:

> Falkland, that you may not have any qualms upon you, take my most solemn oath, which I never violate to *man*, that I will not injure the fair one. Miss Arnold is not a Theodora Williams, she was not born to be the mistress of any one; but I think she will make an admirable wife [...] Once I get her in my net, I shall give her no other cause of complaint than that of detaining her as my prisoner; for I mean to deport myself towards her with the sanctity due to a vestal.[15]

Passing over the fact that 'detaining her as my prisoner' seems like a completely reasonable cause for complaint, we here see Audley setting out his view of women and their role in society. Theodora Williams, who does not have money, is not the type of woman a man like Audley would want to marry. She, therefore, is 'born to be the mistress', while Dolly has claims to comparatively better treatment because of her position, family, and connections. Her virginity is protected by her social class. Oaths are explicitly only binding on men, because men are the only persons with whom honour has currency. Audley himself uses a specious loophole whereby oaths to women are not binding because nobody abides by them, and therefore since nobody abides by them, no woman can reasonably expect that they will be abided by; therefore no women expect oaths to them to be kept, and therefore oaths to women do not have to be kept because there was no belief in their being kept in the first place (and if there was, it is not a reasonable belief). It's a very convenient bit of fast-talking. As he says,

> I know what it is to swear roundly, in order to make a woman believe that I shall love *her,* and *only* her, as long as live; and I have made many a damsel (by way of carrying on the farce) swear as many to me in return; but it never once entered into my imagination that she expected I should *keep* those oaths, no more I expected that she should keep hers, longer than we liked each other. If these be what you call *vows,* I have made and broke as many of them as most private gentlemen in England.[16]

It is this logic which leads him to reason that Theodora Williams is being entirely unreasonable in her expectations that he acknowledge her as his wife. Theodora, a young woman Audley promises to marry, stages a sham wedding to, engages in sex with, and then declares his mistress, does not agree with his views. When she uncovers the fact that it was actually Audley's servant who conducted the ceremony rather than someone licensed to do so, she becomes uneasy about the legality of their marriage, and 'I went to bed in great affliction, considering myself, though very innocent in my intention, as living in an unlawful state.' She hears Falkland laugh along with Audley at the idea that she had been taken in 'by the old bait, a promise of marriage'.[17] Her attempts to convince Audley to make good on his promise are in vain (though he does legitimise her and name her his wife on his deathbed), and in the end her family friend Mr Main removes her from Audley's house. Here, we see the root of what Audley's sophisticated excuses come to mean – that women will not engage in sexual acts with him unless they believe that they are or soon will be married (which would remove any stain on their reputation). Because he knows that these are the only conditions under which they will agree to have sex with him, he fabricates those conditions in order to obtain their consent – meaning that he removes from them the ability to give meaningful consent, since they are not consenting to the situation at hand, but to an elaborate farce. Consent is not something which exists out of context.

The law stating that consent is given with marriage does just this – removes any kind of context from the situation. Such a methodology is now legally recognised as deeply flawed, but can clearly be seen to have been recognised as problematic much earlier than the 1990s and the criminalisation of marital rape. Theodora is consenting to sex as a married woman, and Audley is aware that she would not consent were she to know that they were unmarried. He is aware that this kind of action is wrong, as it is not something he believes is appropriate for the woman he *actually* intends to marry, but he does not view it as problematic in Theodora's case because he sees it as the type of treatment she ought to expect. Class and money determine one's right to an informed decision. Theodora, then, has had her capacity to consent compromised by Audley, as have numerous other women from the sounds of his boasting. As Audley says, in Dolly's case,

> If I meant nothing but a little amour, I should have better hopes of it; for, with reverence to chastity be it spoken, a lady may fall into such a scrape contrary to her intentions; and many a poor innocent has slipped unawares into the trap, where she has been content to stay, rather than like the silly mouse tear herself in endeavouring to get out: but this, you know, is out of the question.[18]

That these types of encounters lack informed consent is clear – they occur 'contrary' to the woman's 'intentions' and involve her falling victim to his schemes 'unawares'. Though Audley is being metaphorical here, the image of the mouse in the trap makes explicit the idea that the woman will be harmed by freeing herself from him and his scheme. She must either submit or suffer. The same bind faces Dolly, where she must either decide to go along with his plan or face the social consequences, but in her case Audley is not willing to actually become physical until after the marriage has been officiated. Audley, then, thinks that it is quite easy to trap women into sexual affairs, whether they want to have them or not. It is this behaviour that is censured by Sheridan, and that makes Falkland's acceptance of Audley and his schemes particularly troubling. Falkland, after all, has been raised as something of a brother to Dolly, and she is the sister of the woman he intends to marry. (Yes, it is a bit weird – the family thought that the more they tried to make them like real siblings, the less chance there would be of them getting married. They did not manage to carry off the idea.) He clearly trusts that Audley will not ruin Dolly's reputation (even though the over-keen marriage would damage it a little), which means that he trusts that Dolly will capitulate and compromise the morals that are one of the core features of her character.

Sheridan gives us a contrast of what male behaviour should look like in the character of Lord V–. Lord V– is the man who wants to marry Cecilia and who, unlike Falkland, has the full backing of her family. They attempt to compel her to accept him in a myriad of ways, most of which are distressing to Cecilia, but which are not outside the realm of what was socially acceptable familial pressure. It was not unexpected for families to put pressure on women to agree to marry the person the family has chosen for her (we saw this with Clarissa earlier, we'll see it again later in *Mansfield Park* in Chapter 11). However, Lord V– has absolutely no intention of marrying Cecilia without her express consent, regardless of the views and desires of her family. He's in love with her, but says that 'if the sentiments of the lady herself, said I, are averse to me, I am not a lover so void of delicacy as to seize an unwilling hand, joined to mine merely by the authority of parents'.[19] He explicitly views the consent of the family as inadequate in the acceptance of the marriage proposal, and it is Cecilia's word which is given priority and authority through his actions. He goes further than this, and when Cecilia confesses to him that she has feelings elsewhere,

> He interrupted me here with some vivacity, And can you think so meanly of me, Madam, said he, as to believe that after the declaration you have just made, I would like a ravisher seize your reluctant hand? No, Madam, precious as I should esteem the gift were it voluntarily bestowed, I would not accept it when forced on me by the authority of a parent.[20]

Lord V– is Sheridan's model of correct male behaviour, and here he draws the absolute parallel between the man who marries with familial consent against the will of the woman involved and the man who commits an act of sexual violence against her. He describes the process which would lead Cecilia down the aisle as being 'forced', demonstrating an understanding that parental pressure and familial authority constitute a kind of coercion that can actively damage a person's capacity to give or withhold their consent freely. He actively supports Cecilia's words with his actions, refusing the union that he wants. The value he places on Cecilia's active desire to marry him forms a sharp contrast both to Audley's entrapment and Falkland's acceptance of it.

And Sheridan does indicate that familial pressure can be overwhelming. Cecilia goes from favoured child to black sheep, and is forced to endure isolation and constant criticism. This dialogue between Cecilia and her family – especially her mother Sidney – is particularly interesting given this novel's status as a sequel. While Sheridan's initial novel dealt with the question of duty and familial obedience, representing parental authority as an overwhelming power (and showed how much those things hurt young Sidney), the sequel shows an ultimately flawed attempt to move away from that model in the next generation. In writing to her mother, Cecilia says that 'Both Sir George and lady Sarah speak of him as a desirable alliance; but remember I tell you, mama, I do not like lord V–, and I am sure you will never constrain your own poor Cecilia.'[21] It is her hope that, in telling her mother her views about this suitor, her mother will stand by the promise she made to both her daughters: not to do as her own mother did and push them into a union they do not want.

However, while Sidney obeys the letter of this promise, she does not obey its spirit. She responds to Cecilia by acknowledging the force a mother's desires can bring to bear on an obedient daughter, suggesting that Cecilia should not regard her views as absolutes.

> *Advice* from a mother was always considered by *me* as a *command*: yet I do not desire you to regard it in so severe a light. We have been educated differently [… I] though tenderly beloved by my ever honoured mother, had, nevertheless, my neck early bowed to obedience; and this it was which constrained me to yield up my nearest

> wishes, and as it were, mold [*sic*] my heart to the will of her whom I thought I owed all my duty.[22]

She also suggests, by saying she 'thought' she owed all her duty to her mother, that this is a view she has come to disagree with, and therefore Cecilia in turn does not owe all her duty to Sidney. But Sidney distrusts Cecilia's motivations in refusing Lord V–, and does not believe that her generally well-behaved and dutiful daughter has a valid reason for her choices – 'sure I am 'tis impossible you can have any *rational* objection to him' – and she also does not believe that dislike might be a valid reason (as it happens, Cecilia does not dislike Lord V– specifically, but that is beside the point).[23]

In isolation, this might not sound so serious. It is essentially the first discussion about the matter that Cecilia and Sidney have had. If Sidney wants to make sure that her daughter has thought this decision through, there is nothing intrinsically wrong with that. But as the matter progresses, Cecilia only gets more certain in her views, and more emotionally distressed by the attempts to make her change her mind. Her uncle Sir George writes to his sister Sidney repeating Cecilia's cry that 'my mama … would not press me to what I dislike', relaying her distress and discomfort at his suggestions, and displaying the trust she has in her mother's word. Yet the context of Sir George's letter is to warn Sidney that 'I am afraid this indulgence of yours may be productive of consequences as disagreeable in their effects as the too ready submission of her mama was upon another occasion.'[24] Sidney's response draws on the same rhetoric as her initial reply, and explicitly gives Sir George permission to continue to distress her daughter, excusing this conduct on the basis that her daughter's opinion cannot be valid because it conflicts with her own.

> A *reasonable* cause of dislike she cannot have; I therefore am in hopes that time and a little perseverance on my lord's side will overcome her reluctance […] The *authority* of a parent I never will exert; too

> dearly have I myself experienced the consequences of such a proceeding; but as far as remonstrance, advice, and admonition goes, I have not been sparing. I am under a promise to both my children never to urge their acceptance of a man whom they did not like; but *my* punctilio does not bind *you*. You are therefore at liberty to use every means (absolute force excepted) to prevail on Cecilia to receive as she ought so advantageous an offer.[25]

In one paragraph she both acknowledges the damage that parental authority caused her, and her commitment never to use it herself, and yet goes on to expressly permit her brother to impose on her daughter as much as he likes in order to convince her to change her mind. She makes the decision that her daughter cannot have a 'reasonable' cause of dislike – meaning that she herself sees no reason for the match not to take place and therefore assumes that, rather than the possibility of there being a reason she is not currently aware of, there can be no valid reason. Simple dislike from Cecilia, without a specific 'legitimate' reason, is also not regarded as valid. She specifically refers to her promise as a 'punctilio', which perhaps carries more resonances of a technicality than Sidney intends. After all, what good is a promise 'never to urge' if it does not prohibit 'remonstrance, advice, and admonition' and the clear endorsement of harsh tactics on her behalf, even if without her name? That she specifies 'absolute force excepted' brings home that she truly is advocating any other medium of coercion – including, apparently, the threat of force. Though she herself was the victim of overbearing parental authority, Sidney here demonstrates that even a well-meaning or apparently enlightened person can fall into the trap of exerting familial pressure – and from Cecilia's clear expressions, we can see that this distresses her just as much as it distressed her mother. Sidney attempts both to enforce her own will and maintain a position of support for her daughter's decision-making capacity – but this does not and cannot succeed. Cecilia makes this clear when talking to her namesake, saying 'Ah, Madam, you don't know what *sort* of persuaders my uncle and aunt are. Their requests are commands, and their persuasions are threats, and I dread even downright violence from their authority.'[26]

At the root of this confusion, perhaps, is the question Sheridan herself is attempting to wrestle with: how does one balance duty and proper familial obedience against freedom of choice and an independent mind? In both this novel and its predecessor, Sheridan establishes the importance of the capacity to choose, and the misery that can be created by familial diktats, but also stresses that duty and obedience are important virtues for young women to have. In this speech of Sidney's we are presented with Sheridan's dilemma – Sidney wants to give her daughters freedom to choose, and has promised them that she will respect their wishes when it comes to choosing a husband. Yet she firmly believes that what her daughter is doing is not the best course of action, and so she wants to influence Cecilia in order to bring her around to her own way of thinking. The ideal outcome of this situation would be one where Cecilia voluntarily changes to share the same view as the rest of her family; if their views are aligned, then the situation works smoothly. The Harlowe family in Richardson's *Clarissa* insist that obedience does not carry any merit until the fulfilment of it runs counter to the performer's own desires. While Sheridan does not go as far as that, she is forced to contrive a rather convoluted ending in order that Cecilia ends up marrying the 'right' person.[27]

When Dolly reveals her engagement to Falkland – and therefore essentially her marriage – Cecilia realises that she herself can never marry him. To do so would involve her having to fundamentally alter her beliefs and betray her beloved sister. She won't do it. Her sister is more important to her. Falkland finally offers to go through with marrying Dolly as he promised, but she decides to join a convent instead, rather than marry the man who has hurt her sister. Here, Sheridan demonstrates the clear bonds of loyalty and principle which govern the relationship between the two sisters, in sharp contrast to Audley and Falkland's sketchy morals and false promises. Both sisters are in love with the same man, but ultimately they each choose not to have him. They choose each other and themselves instead. Audley, who dies at the end of the novel, tries to make amends for his actions and acknowledges Theodora as his wife, giving her back her legitimacy and social standing.

These powerful resolutions are undercut slightly by Sidney's making a dying request that Cecilia marry Lord V–. Though she waits until Cecilia has declared that she will never marry Falkland, Sidney does still require a deathbed promise from her daughter, which she then immediately transfers to a clause in her will, codifying both her desire and her daughter's promise. In an echo of the practicalities of the marriage contract, the daughter who fought so hard for her right to choose a partner ends the novel bound by a legal document which effectively removes her ability to modify her consent.

Across these novels, predatory men are rightly criticised – but so too are the actions of the society which enables them, which closes its doors to the victims but allows the perpetrators to continue their lives as normal. In thinking about the audience of courtship novels, it is important to see this group. The novels are not necessarily trying to change the minds of potential rapists (as they show, the only thing that really impacts whether a rapist rapes is whether they want to). They're not trying to persuade them not to violate women. But through the portrayal of the harm created by a lack of rehabilitation and the inaction of those bystanders around them, the novels work to align the reader with the victim's needs, promoting the idea that they deserve to be supported and sheltered by their peers. The novels emphasise that the stakes are higher the lower class you are, because there is a degree of protection given by being a potential wife. Coercion and pressure are highlighted as dangerous and damaging tools, ones which often rely on the threat of social backlash and public perception. If there is anyone whose behaviour these novels are trying to change, it is the bystanders, the rape-permissive society that loads the bulk of the social stigma on to the victims, while allowing the rapists to assimilate back into the drawing rooms as gentlemen. It's the 'boys will be boys' mentality that does no one any favours. But change the fallout and you can dramatically change the scale of harm that rape does to victims.

PART IV

MARRIAGE

10

Elinor, or Honouring Engagements

Jane Austen's books are still read and re-imagined as silly, frivolous stories for and about silly, frivolous women, but there are desperate stakes on the table. Austen, who never married herself, writes about women living in cages built by men, trying to survive as best they can, which is precisely what makes the stories so exciting and, to me at least, so frightening.

– Laurie Penny[1]

Impropriety! Oh! Mrs Weston – it is too calm a censure. Much, much beyond impropriety! – It has sunk him, I cannot say how it has sunk him in my opinion. So unlike what a man should be! – None of that upright integrity, that strict adherence to truth and principle, that disdain of trick or littleness, which a man should display in every transaction of his life.

– Jane Austen, *Emma*[2]

Jane Austen's *Sense and Sensibility* (1811) is a novel full of contrasts. Elinor and Marianne, the two protagonists, have very different approaches to life – and to men. One is looking for constancy, stability, kindness; the other for passion, a deep emotional connection, a vivid approach to life. But both sisters wind up falling in love with men who lie to them. In the comparisons she draws between Edward Ferrars and John Willoughby, Austen explores what it looks like when questions of verbal and behavioural consent are applied to men.[3] How meaningful is consent when it's made under false pretences? And what information is it fair to withhold from someone you're marrying?

Edward Ferrars, the man Elinor loves, is secretly engaged to Lucy Steele. They got engaged young, but even though Edward now regrets the engagement and would much rather marry Elinor, he intends to keep his promise. He thinks it is the right thing to do. When his family eventually find out, they are furious, and quickly disown him. Despite his family's objections, and the dramatic reduction in his finances, Edward insists on standing by Lucy. He winds up disinherited, engaged to a woman he doesn't love, sad that he is not engaged to the woman he *is* in love with, but with the consolation that he has done the honourable thing. Our view of this original relationship with Lucy comes largely from Elinor, who's going to put Edward in the best possible light, but it's important to recognise the point that scholar Claudia Johnson makes, that Edward 'forms an early attachment to Lucy out of the idleness endemic to landed gentry'.[4] It's not really a love match – he fell into it because he didn't have anything else to do. Not exactly a romance for the ages. It's important to Edward's decision making that he believes Lucy is very much in love with him. He says he doesn't want to let her down – he will do his best to act as though he's in love with her, trying to make her experience of the relationship as close as possible to the one she thought she had consented to. He isn't planning on telling her that he doesn't love her any more, and justifies hiding the change in his feelings on the grounds that telling her the truth, or asking her to let him marry Elinor, would be selfish.

In doing this, he removes the choice from Lucy to consent to her situation. Pretending to be in love – or being married to someone who only pretends to be in love with you – is hardly a romantic ideal. But because our view of Lucy is coloured both by Elinor's dislike of her and the narrator's insights into her scheming, we are less critical of Edward than we might be. It's clear that communicating with Lucy would not have resolved the issue, since she's motivated by money and status rather than love, and was already doing at least a bit of play-acting of her own about her feelings for Edward.[5] Had he asked her to dissolve their engagement on the grounds that he wasn't in love with her, it seems unlikely that she would have accepted. Certainly Edward seems to believe this, and therefore also believes that the engagement would remain in place even if he disclosed his feelings – and his failures – to Lucy. When he does tell her that the circumstances of their relationship have changed, it's to tell her about the change in his financial status after he gets disowned. And on those grounds Lucy is very happy to jump ship to the brother who gets his inheritance. Nevertheless, we can see that there are actually a lot of similarities between Lucy and Edward. Lucy's actions in pretending to love Edward are – in effect – the same as Edward's in pretending to love Lucy. The crucial difference lies in their motivation. Where Lucy is acting because she wants to improve her situation in life, Edward doesn't want to hurt the feelings of the woman he believes he's failed. We are far more disapproving of her than of him. Edward's position as Elinor's love interest, and Lucy's general dislikeability, are powerful tools that encourage us not to question this quite as closely as the narrator suggests we maybe should.

Edward is acting simultaneously from a place of cowardice and arrogance here, not selfless chivalry. Taken at face value, continuing his engagement by pretending to be in love is an act of kindness and honour, which he is willing to go through with even though it requires sacrifice. Lucy is a person he views as worthy of honouring his word to, even when it no longer benefits him in the ways he anticipated, and when his personal opinion of her has sunk. There is a kind of respect here, which many of the male characters we've encountered across these novels lack. But in performing this charade and not communicating honestly with Lucy, Edward removes her ability to give meaningful consent to the marriage. She is unaware of the situation she would be committing herself to. (The same could absolutely be said in reverse, but we're not encouraged to defend Lucy's behaviour.) In doing this, Edward makes an assumption about what Lucy feels and wants, and acts accordingly, without giving her a chance to weigh in on the matter. It's a completely different matter when it's his finances that have changed, rather than his feelings.

> 'I thought it my duty,' said he, 'independent of my feelings, to give her the option of continuing the engagement or not, when I was renounced by my mother, and stood to all appearance without a friend in the world to assist me.'[6]

Though he sees a significant shift in financial status as a reason for asking Lucy if she would like to continue their engagement, he does not appear to view a significant change in his own attachment to her as meriting the same kind of frank communication. Had Lucy actually been motivated by love she might well have preferred to 'free' the person she cared for; to hope for a relationship where she is loved in her own right, rather than as some form of sacrificial duty. Regardless of what she *might* have chosen, Edward acknowledges that a change in at least some kinds of circumstance warrants a re-examination of the agreement. Consent can be withdrawn if what you had agreed to is different enough. Conveniently, Lucy's motivations and his altered financial expectations allow him to exit an engagement he no longer wants, without requiring him to admit to any wrongdoing himself. He didn't choose to cut himself off, and hasn't made explicit that his feelings have changed; the change he admits to isn't his fault, and he hides the one that he is responsible for. Once again he positions himself in the role of the chivalric knight, offering Lucy the chance to throw him over, without acknowledging his role in why she might wish to do that.

Edward's belief that Lucy would be irretrievably hurt by the loss of him shows more self-confidence than his character typically displays. He's reading the situation as Lucy intends him to, and therefore has correctly interpreted the role she is performing (rather than the situation as it is), but he is personally able to fall in with the belief that he is essential to her happiness. He's acting from the evidence of a four-year-long secret engagement – not an insignificant period of time – and believes that Lucy will remain permanently attached to him. Unlike other male characters across the courtship novel genre, he doesn't view women as inherently fickle.[7] However, if we contrast this hypothetical Lucy scenario with Elinor, whom we know really does love Edward, we see that his view of his own importance is still overstated. One of the key elements of Elinor's character is that despite her personal grief at the losses she suffers, she refuses to look at the future with bleak hopelessness. Rather, she sees heartbreak as a burden she should work to overcome.[8] Though she would very much like to marry Edward, and believes he would make her happy, she's not going to be miserable forever without him – not if she can help it. When Lucy makes the choice that ultimately gets Edward what he wants – choosing to marry his brother and leaving him free to marry Elinor – he judges her for her decision:

> even now, I cannot comprehend on what motive she acted, or what fancied advantage it could be to her, to be fettered to a man for whom she had not the smallest regard, and who had only two thousand pounds in the world.[9]

At this point he is convinced that Lucy is 'capable of the utmost meanness of wanton ill-nature', and therefore the idea of her wishing to honour her side of the engagement doesn't enter into his calculations of her comparable actions.[10] Yet without the idea of honour – and guilt – he can't understand her decision, perhaps failing to consider the material difference between being securely married to a man with two thousand pounds and being the unmarried daughter of a professional tutor.

But what happens if we apply Edward's assessment of Lucy to himself? Had the marriage occurred, he would have been 'fettered' to Lucy, with honour (and cowardice and guilt) as the compelling factor. Austen's treatment of the ethics of this love triangle is a little convoluted, but still conveys the idea that in these situations, the question of who is acting rightly is complicated. Edward treats both Elinor and Lucy poorly, and it is only because Lucy is scheming for herself that we don't feel bad about the way he acts towards her. But if she had been the person he thought she was when he was busy falling in love with another woman, had she really been devoted to him, it would be much harder to make excuses for him. We might not like Lucy, but her actual character doesn't alter the fact that Edward was misbehaving, and doing so when he believed the best of her. If we view Elinor as being injured by Edward's treatment of her, then we must also accept that the Lucy Edward says he believes in would have been injured in the same way, had he allowed her to see his changed feelings towards her. But if we judge Lucy for pretending to love Edward, then we must also ask whether Edward is wrong in pretending to love Lucy. And if Edward believes that it is reasonable for Lucy to marry a person while being unaware of the fact that he doesn't care about her, then we must also question whether he's justified in his criticism of her for acting as though she loved him. Edward's honouring of his engagement is represented in positive contrast to the way rakish Mr Willoughby ruins women and leaves them unmarried, but his choices are by no means unambiguously good.[11] His willingness to deceive Lucy as to his feelings for her comes from a belief in his own importance to her, as well as from his general reluctance to take responsibility for actions which might displease someone. If Lucy had not been able to procure a better offer, Elinor believes that she would have married Edward as a preferable alternative to being single. Though this is presented in a way that suggests that it adds to Lucy's crimes, if Edward felt it reasonable for her to alter her engagement due to financial changes, and believed it was reasonable to fabricate feelings of attachment to another person, then the practical steps of Lucy's actions are far more aligned with Edward's behaviour than Elinor would like to think.

A key part of Edward's resolve and concern stems from cowardice. Throughout the novel we are reminded of the fact that he is a constant disappointment to particular members of his family. They want him to distinguish himself in professions or lifestyles which he either doesn't like or doesn't have the aptitude for. But though he expresses that he would like to be busy, and to have his own profession in a lifestyle that would suit him, he's not willing to contradict his family's wishes in order to achieve it.[12] When it comes to maintaining the engagement, however, he has a reason that he can hold on to which enables him to defy their wishes while feeling morally secure. Through standing by his word to Lucy, he finds himself in a situation where he is able to take on the kind of lifestyle that, though less affluent, is more suited to his character – but he also had the ability to do this at any previous point, and chose not to. His unwillingness to defy his family for his own sake may be read as a sense of duty or a sense of diffidence, but in either circumstance, the secret engagement functions as a trigger to release him. In his unwillingness to reveal his feelings to Lucy – or to put it another way, to be honest with his potential wife – he shows an unwillingness to confess his own flawed behaviour. Rather than confronting or owning his mistakes, he tries to conceal them. He recasts himself in the role of the noble martyr, focusing on the idea of sacrificing his own happiness for Lucy's, rather than on the fact that he and his behaviour are the reasons why any sacrifice was needed in the first place.

The most interesting part of his behaviour, though, is in the contrast his actions provide with those of Willoughby, demonstrating the different ways that promises can be made and broken. Critic Barbara Seeber rightly points out that 'the similarities between Edward's and Willoughby's conduct are striking', and the two are eminently comparable.[13] That being said, the different treatments and specifics of each allow Austen to explore the question of honour and pledged faith across a range of circumstances. Though secretly engaged to Lucy, and therefore with his word pledged to her and his honour also engaged, Edward spends significant time with the Dashwood family, behaving in a way that makes everyone believe he is attached to Elinor. Elinor herself tells him off about this once they've got together: 'Elinor scolded him [...] for having spent so much time with them at Norland, when he must have felt his own inconstancy.' She rebukes Edward 'because – to say nothing of my own conviction, our relations were all led away by it to fancy and expect *what*, as you were *then* situated, could never be'. Not only does Edward injure Elinor by making her believe that he cared for her when he knew that he couldn't honourably pursue her, but he causes her difficulty with his relations, who then slight her because they believe she is aspiring to marry Edward. Their behaviour towards Lucy (who they don't believe could be intending any such thing) is far more cordial and pleasant, and is often used as a deliberate contrast to make Elinor feel their dislike.

Edward's defence is 'ignorance of his own heart' and 'mistaken confidence in the force of his engagement'. He says that

> I was simple enough to think that, because my *faith* was plighted to another, there could be no danger in my being with you; and that the consciousness of my engagement was to keep my heart safe and sacred as my honour. I felt that I admired you, but I told myself it was only friendship; and till I began to make comparisons between yourself and Lucy, I did not know how far I was got. After that, I suppose, I *was* wrong in remaining so much in Sussex, and the arguments with which I reconciled myself to the expediency of it, were no better than these: – The danger is my own; I am doing no injury to anyone but myself.[14]

Edward believed that because he had engaged himself, he *could* not incur other feelings. The binding nature of his word would provide a theoretical protection against the emotions that he could not acknowledge feeling. This policy results in him keeping a promise in word, but not in action; though he has given Lucy his word and pledged himself to her, he does not act in a manner which upholds that engagement. Instead, he continues on a course of action which ultimately diminishes the affection he feels for his fiancée. Once aware of his feelings for Elinor, he still does not take the honourable step of removing himself from her (either geographically or emotionally), and justifies this by the obviously faulty logic that he is only risking himself. By risking the feelings of both women in this way, Edward again ignores the substance of his promise to Lucy in favour of the letter of it. His promise is to marry her – and this he will do – but he completely fails to moderate his conduct so as to maintain his regard for her or protect her from the loss of his affection. Edward will wed Lucy and pretend to love her, but he doesn't act as though he was engaged. He adheres to the letter of his promise, not the spirit. He is unwilling to spend less time with Elinor because he doesn't want to spend less time with her, and so he justifies his behaviour in order to convince himself that his actions are acceptable and do not contradict his promise. With all his later talk of sacrificing himself, the true sacrifice – and perhaps the most honourable thing to do – would have been to remove himself earlier from his regular interactions with Elinor. He does not treat fairly with either her or Lucy, risking the feelings of both for his own happiness. What he does do is agree that he will carry out the material effects of his word; when all is said and done, he intends to marry Lucy, even though at that point he would prefer not to.

Consider the similarities with Willoughby's description of his early motivation in spending time with Marianne:

> When I first became intimate with your family, I had no other intention, no other view in the acquaintance than to pass my time pleasantly [...] Careless of her happiness, thinking only of my own amusement, giving way to feelings which I had always been too much in the habit of indulging, I endeavoured, by every means in my power, to make myself pleasing to her, without any design of returning her affection.[15]

Though Willoughby is more intentional and deliberate in his conduct than Edward, they are nonetheless strikingly similar – 'careless of her happiness' could well describe Edward's behaviour towards either of his ladies. Rakish Willoughby even finds himself falling for Marianne in spite of himself, finding himself 'by insensible degrees, sincerely fond of her', and interestingly he notes that 'the happiest hours of my life were what I spent with her when I felt my intentions were strictly honourable, and my feelings blameless'.[16] In contrast to Edward, Willoughby deliberately never pledges his word:

> 'Engagement!' cried Marianne, 'there has been no engagement.'
>
> 'No engagement!'
>
> 'No, he is not so unworthy as you believe him. He has broken no faith with me.'
>
> 'But he told you that he loved you?' –
>
> 'Yes – no – never absolutely. It was every day implied, but never professedly declared. Sometimes I thought it had been – but it never was.'[17]

Though everyone believed that Willoughby and Marianne were engaged because of the way that they acted, Willoughby has held back from absolutely putting a promise or intention into words. In explaining himself to Elinor while Marianne is in the grip of her illness, Willoughby reflects on his behaviour towards Marianne, his new wife Sophia, and the young woman Eliza, whom he left pregnant and unmarried. He says of Marianne

> Even *then*, however, when fully determined on paying my addresses to her, I allowed myself most improperly to put off, from day to day, the moment of doing it, from an unwillingness to enter into an engagement while my circumstances were so greatly embarrassed. I will not reason here – nor will I stop for *you* to expatiate on the absurdity, and the worse than absurdity, of scrupling to engage my faith where my honour was already bound.[18]

If we contrast this 'scrupling to engage my faith where my honour was already bound' with Edward's thinking that 'because my *faith* was plighted to another, there could be no danger in my being with you', we see Austen's mirrored approach in portraying compromised honour and promises. While Edward gives his word but fails to moderate his behaviour, Willoughby ducks the obligations created by his behaviour on the grounds that he has not given his word. All of Willoughby's actions – even at least theoretically his intentions – are that he will marry Marianne, but he holds back committing his word because his word to her would be binding. Here is an example of where behavioural consent is effectively endorsed: by his behaviour, Willoughby has performed all of the practices of an engaged man. He calls regularly on Marianne, he has a lock of her hair, they drive out and spend the day together unchaperoned, and he even shows her around the house he hopes to inherit. The only piece missing is the specific verbal solicitation of Marianne's hand. Willoughby explicitly withholds this, because this step will engage his 'faith', but he acknowledges that he had created the expectation that he would seek this engagement by his actions. His 'honour' is pledged by his conduct. Elinor, Mrs Dashwood, and the rest of their society view Willoughby as having mistreated Marianne, because he effectively jilts her: in their view, his behaviour has signalled his consent to the marriage. This also demonstrates another way that behaviour can be used to mislead – by behaving as though he will marry her, Willoughby creates an expectation that he will, and therefore Marianne thinks it is acceptable to perform actions which are not socially sanctioned for non-engaged couples. This appears to be Willoughby's dangerous strategy; a means of deceiving without words to dispute.

Like Edward, Willoughby also lies to the woman he *does* promise to marry. In describing his brief courtship of Sophia Grey, he asks Elinor that 'If you *can* pity me, Miss Dashwood, pity my situation as it was *then*. With my head and heart full of your sister, I was forced to play the happy lover to another woman.'[19] Like Edward, Willoughby pretends, and like Edward, Willoughby's fiancée responds possessively to the threat of another woman. It is difficult to read her feelings towards Willoughby, as the only details we have of the situation are given by Willoughby himself, but her feelings for him are suggested even as he criticises her and her actions. Sophia has cause for suspicion, as '[s]ome vague report had reached her before of my attachment to a young lady in Devonshire, and what had passed within her observation the preceding evening had marked who the young lady was, and made her more jealous than ever'.[20] From this we can ascertain that although Willoughby was 'play[ing] the happy lover', his potential bride felt jealousy regarding his former attachment, which was only intensified by seeing the person concerned. When Marianne writes to Willoughby, asking him to explain why he was suddenly acting as though he didn't know or care about her, Sophia reads her letter.

> Affecting that air of playfulness which is delightful in a woman one loves, she opened the letter directly, and read its contents. She was well paid for her impudence. She read what made her wretched. Her wretchedness I could have borne, but her passion – her malice – At all events it must be appeased.[21]

We can see from this both that Sophia is upset by Marianne's letter, and that Willoughby does not care about this fact. He 'could have borne' her 'wretchedness', but it is anger rather than grief or sadness which moves him to action. He does not act in order to heal or repair, but to salvage the engagement to Sophia that he perceives as being financially necessary to his way of life. 'In honest words, her money was necessary to me, and in a situation like mine, anything was to be done to prevent a rupture.'[22] Sophia's anger, her 'passion' and 'malice', is what causes Willoughby to break off his contact with Marianne – not any notion of honour. While this is not done in a kind way, it is nonetheless done – and it is something that it's unlikely that Willoughby would have done himself, given his policy of avoidance.

Elinor rightly challenges Willoughby on the idea that he was 'forced' to pretend attachment to Sophia in this way, saying that

> You have made your own choice. It was not forced on you. Your wife has a claim to your politeness, to your respect, at least. She must be attached to you, or she would not have married you. To treat her with unkindness, to speak of her slightingly is no atonement to Marianne.[23]

Willoughby's sole response to these charges is to tell Elinor that 'She does not deserve your compassion. – She knew I had no regard for her when we married.'[24] Here, apparently, Sophia forfeits her right to respect because she married Willoughby knowing that he didn't love her. For some reason, Willoughby believes that this makes the situation her responsibility, despite his initial pretence and his own willingness to go through with the marriage. His absolution of his own responsibility is as specious here as it is elsewhere. We can see the distinction between a coerced choice and meaningful consent. Willoughby is presenting his narrative as though his decision to pursue and marry Sophia was forced upon him, influenced by circumstances which meant that he could not make another decision. But unlike the coerced choices discussed earlier in this book, Willoughby *does* have a meaningful alternative – and furthermore he is the root cause of his own 'coercion'.

Willoughby's argument is that he has an expensive lifestyle, has grown used to this, and has run up debts. He needs a wife who comes with a significant sum of money attached to her, in order to ensure that his debts can be paid and his lifestyle can continue. He is due to inherit the fortune of his aunt, but this inheritance is dependent on his continuing in her favour. Though attracted to Marianne, he is concerned about the fact that she does not come with a fortune, and he worries that marrying her will cause his aunt to cut him off, which would leave him without the means to live the lifestyle that he wants. His resolution to marry Marianne anyway, and attempt to ensure that there is no breach with his aunt, would, if successful, put him in the position of being both theoretically happy and ultimately wealthy. His delay in proposing is owing to a desire for a better material prospect – if Marianne had had money, there would have been no delay. However, at no point does Willoughby contemplate the possibility of retrenching on his own expenses, attempting to live more moderately, or getting a job, as Edward does. Edward, who is not motivated by money, is not as influenced by the threat of being cut off; the comparison further undermines Willoughby's suggestion that such a threat is the same as being forced. Lack of money can be a coercive factor, but a desire for extravagance is not the same thing as an unfree choice.

Willoughby also has another option presented to him. His aunt, who does not approve of his libertine lifestyle, finds out about Eliza, the young woman he got pregnant and then abandoned.

> By one measure, I might have saved myself. In the height of her morality, good woman! She offered to forgive the past, if I would marry Eliza. That could not be – and I was formally dismissed from her favour and her house.[25]

This is unusual, as here we see an example of a wealthy relative openly accepting a 'fallen' woman into the family, without causing disinheritance. She clearly puts the responsibility on Willoughby, and her morality requires him to make amends for his actions and their consequences. In marrying Eliza, Willoughby would have been making social and financial amends to a person whose suffering he had occasioned, and he would have kept the prospect of his aunt's fortune. If he were going to marry anyone, she is the first character we are aware of to have claim on him.[26] But Willoughby dismisses this option without consideration, simply saying that 'that could not be'. This is not the same as a coerced or forced choice. Though he presents himself as one whose situation arises because he is forced into having to marry Sophia, he actually has multiple options, and picks the one that best suits his financial aspirations.

This section dealing both with Willoughby's response to Eliza, and his aunt's forgiveness if he were to marry her, is an important coda to the broader discussion of honour through word versus deed that the duality of Edward and Willoughby creates. Forgiveness for mistakes is unusual, but here it is forgiveness coupled with the demand for an action which tries to atone for past wrongdoing. Willoughby's aunt disowns him, not because of his relations with this young woman, but because she can't condone his abandonment of her. This is more fallout for the seducer than is often found in a seduction narrative. Here we have one female character standing by a disgraced and unknown woman, dismissing her heir because she finds his conduct unacceptable.[27] Willoughby tries to justify himself by saying that he

> acknowledge[s] that her situation and her character ought to have been respected by me. I do not mean to justify myself, but at the same time cannot leave you to suppose that I have nothing to urge – that, because she was injured, she was irreproachable, and because I was a libertine, *she* must be a saint.[28]

He cites 'the violence of her passion, the weakness of her understanding' as reasons why he is less responsible, though any weakness in her understanding would simply make her less able to give meaningful consent, and not more culpable.[29] When we talked about the idea of the perfect victim earlier in this book, we mentioned what academic Sandra MacPherson describes as 'the invidious – and antifeminist – cruelties of constructive intent', whereby people assign blame to the victim after the fact, claiming that their actions signalled consent. She argues that this view 'cultivat[es] the obverse idea that blameable persons are not innocent, and if they are not innocent they have not been harmed'.[30] In this instance, Austen does not give us any details of Eliza's behaviour – which tells us that it's not something we need to consider when assigning blame to Willoughby. Harm being done to Eliza is more important than whether Eliza's behaviour was 'irreproachable'. As Elinor says,

> Your indifference, however, towards that unfortunate girl – I must say it, unpleasant to me as the discussion of such a subject may well be – your indifference is no apology for your cruel neglect of

> her. Do not think yourself excused by any weakness, any natural defect of understanding on her side, in the wanton cruelty too evident on yours. You must have known, that while you were enjoying yourself in Devonshire, pursuing fresh schemes, always gay, always happy, she was reduced to the extremest indigence.[31]

This is really important. Elinor is a lot more lenient with Willoughby than she knows she should be because he's so charismatic, but she still describes his behaviour to Eliza as 'wanton cruelty'. By highlighting the state his actions have reduced Eliza to, rather than getting into a discussion about the responsibility for their sexual relationship, Elinor echoes and inverts Willoughby's point: it does not matter whether Eliza was a saint; Willoughby still acted like a libertine. Moreover, it is his 'cruel neglect' which is the damaging factor. Though Willoughby characteristically handwaves responsibility by suggesting that Eliza could easily have found a way to contact him, he didn't consider her circumstances after he left her. He simply left, and then suggests that the burden of communication should have been entirely on her – yet he also knew where to find her. Though Elinor doesn't push him on this point, we see that Willoughby consistently refuses to take responsibility for the actions that his honour engages him to, but his faith does not.[32]

Sense and Sensibility is not the only novel where Austen reflects on how men promise and uphold things with their words and actions. In *Emma* (1815), we also have a secret engagement, this time between Frank Churchill and Jane Fairfax. Like Willoughby, Frank is the heir of his aunt, and like Edward, he conceals his engagement for fear of disinheritance upon discovery. Like Lucy, Jane Fairfax is comparatively poor; the marriage will greatly improve her economic situation in the world, and prevent her from having to work as a governess. Like Edward, Frank displays an attachment to the novel's protagonist, and like Willoughby, he doesn't intend to follow through on any attachments he might create by acting this way. Frank deliberately acts as though he's interested in courting

Emma, in order to help conceal the relationship between himself and Jane.

Frank Churchill is engaged by his word to Jane, and also by his actions: he buys her thoughtful and expensive gifts (the pianoforte), they correspond, and he frequently calls on her and her family. He performs an interest in Emma by calling on her, dancing with her, and apparently distinguishing her at social events. In his more private performances to Emma, he makes Jane Fairfax the centre of their conversation, but situates her as the focus of a joke between the two of them. Throughout, Frank speaks in a kind of double-talk, which presents one meaning outwardly, and reveals another to those aware of his situation – even if that is only himself. When Emma tells him of her mistaken deduction that Jane is in love with an Irishman called Mr Dixon, Frank delights in dropping hints and making reference to this supposed attachment. After a particularly pointed comment about the music provided for the new pianoforte including 'Irish airs', Emma attempts to check him:

> 'You spoke too plain. She must have understood you.'
>
> 'I hope she does. I would have her understand me. I am not in the least ashamed of my meaning.'
>
> 'But really, I am half ashamed, and wish I had never taken up the idea.'
>
> 'I am very glad you did, and that you communicated it to me. I have now a key to all her odd looks and ways. Leave shame to her. If she does wrong she ought to feel it.'
>
> 'She is not entirely without it, I think.'
>
> 'I do not see much sign of it.'[33]

Here, Emma is concerned that she has been unkind to Jane by speaking of the speculated attachment to Mr Dixon – she is worried that she has 'transgressed the covenant of woman by woman' in betraying this idea to Frank.[34] She feels ashamed of her own actions, and wants to keep Frank from making his jokes too recognisable and pointed – while Frank is determined to use this circumstance to allow him to communicate with Jane in public without giving away their engagement (and while indulging his sense of humour). In saying 'I have a key to all her odd looks', he both implies to Emma that he now can decode Jane's behaviour, and puns to himself and the reader through his use of 'key' that he now has a means of unlocking the behaviours in Jane that, if he caused them openly, would throw suspicion on to himself. Frank wants Jane to understand that *he* has given her the piano as an offering of love, and by seizing on the convenient pretence of Mr Dixon, he can speculate publicly on the meaning behind the gift, explaining without implicating himself. Frank's comments on shame, similarly, are misinterpreted by Emma. Frank wants her to think that – just as he says – Jane deserves to be embarrassed if she acts wrongly. In reality, he does not think she is acting wrongly, and therefore is actually saying that he does not want her to, and does not believe she will, feel shame. Jane and Frank have different thresholds for shame, and while Frank doesn't see anything to criticise in Jane's behaviour, Jane decidedly does. When Emma points out that Jane *does* seem to feel some shame, she is seeing more clearly than Frank – he, like Emma, is unable to see what he does not wish to.

Frank uses the shared joke with Emma as a vehicle for his speaking to or dancing with Jane. With their inside joke as ostensible motivation, he suggests to Emma that he will tease Jane about some aspect of her relationship to Mr Dixon, or some aspect of her personality, to help him take these actions without arousing suspicion. It's clear that Frank prioritises Jane with his attentions too: though he performs and pretends courtship to Emma, he disguises his preference for Jane as jokes and coincidences.

> In he walked, the first and handsomest; and after paying his compliments en passant to Miss Bates and her niece, made his way directly to the opposite side of the circle, where sat Miss Woodhouse; and till he could find a seat by her, would not sit at all. Emma divined what every body present must be thinking. She was his object, and everybody must perceive it.[35]

Frank pays his compliments first to Jane Fairfax (so far from Emma's suspicion as not even to merit being named in this section), but it is 'en passant', so while technically she is the first person he seeks and greets, it is done in a manner which implies that he was heading towards Emma but did not wish to be rude and slight the acquaintances he was required to walk past. Similarly, his insistence on sitting next to Emma gives the impression of his wanting to be close to her, but more importantly allows him to sit directly opposite Jane – and therefore have a perfect excuse for staring at her. Crucially for Frank, 'every body must perceive' that Emma is his focus – it is a performance, not just for Emma, but for the whole room.

Not all of his jokes are so successful at performing a double function, however. By the time of the Box Hill picnic, when communication between him and Jane is at a particular low, he flirts conspicuously with Emma, saying things which are designed to wound Jane. Though at this time Emma doesn't believe Frank's flirtation with her is serious, she nonetheless responds, and again misreads the situation.

> When they all sat down it was better; to her taste a great deal better, for Frank Churchill grew talkative and gay, making her his first object. Every distinguishing attention that could be paid, was paid to her. To amuse her, and be agreeable in her eyes, seemed all that he cared for – and Emma, glad to be enlivened, not sorry to be flattered, was gay and easy too, and gave him all the friendly encouragement, the admission to be gallant, which she had ever given in the first and most animating period of their acquaintance; but which now, in her own estimation, meant nothing, though in the judgement of most people looking on it must have had such an appearance as no English word but flirtation could very well describe. 'Mr Frank Churchill and Miss Woodhouse flirted together excessively.' They were laying themselves open to that very phrase – and to having it sent off in a letter to Maple Grove by one lady, to Ireland by another. Not that Emma was gay and thoughtless from any real felicity; it was rather because she felt less happy than she had expected. She laughed because she was disappointed; and

> though she liked his attentions, and thought them all, whether in friendship, admiration, or playfulness, extremely judicious, they were not winning back her heart.[36]

Austen's text here draws out the distinction between what Emma does and what Emma feels, and in this instance Emma's view is that the appropriateness of her behaviour depends on the meaning or feeling behind it. Because she does not believe that either she or Frank is serious, she sees no harm in it. However, in the potential response of the two letter writers, the narrative voice identifies that Jane views this as a flirtation, and that *that* is the purpose of Frank's behaviour. His request that Emma choose his wife for him, that she be like herself – specifically 'lively', one of the main contrasts emphasised between the characters of Emma and Jane – and with hazel eyes, is clearly a barb for Jane.[37] He 'has so little confidence in my own judgement' that he requests a person both like Emma and unlike Jane, and in doing so suggests to Jane that he regrets their engagement and would prefer another woman. This whole outing hurts Jane, and ultimately brings her to decide to end the engagement to Frank and take up the role of a governess instead. Jane believes she is in the position occupied by Lucy in *Sense and Sensibility* – that of having her fiancée no longer care for her. While we can only speculate about Lucy's potential actions, here we see an example of the unloved party deciding to make their own more difficult way in the world rather than hold to an engagement with someone who they don't think loves them.

If we consider the Box Hill exchange between Frank and Jane, we see a vastly different situation from that of Edward and Lucy, though many of the circumstances of their situations are comparable. Frank declares that

> as to any real knowledge of a person's disposition that Bath, or any public place, can give – it is all nothing, there can be no knowledge. It is only by seeing women in their own homes, among their own set, just as they always are, that you can form any just judgement.

> Short of that, it is all guess and luck – and will generally be ill-luck. How many a man has committed himself on a short acquaintance, and rued it all the rest of his life![38]

His implication is that Jane is different from the woman he had thought her when they met, and that he has committed himself to a course of action that he will regret. These fears about a foolish engagement being of material detriment to one's own happiness are explicitly shared by Edward. Edward, however, would never speak so publicly in this manner – though we might question his actions in pretending to love Lucy, he would think it inexcusable to speak in this way, even if she were to be the only one who understood him. (Edward also met Lucy in her home, and in having an engagement of four years rather than several months he theoretically has more knowledge of her character.) But this is not honesty from Frank either – it is hurt feelings and miscommunication, and Austen definitely doesn't present it as a good way to conduct a relationship.

Still, contrast Jane's response to Lucy's actions, and indeed to Edward's:

> I was only going to observe, that though such unfortunate circumstances do sometimes occur to both men and women, I cannot imagine them to be very frequent. A hasty and imprudent attachment may arise – but there is generally time to recover from it afterwards. I would be understood to mean, that it can only be weak, irresolute characters, (whose happiness must be always at the mercy of chance,) who will suffer an unfortunate acquaintance to be an inconvenience, an oppression forever.[39]

The choice of the word 'acquaintance' here is telling, as the word itself does not fit – you don't form an engagement with someone you see as an acquaintance. This takes Frank's suggestion that he doesn't know her and depersonalises it further, placing herself both at a greater emotional distance, and as one easier to break with. She's telling him that he is free to break with her if she is a source of regret to him – touching on the questions of courage and resolution discussed earlier in this chapter. Jane suggests that Frank has only to act in order to have his life return to a direction he would prefer, to free himself of their connection. However, Frank is not the one who takes the action following this discussion. After Frank tells Emma that she can choose him a wife as long as she chooses someone just like her, Jane leaves to begin the process of engaging herself as a governess. She doesn't tell Frank about her plan – he hears of it by accident days later. Instead, Jane lets go of the engagement, though it saddens her greatly, and though the prospect of going into employment as a governess is something she dreads.[40] She displays the precise strength and resolution of character that Frank (and Edward and Willoughby) was supposed to display, but lacked. And though Frank does not actually want to break with Jane, here we see the dangers and difficulties of performative consent – able to primarily communicate by action when in public, by playing other parts, and speaking double, they find themselves deceived by each other's performances.

The engagements – both secret and public – in *Sense and Sensibility* and *Emma* set out the ways in which male characters separate out the ideas of promises given through words and promises given through actions to try to explain away their questionable behaviour. Characters make excuses for themselves, claiming that because they have given their word their behaviour is unimportant, or because they have avoided asking the specific 'Will you marry me?' question, they have also avoided performing an engagement through their behaviour. Austen makes the importance of both of these forms of consent clear – and also the fact that they can operate individually, regardless of what a character intends. It's refreshing to find the focus on interrogating behaviour or promises applied to the men. Where Edward is let off the hook for his actions because Lucy is so unlikeable, and Willoughby charms even as he tries to dodge responsibility, Emma at least seems to conclude that the best husband is the man who is careful with any kind of consent. In a novel full of misunderstanding about who people are actually interested in courting, rife with misreading behaviour, it seems telling that the way Emma describes the man she thinks of as best is as 'the last man in the world, who would intentionally give any woman the idea of his feeling more for her than he really does'.[41]

11

Fanny, or The Price of Refusal

'Why?' I remember asking my sergeant. 'Why won't she get in the ambulance? I don't understand.'

'Get used to it,' he replied, sighing. 'It's what they're like.'

By they he meant victims of domestic abuse […] He was used to seeing victims refuse help, often time and again. He, like many others before and after him, made the assumption that as an adult woman, she had the ability and the choice to just get up and leave […]

The starting point I use when attempting to interpret people's behaviours is that most people will act in what they think are their own best interests. So instead of asking: Why won't she get in the ambulance? I would for instance, ask: Why was it in her best interests not to get in the ambulance?

– Jane Monckton Smith[1]

Recognising the psychological power that an abuser can wield over his victim is key to defeating the myth that domestic violence only happens when wives and girlfriends are beaten and raped.

– Helena Kennedy[2]

Let him have all the perfections in the world, I think it ought not to be set down as certain, that a man must be acceptable to every woman he may happen to like himself.

– Jane Austen, *Mansfield Park*[3]

If there was ever a character who frustrated readers by refusing to get in the metaphorical ambulance, it's Fanny Price. However, that refusal is not only in her best interests, it's a fundamentally important decision that highlights the damaging impact of long-term psychological abuse.

Jane Austen's *Mansfield Park* (1814) begins with a stylised tale of three sisters: one who marries for money, one who marries for love, and one who marries for convenience. Lady Bertram, who marries well, finds herself reasonably happy and very well-to-do. She is vapid, well meaning, and childish, spending most of the novel heavily dosed with laudanum. However, as a result of her station and income, this does not materially matter – she has people to see to things for her. The closest thing to a consequence that Lady Bertram experiences is when her ineffectual parenting helps facilitate behaviour in her children which she disapproves of. The eldest sister also expects to marry well, but ultimately marries a clergyman when no better offer arises, and attaches herself to the grand estate of Mansfield Park via the clergy living position. Mrs Norris is self-interested and spiteful, and continually casts herself in the role of victim or martyr in her externalised narratives. She is, however, also industrious and capable of being practical and economical. The youngest sister marries for love. Narratively, we are conditioned to believe that this should go well, as this tale is told in the style of a fable or fairytale, and love is typically the motivation endorsed by the genre. Ultimately though, Frances's situation is the most difficult of the three. With a husband decommissioned from active service in the navy and fond of drinking, she is poor. They have nine children, and she is constantly borrowing money from her siblings in order to care for the family. The tale indicates that, regardless of the motivations for a marriage, the material situation plays a significant role in determining the ease and potential happiness of the resultant life. When, much later in the novel, we visit the Prices in Portsmouth, this is emphasised, as the narrator and Fanny reflect that Frances 'might have made just as good a woman of consequence as Lady Bertram, but Mrs Norris would have been a more respectable mother of nine children, on a small income'.[4]

We are therefore introduced right at the beginning of the novel to the idea that when thinking about marriage, love should not be the only consideration. It is important to consider a number of factors: the motivation, the practical or financial situation, and also the temperaments of the people involved.

The novel itself follows Fanny, Frances's eldest daughter, who is taken in by the Bertram family, an act of charity on their part to alleviate some of the financial pressure on her mother (the act itself is proposed by Mrs Norris, who can be extremely generous with other people's money). Fanny is shy, timid, and fundamentally terrified upon her arrival. Her cousins are taller, prettier, bolder, and better educated. From her first arrival as a homesick child, she feels that everything she does is wrong, and as she grows she is consistently squashed and put down – most famously by her Aunt Norris, but the abuse is enabled and performed by the entire family. Her cousin Edmund is the only member of the family to take her happiness into account, and it is during these early kindnesses that Fanny falls in love with him.

> In her day, a woman's safety from humiliation depended not on her own worth, but on the solvency and status of her parents, her ingenuity in preventing herself from being compromised or jilted, and her success in disclaiming strength of intellect and emotion.[5]

Critic Rebecca West's description of Austen's era matches Fanny extremely well – Fanny's security and her position at Mansfield are dependent on her doing these things, and she carries them out to the best of her ability. But crucially, Fanny is not always conscious that she is doing these things to protect herself, instead internalising the fear and precariousness of her position, and coming to believe the narrative of her aunt that she deserves none of the security necessary to exert her own will on a situation. *Mansfield Park* is a novel about the effects of silencing and stifling – about domestic and emotional abuse. There is only one point in the novel when we see Fanny actively exert her own will and go against the family

– when she refuses to accept the wealthy and charismatic Henry Crawford's marriage proposal.

The Crawfords arrive as the force of change in Mansfield Park; Mary Crawford intends to make a play for Tom, the heir, but finds herself falling for Edmund (and earns Fanny's jealousy along the way). Henry Crawford flirts with the two Bertram sisters Maria and Julia – particularly the engaged Maria – but ultimately has no intention of marrying either of them. After Maria is married, he turns his attentions to Fanny, and proposes marriage to her. She refuses this proposal, much to the displeasure of the rest of the house, and in a bid to compel her to accept they send her home to Portsmouth to remind her just how precarious her financial status is, and how much her lifestyle depends on them.

Cultural critic Laurie Penny remarks, 'One sure test of social privilege is how much anger you get to express without the threat of expulsion, arrest, or social exclusion.'[6] After a difficult day when she has been greatly fatigued and made unwell by the demands of her two aunts, Fanny is lying on the couch with a headache. Edmund returns home, and on hearing how her day has been spent, understands the state she must be in.

> Edmund said no more to either lady; but going quietly to another table, on which the supper tray yet remained, brought a glass of Madeira to Fanny, and obliged her to drink the greater part. She wished to be able to decline it; but the tears which a variety of feelings created, made it easier to swallow than to speak.[7]

Not only was Fanny unable to protest against her aunts in the early part of the day, but she cannot decline the wine Edmund offers her. It's not that she doesn't want the wine, but that she wants to be able to refuse it; it's expensive, it centres attention on her, it involves acknowledging her own needs. She has been silenced from asking for relief through her indoctrination into the rhetoric of her own unworthiness. Her tiredness, her fatigue, her headache, her sense of her own inferiority, her gratefulness towards Edmund, all contribute to her tears and make her unable to verbalise the response that she believes she ought to make. Fanny will frequently 'swallow' rather than 'speak' when speaking would cause her to go against the wishes of others. She requires the authority of someone like Edmund to apply worth and value to her, because she does not – cannot – do it herself. To do so requires a belief in the validity of her own needs which she has not been permitted to cultivate.[8]

When Fanny is invited out to a dinner as company, Aunt Norris is quick to reinforce that she should do her best to refrain from speaking.

> Fanny, now that you are going out into company without any of us; and I do beseech and intreat you not to be putting yourself forward, and talking and giving your opinions as if you were one of your cousins – as if you were dear Mrs Rushworth or Julia.[9]

The right to an opinion is not extended to her; it is dependent on rank and position. She should, Aunt Norris suggests, be so grateful to have been noticed by the invitation that she should regard it as more than she deserves and not rise so far above herself as to 'talk', give [...] your opinions', or essentially take up space. Perhaps the worst part is that Fanny is conditioned to broadly agree with her aunt. We can see this clearly on a rare occasion when she attempts to carry a point, when her brother William comes to visit. Fanny wants to spend William's last morning alone with him, but her uncle Sir Thomas interferes and invites Henry Crawford along as well.

> She had hoped to have William all to herself, the last morning. It would have been an unspeakable indulgence. But though her wishes were overthrown there was no spirit of murmuring within her. On the contrary, she was so totally unused to having her pleasure consulted, or to anything to take place at all in the way she could desire, that she was more disposed to wonder and rejoice at having carried her point so far than to repine at the counteractions which followed.[10]

It is these quiet observations into Fanny's character that convey to the reader the depth of the conditioning she has received. Getting to spend time alone with a beloved brother she has not seen for many years, who is going back to sea – an active and dangerous profession – is an 'indulgence'. More significantly, it is an 'unspeakable' one. Though the word here is being used to convey how significant the time with William would be to Fanny, it also highlights that it literally is *unspeakable* for her. In this instance, she succeeds in being allowed to join William for breakfast after her uncle instructs her to have a lie-in, but she does not then ask to have him all to herself. Once Mr Crawford has been invited, she does not say anything more on the subject.

The novel is filled with these notes: 'Fanny would rather have been silent, but being obliged to speak, she could not forbear.'[11] Throughout the text Fanny submits, speaks, or is silenced contrary to her personal preferences, and concedes ground to the demands of others. There is, however, one glaring exception. Fanny refuses Henry Crawford's marriage proposal. Having established that Fanny is a character who has been taught to find standing up for herself difficult, I want to talk about the methods of deliberate persuasion and manipulation – of compulsion – that the family use to attempt to pressure her into marrying Crawford. In particular, the cocktail of obligation, familial duty, and the fetishised (feminised) quality of obedience.

Henry Crawford initially begins his courtship of Fanny without serious intentions. However, his decision to pay her attention and attempt to make her love him results in him not only taking more notice of her, but finding value and worth in her. When he decides that he wishes to marry her, he speaks of his intentions to his sister.

> 'Yes, Mary,' was Henry's concluding assurance. 'I am fairly caught. You know with what idle designs I began – but this is the end of them. I have (I flatter myself) made no inconsiderable progress in her affections; but my own are entirely fixed.'[12]

Henry is mistaken here – Fanny is in love with Edmund, and remembers Henry's flirtation with Maria too well to trust him. However, in this same conversation with Mary we are introduced to the prevailing public opinion, which is that Fanny must love him, and even if she does not love him at the moment, her nature will cause her to love him in time. Mary describes her as 'a sweet little wife; all gratitude and devotion'.[13] She asks

> 'What are you waiting for?'
>
> 'For – for very little more than opportunity. Mary, she is not like her cousins; but I think I shall not ask in vain.'
>
> 'Oh! no, you cannot. Were you even less pleasing – supposing her not to love you already (of which however I can have little doubt) you would be safe. The gentleness and gratitude of her disposition would secure her all your own immediately. From my soul, I do not think she would marry you *without* love; that is, if there is a girl in the world capable of being uninfluenced by ambition, I can suppose it her; but ask her to love you, and she will never have the heart to refuse.'[14]

Though incorrect in her brother's case, Mary actually reads Fanny very well. She identifies here where Fanny's love for Edmund comes from – her gratitude to him for the kindnesses he showed to her, particularly in contrast to the cruelties of the rest of the family, and her feeling that he therefore deserves her love in return.[15] Her love is bound up in her sense of gratitude, and she is 'all [Edmund's] own' long before he realises. The mistake that Mary – and everyone else – makes is in supposing that Fanny's heart is as yet unattached.

Henry delivers his proposal attached to the news that he has arranged for William's promotion. Fanny is overwhelmed by the news of her brother's advancement. She 'could not speak, but he did not wish her to speak'.[16] However, this extreme happiness means that Fanny is unaware of Henry's proposal for a while. Though

> he spoke with such a glow of what his solicitude had been, and used such strong expressions […] that Fanny could not have remained insensible of his drift had she been able to attend; but her heart

> was so full and her senses so astonished, that she could listen but imperfectly.[17]

When Fanny does finally come to understand what Henry is saying, 'she was exceedingly distressed, and for some moments unable to speak'.[18] At play here is Fanny's consciousness that Henry Crawford is an unprincipled rake who flirted with both her cousins simultaneously before focusing on the engaged Maria, without any intention of marrying either.

> She considered it all nonsense, as mere trifling and gallantry, which meant only to deceive for the hour; she could not but feel that it was treating her improperly and unworthily, and in such a way as she had not deserved, but it was like himself, and entirely of a piece with what she had seen before.[19]

The situation, however, is complicated for her by Henry's actions regarding William. The sentence above concludes that 'she would not allow herself to show half the displeasure she felt, because he had been conferring an obligation, which no want of delicacy on his part could make trifle with her'. It is this sense of obligation which the family all wish Fanny to feel, which the Crawfords expect her to feel, and which, unfortunately for her, she does feel. They believe that this will make her feel as though she must accept Henry's proposal – that she owes it to him, based on his having asked her. But it is solely obligation from Henry's kindness to William that she feels, and not obligation from his proposal. She cannot see that as anything but a joke or game – and therefore can only view it as an insult. Henry thinks her refusal is merely 'her modesty', misunderstanding the refusal she offers to be what our long-suffering Mr Collins would term 'merely words'.[20] Fanny, meanwhile, believes that 'Mr Crawford would certainly never address her again: he must have seen how unwelcome it was to her', because 'I told him without disguise that it was very disagreeable to me.'[21] At the end of the initial proposal, each feels as though they have carried their opposing points.

Henry returns the next day and makes his intentions known to Sir Thomas, who is delighted. He knows nothing of Henry's flirtations with his daughters, nor of Fanny's feelings for Edmund. All he perceives is an unexceptionable young man whom Fanny does not appear to dislike, asking for the hand of his niece (whose lack of personal wealth means that the choice is financially disinterested). Henry is wealthy, charming, intelligent, personable, and has spent a significant amount of time with the family. Sir Thomas is therefore baffled by Fanny's declaration that she cannot marry him. Their exchange displays the tension between the idea of the appropriate lack of interest of a modest girl, and what is viewed as an inappropriate lack of interest, highlighting the justifications Fanny is allowed to give for her refusal to be viewed as acceptable or legitimate. Their discussion also presents the idea that her entire character is going to be fixed from this one interaction; either she is obliging and obedient always, or she is totally proud and contrary for taking this specific singular stance. We can see this kind of construction across the courtship genre, including in Richardson's *Clarissa*. Clarissa's past behaviour is ignored by the Harlowe family, and her single act of 'defiance' on the subject of her marriage is used to paint a picture of her entire character. The family argue that Clarissa has always *seemed* obedient because she has always wanted to do what they told her; she has in fact been simply following her own will.[22] This defiance supposedly represents her true nature – rather than being a point of deviation from her character's normal pattern, they claim it is just the first instance when her will and theirs have not aligned. Fanny's lifetime of self-suppression and obedience are overwritten by Sir Thomas the moment he encounters her active disagreement.

This kind of gaslighting functions as a tool of emotional abuse in both *Mansfield Park* and *Clarissa*, denying the lived experiences of these young women with a view to manipulating them into accepting the will of the family. The undermining of their sense of reality allows for the assertion that they are ungrateful and undutiful – qualities which are clearly important to these women because of the motivations that have governed their behaviour to this point.[23] Instead of allowing them to advocate for themselves as one who has always followed the rules of their social group, these first instances of self-assertion are horribly inverted into signifiers that they are hostile to the social group – that not only do they not belong to it but that they are damaging to it. This reinforces Fanny's sense of transience and insecurity, as it is stark evidence that the narrative of her gratitude and conduct is perpetually subject to redrafting. It is to be constructed by her uncle, not by her actual behaviour, thereby clearly displaying the message that love and safety can and will be withheld from her when she does not do exactly as she is told.

Sir Thomas expects Fanny to accept Henry Crawford, and upon hearing her declare that she cannot, he is confused.

> Out of your power to return his good opinion! what is all this? I know he spoke to you yesterday, and (as far as I understand), received as much encouragement to proceed as a well-judging young woman could permit herself to give. I was very much pleased with what I collected to have been your behaviour on this occasion; it shewed a discretion highly to be commended. But now, when he has made his overtures so properly, and honourably – what are your scruples *now*?[24]

Sir Thomas does not criticise Fanny for not accepting Henry on his first application, because it was made to her without his express approval. He views it as a demonstration of Fanny's 'discretion' that she waits to have the engagement properly sanctioned by an appropriate figure (himself), rather than giving an answer based on her own feelings. Because of this, her signs of refusal do not translate into signs of rejection; Sir Thomas reads them as markers of modesty and not disinclination, that which in *Clarissa* is described as '*consenting negatives*'.[25] A 'well-judging young woman' in such a scenario as Fanny's does not commit herself until she knows what she is supposed to do, and will subsequently adopt the parental will as her own. Since Sir Thomas wants Fanny to marry Henry, her not accepting is read as a marker for her wanting to accept once his permission has been granted. Because neither Henry nor Sir Thomas can believe that Fanny does not want to marry Henry, they interpret her behaviour through a confirmation bias which suggests that she is amenable.

> 'Refuse Mr Crawford! Upon what plea? For what reason?'
>
> 'I – I cannot like him, Sir, well enough to marry him.'
>
> 'This is very strange!' said Sir Thomas, in a voice of calm displeasure. 'There is something in this which my comprehension does not reach […] you must have been some time aware of a particularity in Mr Crawford's manners to you. This cannot have taken you by surprise. You must have observed his attentions; and though you always received them very properly (I have no accusation to make on that head,) I never perceived them to be unpleasant to you. I am half inclined to think, Fanny, that you do not quite know your own feelings.'[26]

Quite apart from the legalistic echoes of the question 'Upon what plea?', this comment sets out the difficulty Fanny is faced with. She has indeed received Henry's attentions to her – because she was compelled to by social convention, politeness, and the wishes of Sir Thomas himself. She has not made her preference for not receiving these attentions obvious, because that would have been rude, drawn familial displeasure, and committed the cardinal sin of attracting attention. She has, however, done nothing to encourage him; neither giving offence nor seeking further attention, but remaining polite and uninterested. However, because this is exactly how modest women are meant to behave, just as with her refusal of Henry the previous day, this proper behaviour is conflated into evidence of acceptance.

In effect, Fanny has performed social compliance, and it is the fact that she is no longer complying with Sir Thomas's demands which is the issue. Fanny was not previously opposed to Henry Crawford, and did not seek to actively discourage him, therefore

Fanny has no grounds to refuse to marry him, no evidence that she does not 'like him […] well enough to marry him'.[27] Because Sir Thomas could not tell that Fanny found the attentions unpleasant, he believes that she must not understand her own feelings; his observations are not subject to interrogation, but her performance of her feelings is to stand in place of the feelings themselves (and no acknowledgement is given for the constraints imposed upon that same behaviour). Though he suggests that the matter involves something outside of his comprehension, the suggestion serves not to invite a confidence of some previously unknown reason, but to reinforce the notion that the facts speak clearly and that Sir Thomas is aware of those facts. The only explanation he can come up with at this point is that Fanny is in love with someone else – a correct guess, as it happens – but since Fanny denies it, and Sir Thomas wishes to believe it, he adopts the policy of 'chusing at least to appear satisfied' that Fanny is not in love with one of her cousins.[28] Though Fanny is greatly relieved to have avoided betraying her love for Edmund, she has also hidden the only motivation Sir Thomas could understand for her not accepting the proposal.

Fanny is in an unenviably awkward position, as she *does* have reason to think badly of Henry – but she cannot explain his actions without also implicating her cousins.

> 'Have you any reason, child, to think ill of Mr Crawford's temper?'
> 'No, Sir.'
> She longed to add, 'but of his principles I have;' but her heart sunk under the appalling prospect of discussion, explanation, and probable non-conviction. Her ill opinion of him was founded chiefly on observations, which, for her cousins' sake, she could scarcely dare mention to their father. Maria and Julia – especially Maria, were so closely implicated in Mr Crawford's misconduct, that she could not give his character without betraying them. She had hoped that to a man like her uncle, so discerning, so honourable, so good, the simple acknowledgement of settled *dislike* on her side, would have been sufficient. To her infinite grief, she found it was not.[29]

Again, there is a flavour of the courtroom in this description; the 'appalling prospect of discussion, explanation, and probable non-conviction' would not be out of place in a description of a trial – particularly a trial involving elements of sexualised behaviour or potential sexual misconduct. Fanny is aware that not only would she find the discussion and required explanation deeply unpleasant, but that her testimony would probably be rejected. It would, after all, require Sir Thomas to believe that his daughters (including his now married daughter) were acting improperly with this man, instead of the easier option of believing Fanny mistaken. At this moment, she is not even being allowed to be an adequate judge of her own feelings; it is easy to see why she does not believe in the viability of this route. Further, she is bound to a code of honour that is also a code of silence; disclosing this information might make her understandable to her uncle, but it would expose her cousins, which is its own betrayal of family loyalty. The result is that, once again, Fanny cannot speak freely.

To return again to a quotation from Anne Elliot in Austen's *Persuasion*, it is the

> circumstances (perhaps those very cases which strike us the most) [which] may be precisely such as cannot be brought forward without betraying a confidence, or in some respect saying what should not be said.[30]

Many of Fanny's silences involve her keeping quiet about things that 'should not be said', be that her forbidden love for Edmund or the conduct of various members of the family. She cannot bring her evidence to bear on the discussion here, as disclosing her cousins' behaviour would also function as disclosing a confidence, in addition to bringing up a subject that is regarded as unsuitable for 'polite' society. There are two sides to the Anne Elliot quote: that which should not be said because it places someone at risk, and that which should not be said because it is not the done thing. It speaks to the presence of whisper networks like those discussed earlier in relation to the Harvey Weinstein case – that two-tier level of known things whereby, while many things are widely known, only some are publicly acknowledged. Anne's declaration suggests that there is an undercurrent of knowledge which is not acknowledged to be known, but which nonetheless exists. Such networks can function as a safety tool, by protecting the privacy of vulnerable victims or quietly warning people about a potential threat to their safety – or they can operate to allow for public ignorance of the problematic behaviour of individuals. Fanny is clearly a participant in the whisper network, maintaining her silence both because she does not believe that her testimony will be allowed to stand, and from a desire to protect her cousins.

But let us briefly consider Mary Crawford's endorsement of her brother's relationship. She is genuinely pleased with his choice of Fanny, and for all that she has self-interested motivations, she views the match as likely to be beneficial to her brother's character. To her, it demonstrates that the behaviour of his guardian the Admiral (a man she detests, and whose insistence on housing his mistresses in the family home is the reason she has had to move away to Mansfield in the first place) has not had too lasting an influence on him. In the first section of the conversation quoted below, she declares that Henry will be saved from being like the Admiral, almost as though he were being saved from some kind of deadly disease.

> 'My dear Henry, the advantage of you getting away from the Admiral before your manners are hurt by the contagion of his, before you have contracted any of his foolish opinions, or learnt to sit over your dinner, as if it was the best blessing of life! – *You* are not sensible of the gain, for your regard for him has blinded you; but in my estimation your marrying early may be the saving of you. To have seen you grow like the Admiral in word or deed, look or gesture, would have broke my heart.'
>
> 'Well, well, we do not think quite alike here. The Admiral has his faults, but he is a very good man, and has been more than a father to me. Few fathers would have let me have my own way half

> so much. You must not prejudice Fanny against him. I must have them love one another.'
>
> Mary refrained from saying what she felt, that there could not be two persons in existence, whose characters and manners were less accordant; time would discover it to him; but she could not help *this* reflection on the Admiral. 'Henry, I think so highly of Fanny Price, that if I could suppose the next Mrs Crawford would have half the reason which my poor ill-used aunt had to abhor the very name, I would prevent the marriage, if possible; but I know you, I know that a wife you *loved* would be the happiest of women, and that even when you ceased to love, she would yet find in you the liberality and good-breeding of a gentleman.'[31]

Henry's description of the Admiral as a 'very good man' and 'more than a father' is shown by Austen to be questionable, boiling down to the fact that Henry was allowed to do what he wanted (which suggests that, really, he is quite the reverse). Mary's thought that Fanny and the Admiral are diametrically opposed characters confirms this, and further reflects that Mary has a better grasp on Fanny's character than most of the rest of the novel's cast – especially at this point. But most interesting here is Mary's assertion that her valuation of Fanny is enough that it would compel her to speak out against her brother (or in some other way 'prevent the marriage') if she believed he would treat Fanny in the manner that the Admiral treated their aunt. The Admiral's cruelty towards his wife is an underlying shadow in this novel. It is alluded to – when the Crawfords arrive at Mansfield, when Edmund and Fanny discuss Mary's way of talking about the Admiral – but very few specifics are ever mentioned. Furthermore, in Fanny and Edmund's conversations, it is not allowed to have sufficient weight to make it appropriate for Mary to publicly express criticism of her uncle; her refusal to remain within the whisper network by publicly discussing the Admiral's behaviour is a source of censure from both Fanny and Edmund. Whether the true extent of his behaviour is unknown, or is not enough for Fanny and Edmund to consider vocalisation appropriate, we see here a prime example of 'what ought not to be said' being exactly what a woman might need to have said in order to keep herself safe.[32] We also see that Henry, with his lack of serious thinking and his self-absorption, knows about the treatment of his aunt, but is able to maintain that knowledge separate from his characterisation of the Admiral as 'a very good man'.

This secrecy from Fanny, her participation in concealment both of her own feelings and of the actions of those around her, represents a form of duplicity which is also a safety tool. Jenny Davidson, in her book *Hypocrisy and the Politics of Politeness: Manners and Morals from Locke to Austen*, writes that 'In the modest figure of Fanny Price [...] Austen defends those forms of insincerity that are produced by dependence.'[33] We see in Fanny a person aware of the value of truth, aware of the value of principles, who nonetheless is forced to uphold behaviours she does not agree with. She lies to her uncle, conceals things from him, and takes actions which she does not wish to – most notably taking on a role in a play – but it is crucial to remember both her relative dependency on the family and family regard, and the abusive conditioning she has undergone, which for years has asserted that she has no right to disagree.

Barbara Seeber's work suggests that 'It is true that Fanny perpetuates the very ideology that has oppressed her, but her stillness is not one of reactionary conservatism: it is the stillness of somebody who is literally afraid to move.'[34] Fanny has been starved of love, of regard, and of affection. While at Mansfield, we see her disproportionate gratitude when Edmund considers her needs, or when she is not prohibited from acting in the way she would like. A significant part of her attachment to Edmund is drawn from his status as the person most likely to show her affection. When she returns to Portsmouth, we see her longing to be important to her family. She reaches the conclusion that she has no right to importance, and does not fully belong in either household.[35] The tenuousness of her position in the Bertram household is utilised by Sir Thomas in order to attempt to leverage Fanny to marry Henry.

The threat here is not simply one of material resources, but a clear sign that Fanny's access to family and familial regard is dependent on her submission to the will of the family in general, and Sir Thomas in particular. Fanny's 'insincerities' are, as Davidson rightly points out, not censured by Austen, but recognised as a medium through which Fanny has shaped herself to be safe at Mansfield. Fanny might 'perpetuate the very ideology that oppresses her' through her silence and her self-suppression, but she also has nowhere to go that will meet her needs as a victim of this kind of trauma. By taking her character to Portsmouth in the novel, Austen removes the notion of Fanny's returning home as a truly viable alternative – 'just going home' cannot solve Fanny's problems because she is not valued there either.

The overwhelming exception to Fanny's submissive conduct is her remarkable defiance over the question of her marriage. It is highly significant that the thing she is willing to risk her slight portion of familial regard for is the prospect of being important to the person she has the most love for. Not only that, but Edmund represents stability rather than transience; Fanny knows exactly what life with him would be like because she has already lived under his will, and she knows that he will not hurt her. It is nothing short of remarkable that she is able to explicitly refuse to comply with Sir Thomas, a man who has not only terrified her for years, but whom all the inhabitants of Mansfield Park struggle to challenge.[36] Perhaps this is because Fanny's love has been her comfort and secret for years, perhaps it is because her religious principles here override the mastery of Sir Thomas with the mastery of God, perhaps it is because she cannot make a vow she does not believe in – perhaps most of all, because she *is* in love and clings to the thing that brings her happiness. When she thinks of 'how wretched, and how unpardonable, how hopeless and how wicked it was, to marry without affection', there is a clear alternation between the motivations of 'the right thing to do' (where the conduct would be 'wicked' or 'unpardonable') and the motivations of her life being 'wretched' and 'hopeless'.[37] Fanny's ability to stand up for her own life at this moment is the only point in the novel where she considers her own happiness a need, and the only need that outweighs her conditioned submission to the desires and whims of the rest of the family.

Sir Thomas disappoints Fanny by his seeming inability to recognise 'dislike' as sufficient motivation for not marrying someone. He makes an effort to interrogate whether there might be reasons he is unaware of, but as he doesn't want to think about the idea of Fanny being in love with one of his sons, he doesn't look too hard at that particular prospect. After ascertaining that there is nothing Fanny can tell him that he considers justification for her dislike, Sir Thomas concludes that she must simply be unaware of her own feelings. He again situates her understanding (this time of herself) within the scope of his own perception, and so he feels justified in attempting to compel her to accept the proposal. Fanny's refusals are stripped of potency, nullified by the belief that she does not know her own mind.

Austen's portrayal of Sir Thomas's inability to judge his own feelings here offers a wonderful commentary; if he were more willing to entertain the possibility that his niece loved her cousin, Fanny's refusal would make perfect sense to him. Given the choice between the two possibilities he can see, Sir Thomas picks the more comfortable option. Either Fanny is in love with one of her cousins, or she doesn't understand what she wants, has suddenly started acting contrary to how she has been for more than a decade, and can't possibly mean what she says. Far easier to deal with Fanny as a different woman than have a poor relation in love with his son… He tells her that

> It is of no use, I perceive, to talk to you. We had better put an end to this most mortifying conference. Mr Crawford must not be kept longer waiting. I will, therefore, only add, as thinking it my duty to mark my opinion of your conduct – that you have disappointed every expectation I had formed, and proved yourself of a character

> the very reverse of what I had supposed. For I *had*, Fanny, as I think my behaviour must have shewn, formed a very favourable opinion of you from the period of my return to England. I had thought you peculiarly free from wilfulness of temper, self-conceit, and every tendency to independence of spirit, which prevails so much in modern days, even in young women. And which in young women is offensive and disgusting beyond all common offence. But you have now shewn me that you can be wilful and perverse, that you can and will decide for yourself, without any consideration or deference for those who have surely some right to guide you – without even asking their advice. You have shewn yourself very, very different from anything I had imagined.[38]

In this tirade, so overwhelming to Fanny, we see Sir Thomas's biggest issue with her refusal: it means she is not doing what he wants her to do. He had previously thought that she lacked 'independence of spirit', which he found praiseworthy in someone who he thought ought to follow the guidance and mandates of others. Her display of being 'wilful and perverse' is exactly as he says: nothing more than the idea that she 'can and will decide' for herself. In this refusal, she lacks the 'deference' that he feels is his due, a deference which clearly translates into not merely a listening to but an *adherence* to his will. In a previous chapter, he had advised Fanny to leave the ball they were at and go to bed – it is the same kind of advice that Sir Thomas has in mind here: '"Advise" was his word, but it was the advice of absolute power.'[39] In this ball scene, the narrator speculates as to whether Sir Thomas was attempting to advertise Fanny as a good potential wife to Henry Crawford by demonstrating her 'persuadableness' – suggesting a direct correlation between a good wife and an obedient one. The fact that he's ordering Fanny to bed, as a husband would have legal right to do, adds an uncomfortably sexual element to the whole conversation.[40] What we see repeatedly from Sir Thomas is a conflation between the idea of obedience as a general quality, and obedience as an unvarying state of being. Sir Thomas's authoritarian role as master of an Antiguan plantation and keeper of enslaved people is echoed in these interactions; he dehumanises the people he controls. Neither he, his word, nor his will are allowed to be questioned, and it is not enough to usually do as you are told. If it is not universal, it counts for nothing.

In this moment of defiance, Fanny's character is simultaneously viewed as being overly obstinate and eminently persuadable, and part of Sir Thomas is aware of the uneasy dichotomy.[41] The overriding message from Sir Thomas, even from Edmund, is that she ought to do as she is told because it is by surrendering her self-will that she earns the right to be loved. They both know that she usually does as she is told. It is precisely this usual state that makes her deviation from it both so surprising to them, and so offensive. This obedience, submission, lack of independence or 'wilfulness', forms what Sir Thomas and Edmund are both advocating for in a wife.

After being confronted with Sir Thomas's tirade, Fanny bursts into tears. However, these tears have the opposite effect to the one she would have wished.

> Another burst of tears; but in spite of that burst, and in spite of that great black word *miserable*, which served to introduce it, Sir Thomas began to think that a little relenting, a little change of inclination, might have something to do with it.[42]

Somewhat inexplicably, Sir Thomas reads Fanny's crying as a signal that she is 'relenting' or coming around to the idea of marrying Henry. However, Austen's narrator makes it clear that this is not what Sir Thomas is actually thinking:

> He knew her to be very timid, and exceedingly nervous; and thought it not improbable that her mind might be in such a state, as a little time, a little pressing, a little patience, and a little impatience, a judicious mixture of all on the lover's side, might work their usual effect on. If the gentleman would but persevere, if he had but love enough to persevere –[43]

We see from the beginning of this that Sir Thomas can tell that his niece is feeling overwhelmed. He shows a greater knowledge and acknowledgement of her character here, of the fact that she is nervous and shy, and therefore that this situation will be impacting upon her in a particular way. However, the 'state' that Sir Thomas attributes Fanny's mind to being in he sees as a situation to take advantage of in order to work her into accepting the proposal. Her being overwhelmed is proof not of a change of mind, but of someone who is affected by the words of others in a way that he believes can be manipulated in order to make her take the course of action that he wants. The gentleman's 'perseverance' against the wishes of the lady is simply a form of pressure, a means of bearing down on a 'no' that Sir Thomas does not think can stand up to such careful targeting. It is not even a question of whether Fanny will come to believe that she *wants* to marry Henry – it's the suggestion that if they keep at her long enough, and in the right ways, she *will* marry him regardless. Though Sir Thomas later says to Fanny, 'You cannot suppose me capable of trying to persuade you to marry against your inclinations', his entire plan and mode of behaviour in this matter are governed by his belief in what is most likely to make this marriage happen.[44] He believes that if he shows her kindness, and makes her see Henry repeatedly, then he will succeed in doing the very thing that he assures her he would never try.

This notion of perseverance being a natural part of courtship is shared by Henry himself, and is in part what makes him more invested in continuing to pursue Fanny.

> He was in love, very much in love; and it was a love which, operating on an active, sanguine spirit, of more warmth than delicacy, made her affection appear of greater consequence, because it was withheld, and determined him to have the glory, as well as the felicity, of forcing her to love him.[45]

Henry, we are told, does not 'know he had a pre-engaged heart to attack'.[46] The language – 'glory', 'forcing', 'attack' – is that of the fight; a conquest as conquest. There is a suggestion of masculine achievement through female submission, turning a refusal into a barrier to be surmounted, or a foe to be defeated, rather than the word of an equal to be respected. It takes me back to Toni Bowers's statement that 'Courtship's vaunted mutuality still relies on the gradual achievement of female consent to primary male desire.'[47] Bowers highlights the idea that attempting to create a clear divide between rape and seduction is often a misguided effort, as it emphasises the female response as the point of acceptability. Being worn down or pressured into acceptance is still a problematic situation – consent achieved in such a way doesn't represent a meaningful decision, but a reduction of the capacity to enforce or articulate an opposing desire. Courtship operates on a narrative of 'mutuality', but Austen depicts the clear interrelation of courtship and seduction via the character of Henry, a man who treats obtaining female affection as a challenge or game. He sees a refusal as something to be overturned. Such a thought-process lacks the understanding that a refusal is an active decision; it interprets a 'no' as a 'not yet'. With such understanding, there is no way to offer a meaningful refusal. An acceptance is a capitulation; a refusal a challenge.

> Love such as his, in a man like himself, must with perseverance secure a return, and at no great distance; and he had so much delight in the idea of obliging her to love him in a very short time, that her not loving him now was scarcely regretted. A little difficulty to overcome was no evil to Henry Crawford. He had been apt to gain hearts too easily. His situation was new and animating.[48]

Here we see the elision that is often veiled between the previous 'forcing' and this 'obliging' Fanny to love him – fundamentally both are forces of compulsion. Neither term gives the possibility of choice. For Henry, the joy here is in the challenge, the contest, the hunt. He is used to being able to exercise his will, and his power over women, and therefore Fanny's refusal makes him more invested by transforming the game into a greater display of his prowess and skill.[49]

Austen raises the point through Fanny that a lifetime's conditioning to having to submit to the will of others does not make opposition as 'animating' as it might be to one who has had their own way their whole life.

> To Fanny, however, who had known too much opposition all her life, to find any charm in it, all this was unintelligible. She found that he did mean to persevere; but how he could, after such language from her as she felt herself obliged to use, was not to be understood.[50]

Austen further highlights the issues of this personal conditioning with her observations of how Fanny's ability to meaningfully refuse is compromised both by her sense of what she owes to the person she is speaking to, and by her possession of the specific qualities which are deemed desirable in a wife.

> Fanny knew her meaning but was no judge of her own manner. Her manner was incurably gentle, and she was not aware how much it concealed the sternness of her purpose. Her diffidence, gratitude, and softness, made every expression of indifference seem almost an effort of self-denial; seem at least, to be giving nearly as much pain to herself as to him [...] She might have disdained him in all the dignity of angry virtue, in the grounds of Sotherton, or the theatre at Mansfield Park; but he approached her now with rights that demanded different treatment. She must be courteous, and she must be compassionate. She must have a sensation of being honoured, and whether thinking of herself or her brother, she must have a strong feeling of gratitude. The effect of the whole was a manner so pitying and agitated, and words intermingled with her refusal so expressive of obligation and concern, that to a temper of vanity and hope like Crawford's, the truth, or at least the strength of her indifference, might well be questionable.[51]

It is overwhelmingly Fanny's sense of obligation which fights against her refusal – she is so bound up with all of the 'musts' that she feels she has to perform, that she does not manage to convey her own purpose. As Austen points out, the conviction that Fanny really does want to marry Henry derives a part of its strength from the fact that the belief allies with Henry's own wishes and 'vanity'. Nonetheless, we are told that Henry has some justification for thinking that Fanny cares for him, that his perseverance is not unwelcome. Behavioural consent is made even more complicated by the conditioning and behaviour required by social conventions – not to show Henry gratitude for his behaviour towards her brother and his proposal to herself would be considered rude, yet by displaying the aforementioned gratitude, Fanny conveys the impression that she is interested marrying him. We are right back with Husak and Thomas – there is no way that Fanny can behave where her behaviour will be socially appropriate, but not provide 'evidence' that she wants to marry Henry: 'Fanny, meanwhile [...] was trying, by everything in the power of her modest gentle nature, to repulse Mr Crawford and avoid both his looks and enquiries; and he unrepulsable was persisting in both.'[52] Fanny's personality and conditioning, her 'habits of ready submission', make the act of refusing actively difficult for her.[53] She struggles both to bring herself to perform the act, and even more so to have the act recognised when she does. This in turn results in the persistence being more actively coercive: because it requires more from Fanny to refuse, the continuous applications on her to accept are actively draining, designed to wear her down into a state where she cannot continue to say no. As we can see in microcosm, it is an effective design; Fanny is 'wearied into speaking', in sharp contrast to all the moments in the novel where she finds that she must be silent.[54]

Perhaps the most difficult attempts at 'persuasion' for Fanny to hear are those which come from Edmund. Though he begins by telling his cousin that he believes her to be in the right, because marrying without love is fundamentally the wrong thing to do, he moves on to a line of reasoning designed to guilt-trip Fanny into taking the course of action that he personally has decided would be best for her (and which coincidentally would also be best for him).

> So far your conduct has been faultless, and they were quite mistaken who wished you to do otherwise. But the matter does not end here. Crawford's is no common attachment; he perseveres, with the hope of creating that regard which had not been created before. This we know, must be a work of time. But (with an affectionate smile), let him succeed at last, Fanny, let him succeed at last. You have proved yourself upright and disinterested, prove yourself grateful and tender-hearted; and then you will be the perfect model of a woman, which I have always believed you born for […] I cannot suppose that you have not the *wish* to love him – the natural wish of gratitude. You must have some feeling of that sort. You must be sorry for your own indifference.[55]

Here, more explicitly even than Sir Thomas, we see the qualities desirable in the 'model of a woman': that she be grateful to the man who proposes to her, and should therefore want to accept him purely as a result of his wanting to marry her. The suggestion that there is an intrinsic debt between proposer and recipient, where the recipient inherently owes the proposer a positive response because they have made the proposal, is an idea Austen contends with across her novels. Belief in the idea that a man is entitled to success with his chosen woman is almost a guarantee that the proposal will fail – Mr Darcy, Mr Collins, Henry Crawford, Mr Elton, John Thorpe, even to some degree Captain Wentworth, all run aground on this. Edmund also believes that a woman must be 'tender-hearted', in the context of Fanny needing to cease the 'cruelty' of refusing a man who really wants to marry her. Edmund sees a proposing man as one who wishes to 'get your heart for his own use', while Fanny wants a man who respects her heart the way it is.[56] Edmund suggests that she has lost her mind, or at least her power of rationality: 'Never, Fanny! – so very determined and positive! This is not like yourself, your rational self'; 'you must prove yourself to be in your senses as soon as you can, by a different conduct'.[57] The only 'rational' choice is to fall in with the male proposer and the will of her relatives. *Mansfield Park* makes clear the pain that can be given by unwelcome proposals, and demonstrates the nuances of emotional abuse that lie in the apparently romantic notion that if you persevere long enough, you will wear down someone's will to resist until they can no longer refuse.

Fanny articulates some of this to Edmund, in one of her more outspoken moments.

> 'I *should* have thought,' said Fanny, after a pause of recollection, 'that every woman must have felt the possibility of a man's not being approved, not being loved by some one of her sex, at least, let him be ever so generally agreeable. Let him have all the perfections in the world, I think it ought not to be set down as certain, that a man must be acceptable to every woman he may happen to like himself. But even supposing it is so, allowing Mr Crawford to have all the claims which his sisters think he has, how I was I to be prepared to meet him with any feeling answerable to his own? He took me wholly by surprise. I had not an idea that his behaviour to me before had any meaning; and surely I was not to be teaching myself to like him, only because he was taking, what seemed, very idle notice of me. In my situation, it would have been the extreme of vanity to be forming expectations on Mr Crawford [...] How then was I to be – to be in love with him the moment he said he was with me? How was I to have an attachment at his service, as soon as it was asked for? His sisters should consider me as well as him. The higher his deserts, the more improper for me to have ever thought of him. And, and – we think very differently of the nature of women, if they can imagine a woman so very soon capable of returning an affection as this seems to imply.'[58]

Through Fanny's cautious language, Austen helps to highlight the ridiculousness of the assumption that a man *must* be agreeable to any woman he happens to want to marry. The idea that there must at least be the possibility of one woman in the whole world not wanting to marry Henry is hyperbolically careful; Fanny's point in essence is that if you can conceive that one woman might not want to marry the man, then you must be able to at least entertain the idea that a specific woman might not want to marry him, without resorting to the explanation that she is out of her mind. She also points out that, on the gratitude model, she is to begin having feelings only after the man has declared his own, meaning that she is expected to move from no feelings to exceptionally strong feelings in the time it takes a man to give his proposal. If we think about Henry, and the length of time it took him to realise that he was interested in Fanny, we see a stark contrast in the amount of time he had to contemplate such things versus the amount allotted to Fanny. She describes the situation as 'an attachment at his service', again situating the relationship and her regard as tools to be owned or used by the proposer-figure. Her comment that 'his sisters should consider me as well as him' is particularly poignant, calling attention to the fact that most of these discussions only take women into account in practical terms – what their situation would be, how much money they would have, that they would actually have a husband – and fail to think about their emotional state as a valid concern. How, Fanny asks, is she to go from being unworthy to think of a man as a potential husband to being completely in love with him in a matter of moments? Love, she suggests, is not a feeling born of brief meetings, but grows from a knowledge and understanding of each other – a suggestion which is echoed in Austen's other novels.

In the case of Fanny's attachment to Edmund, her love for him predates his own for her by many years, and for virtually all of the novel. While she responds to his kindness and attention, she cannot *respond* to a non-fraternal love, or desire, because it's not present. Fanny's feelings are not romantically responsive. And as she places Edmund on a high pedestal of masculine behaviour, her comment regarding the impropriety of her aspiring to a match with Henry Crawford also contains a comment on her own behaviour in terms of her feelings towards her cousin. Unlike Henry, or Edmund, Fanny has no sense that where she has feelings, they must be reciprocated. She does not actively aspire to marry Edmund – she simply does not want to marry someone else, choosing to remain single and economically unstable rather than attach herself to someone other than the person she loves. She is not the only Austen heroine to be the first to develop feelings. Catherine Morland of *Northanger Abbey* falls for Henry Tilney, and we are explicitly told by Austen that his regard for her begins from a feeling of flattery at her preference, and an enjoyment of it. In the case of Catherine, her feelings are obvious to all around her (though she does not believe she is betraying anything), and so Tilney is able to respond to them. Unlike Fanny, Catherine is naïve, outspoken, and somewhat tactless. Fanny is careful not to betray her feelings, and succeeds in concealing them from everyone involved – which, it should be noted, includes characters with sharp eyes and a sense for schemes, particularly Mary Crawford and Aunt Norris. But where Fanny is unimportant, she is overlooked. Catherine, in contrast, is the recipient of misplaced celebrity. In both of these cases, the love of the female character does not wait for the romantic notice of the male love interest to begin, and Austen makes no issue of that. Indeed, in the case of Catherine, it is precisely her attraction to Tilney that makes him consider her in the first place. And while sanctimonious Edmund is a far less charming character than Henry Crawford, and many readers would prefer Fanny to get a happy ending with Henry rather than one with Edmund, the fact remains that Fanny is allowed to get her own way in this – the one matter where she truly insists.

Mansfield Park receives criticism for the romance between Edmund and Fanny, with some scholars suggesting that the fact that the eventual coupling-up takes place off the page suggests that Austen lost control of her material and couldn't write their love story plausibly because they lack chemistry. Other critics question the nature of the relationship, suggesting either that Fanny and Edmund have a largely platonic marriage, or that the relationship is incestuous because of their sibling-like bond and the way they grew up.[59] The romance between Edmund and Fanny is troubling, and does not read like a great and triumphal love story. The arguments for its incestuous nature are compelling, but regardless of the view you take on that particular issue, it is first and foremost a relationship which has grown out of a situation of domestic and emotional abuse. To criticise Austen for the fact that this relationship isn't sufficiently 'romantic' is to make an assumption about the story that she's telling, and to ignore the one on the page. The novel is *not* a great love story: it is a series of failed love stories; a detailed examination of the conditions required to make a marriage work; an examination of the nature of abusive relationships. Fanny does not end up with a reformed rake, a handsome gentleman, or indeed a particularly likeable character. Like many domestic abuse victims, she's not always seen as particularly likeable herself. But she does end up being allowed to uphold her one decision – a decision which, it must be said, gives her the greatest chance for security and safety out of any of those offered in the novel. She gets to make the choice that she finds in her best interests, and no one is allowed to convince her otherwise – not even her readers.

12

Anne, or Negotiating the Future

> My child, let me not have the grief of seeing you unable to respect your partner in life.
>
> – Jane Austen, *Pride and Prejudice*[1]

> I could no more speak the truth of him than if he had been your husband. My heart bled for you as I talked of happiness. And yet, he is sensible, he is agreeable, and with such a woman as you, it was not absolutely hopeless. He was very unkind to his first wife. They were wretched together. But she was too ignorant and giddy for respect, and he had never loved her. I was willing to hope that you might fare better.
>
> – Jane Austen, *Persuasion*[2]

In a novel about courtship we expect the couple to get together at the end, and ideally to live happily ever after. One thing that Austen's novels are so good at is highlighting that it's not just a case of meeting someone, immediately falling for them, and riding off into the sunset together. Her characters make mistakes when they fall in love. Sometimes they fall for the wrong person first. Sometimes they fall for the right person, but the timing or the circumstances are wrong. But what Austen shows us is that those factors – things like timing or position or lifestyle – are legitimately important to a person's future happiness. You aren't just marrying an individual, you're marrying a life. And that life includes where you will live, and how you will live – and if you can't live happily with the realities of those, the fact that you love the person might not be enough. She doesn't suggest that you should marry someone just because they've got money, but she does advocate making informed choices about the kind of life you want. Sounding out what each other thinks, how they react, what their priorities and tempers are like. Her novels seem to say that if your partner can't give you what you need, or won't respect you, you might be better off staying single – and that's something you need to find out before you end up married to them.

Anne Elliot does not think she is better off single. *Persuasion* was Austen's last completed novel, published posthumously in 1817, and has her oldest and probably wisest heroine. Anne is 27 when the main events of the novel take place – about the same age as *Pride and Prejudice*'s Charlotte Lucas. When she was a teenager she refused to marry the love of her life. She fell in love with Frederick Wentworth when she was 19, he fell in love right back, and the two of them planned to get married. Anne, however, ended up refusing him based on the advice she received from her dear friend (and substitute mother) Lady Russell. In the years that pass between her refusing him and the main events of the book, Anne ends up regretting her decision. She never meets anyone who can hold a candle to Frederick, and she's unhappy and undervalued in her home life. When Frederick reappears – now a successful navy captain – Anne finds that all her old feelings haven't changed. It will come as no surprise to hear that, at the end of the book, they finish up together.

What I find really interesting about *Persuasion* is the way Austen approaches the question of whether Anne did the right thing in turning him down when they were both young. Austen gives us Lady Russell's thought process in recommending that Anne say no, and it's clear that she's motivated by wanting the best for Anne and her future.

> Anne Elliot, with all her claims of birth, beauty, and mind, to throw herself away at nineteen; involve herself at nineteen in an engagement with a young man, who had nothing but himself to recommend

> him, and no hopes of attaining affluence, but in the chances of a most uncertain profession, and no connexions to secure even his farther rise in that profession; would be, indeed, a throwing away, which she grieved to think of! Anne Elliot, so young; known to so few, to be snatched off by a stranger without alliance or fortune; or rather sunk by him into a state of most wearing, anxious, youth-killing dependence.[3]

If you don't know that he's going to be successful, it's a very reasonable set of fears. In the last chapter, we talked about Henry Crawford endearing himself to Fanny by buying her brother's naval commission – using his influence and his income to make it possible for William to advance to a higher rank. Without his interference, William would have struggled to become an officer. Lady Russell here is looking at Frederick Wentworth, and sees that he has no one to pay for his advancement, meaning that unless he is extremely lucky, he'll struggle to rise through the naval ranks. She looks at him and sees that being a sailor is very risky – the sea is dangerous at the best of times, even more so when you're both on the sea and at war. To her, this looks like a match that is going to see her young friend struggle for money. It's not about wanting a fortune for the sake of being rich. It's about worrying what would happen to Anne if she got stuck being poor. She thinks Anne deserves the best, and has all the ingredients that should allow her to live happily and comfortably. She's pretty, she's clever, she's of a good family – why shouldn't she have the best quality of life? Lady Russell is made nervous by the fact that Frederick's main plan for his future career is that he's going to be lucky. And, honestly, who can blame her? She thinks he's reckless, and impetuous, and she wants Anne to be sensible and wait for a safer offer to stake her future on. Anne, we are told, 'was persuaded to believe the engagement a wrong thing', but crucially, she believed it was wrong for Frederick as well as for herself: 'Had she not imagined herself consulting his good, even more than her own, she could hardly have given him up.'[4]

Obviously, Frederick does end up being lucky – something that Anne knows because she keeps track of his career (and whether it looks as though he has married anyone else) while they're apart. No sooner do we hear about her refusing him as a teenager then we hear what she has come to think about it now she's 27. And at 27 Anne is unhappy.

> She was persuaded that under every disadvantage of disapprobation at home, and every anxiety attending his profession, all their possible fears, delays and disappointments, she should yet have been a happier woman in maintaining the engagement than she had been in the sacrifice of it[5]

In weighing up what she needs in her life for her to live well, Anne judges that she would rather take the risks and dangers of a life with Frederick than the life she has had without him. Her judgement is that the material things and the sense of security were less important than feeling loved and being with someone who valued her in a way that her own blood relatives do not. Now, Anne thinks that she holds these views 'without reference to the actual results' of Frederick's fortune, but Austen does make it clear that she knows about it – and it's much easier to believe that you would have been happy struggling when you know that it's something you wouldn't have had to do.

By the end of the novel, when all the hurt feelings are soothed and all misunderstandings are smoothed over, Anne gets a chance to think again about this decision. When she tells Frederick off for thinking that she would be persuaded to marry her (very inferior) cousin William Elliot, she tells him 'If I was wrong in yielding to persuasion once, remember that it was persuasion on the side of safety, not of risk.'[6] She's very clearly able to recognise that marrying Frederick at that time would have been a risky move, and that she wouldn't have had any assurances of his doing well. She's also had enough time without him to know that he is an element she considers essential for her own happiness. She's able to make a more informed decision about the kind of life she wants to have. She tries to talk him into forgiving Lady Russell, wanting the two people she loves best to love each other as well, and in doing so, offers her final reflection on this question that has influenced both of their lives for the last near-decade. Anne concludes that she did the right thing in listening to Lady Russell, but that Lady Russell's advice was bad – too full of the negative possibilities and not representative enough of the possibilities for joy. But, she says,

> it was perhaps one of those cases in which advice is good or bad only as the event decides [...] I was right in submitting to her, and that if I had done otherwise, I should have suffered more in continuing the engagement than I did even in giving it up, because I should have suffered in my conscience.[7]

Anne is absolutely trying to broker peace here and make everybody happy, but her points are still very self-aware. If Frederick had been less lucky, or if she had been in a position to fall in love with other men, she might have looked on the decision differently. Hindsight is a wonderful tool in judging what we should have done. But we can see that, across all these discussions, what Anne is really doing is weighing up the ingredients she needs for her happiness. She needs to feel good in her conscience. She needs to have Frederick in her life. And though Anne herself does not explicitly say that she needs money, Austen suggests it for her. The novel is full of the challenges of running out of money – whether it's Anne's father and sister living beyond their incomes, leading to Anne having to leave the beautiful home she loves so that they can rent it out, or seeing what life is like for the old schoolfriend who lost her fortune. Whether the choice to marry – or to refuse a proposal – is a good one depends on whether it will bring you to the kind of life you need, with the kind of person you want to live with.

This message that happiness must be negotiated for between a combination of factors can be seen all across Austen's work. *Mansfield Park* opens with the tale of three sisters who each marry for different reasons. This too emphasises that it's not just whether you marry for love that's important, but what that will mean for your future. Mary Crawford and Edmund Bertram don't end up getting married to each other, but in many ways this is a good thing – and not just because Fanny wants to marry Edmund. Mary falls for Edmund in spite of herself, having planned to try to marry his older brother, heir to the family estate and fortune. Mary doesn't believe that love is forever. Her experiences in life have made her too cynical, and we see from her advice to both her brother and Fanny that her idea of a good marriage includes thinking about how the wife will be treated after the couple aren't in love any more. She doesn't know if Edmund will love her forever, but she does know that she doesn't want to spend her whole life in a small vicarage, isolated from society. Society is important to her. Her fashionable lifestyle is important to her. We can see from her stay at her sister's that she doesn't need to spend all her time in fashionable company, but we are also shown that when she's in the country, she's dependent on the limited social circle at Mansfield. Part of the reason she socialises so much with Maria and Julia, and ultimately with Fanny, is that there aren't that many other young people of her station nearby. They are her main options for company. Nevertheless, she tells Fanny that

> I am conscious of being far better reconciled to a country residence that I had ever expected to be. I can even suppose it pleasant to spend *half* the year in the country, under certain circumstances – very pleasant. An elegant, moderate-sized home in the centre of family connections – continual engagements among them – commanding the first society of the neighbourhood – looked up to perhaps as leading it even more than those of larger fortune, and turning from the cheerful round of such amusements to nothing worse than a tête-à-tête with the person one feels most agreeable in the world. There is nothing frightful in such a picture, is there Miss Price?[8]

Though she is ostensibly imagining Maria's life with her new husband Mr Rushworth, Mary is clearly imagining what her own situation would be if she married Edmund. At this point, she doesn't know that he is planning on becoming a clergyman, so this lifestyle seems like a reasonable possibility to her. She's rationalising that this kind of life could make her happy. Effectively, what Mary is suggesting here is that for half the year she would live in town, and for half the year she would live like Emma Woodhouse, at the centre of a small but cheerful community in the country. Being around people is a crucial part of her plans for happiness, as is having an important place in the social pecking order.

Though she characterises herself as practical and mercenary, Mary's general disdain for Mr Rushworth and habit of considering Maria's marriage as something to pity tell us that she would not be happy marrying a man she found stupid, no matter how much money he has. (Indeed, at the end of the novel, the narrator tells us that she is 'long in finding' someone who could offer her 'domestic happiness', despite the suggestion that there were lots of potential candidates.)[9] Her attraction to Edmund comes from his personality and the ways he challenges her. It's not based on his money – the money was why she initially planned on trying to marry his brother, the heir. But money isn't of no concern. When she understands that Edmund is going to go into the clergy, she also understands that he's going to be tied to a particular kind of lifestyle. Moving from her sister's house into Edmund's modest new residence would reduce her capacity to socialise, and Mary isn't prepared to accept a lifestyle where she is confined to one small place without a variety of things to do or people to spend time with. Edmund, however, isn't planning on living any part of his life regularly in town. He wants exactly what he has set up for himself, and he isn't planning to compromise on that. Many of Mary and Edmund's conversations therefore see the pair testing out their ideas about what a good married life would involve. They each want the relationship to work, but their inability to agree on what kind of life they should have is a significant part of what ultimately makes the relationship fail.[10]

Austen does not generally write favourably when wealth is the sole motivator for marriage – we look down on fortune-chasers like Willoughby, Mr Elton, William Elliot. But Charlotte Lucas, who marries Mr Collins largely because she wants financial security, is treated more kindly. We get a brief window into Charlotte's viewpoint to make sure we understand her decision making:

> Her reflections were in general satisfactory. Mr Collins, to be sure, was neither sensible nor agreeable: his society was irksome, and his attachment to her must be imaginary. But still he would be her husband. Without thinking highly either of men or of matrimony, marriage had always been her object: it was the only honourable provision for well-educated young women of small fortune, and, however uncertain of giving happiness, must be their pleasantest preservative from want. This preservative she had now obtained; and at the age of twenty-seven, without having ever been handsome, she felt all the good luck of it.

Elizabeth can't understand how Charlotte could bear to tie herself to such a ridiculous man – she certainly couldn't – but Elizabeth is a lot younger and a lot more attractive than Charlotte. We and Elizabeth both get to visit Charlotte, and see that though Charlotte doesn't have a lifestyle that Lizzie would want, she does have one which she prefers to the alternative of living off her brothers' support. She chose the marriage, and 'had chosen it with her eyes open; and […] she did not seem to ask for compassion. Her home and her housekeeping, her parish and her poultry, and all their dependent concerns, had not yet lost their charms.'[11] It's not the romantic ideal, but there's nothing to suggest that Charlotte is less happy than a couple like Mr and Mrs Bennet, who married based on attraction. Mr Bennet was 'captivated' by his wife's looks, but her 'weak understanding and illiberal mind had very early in their marriage put an end to all real affection for her'.[12] At least Charlotte knows what she is getting into.

Mary Crawford isn't looking simply for stability. She's actively and unashamedly looking for a rich husband, but her views on marriage are still related to Charlotte's. Where Charlotte believes that 'Happiness in marriage is entirely a matter of chance', Mary suggests that 'A large income is the best recipé for happiness I ever heard of', on the basis that 'there is not one in a hundred of either sex, who is not taken in when they marry'.[13] Where Charlotte believes that you can't guarantee happiness, but can make choices for stability and respectability, Mary believes that people misrepresent themselves to potential partners, and therefore you can't trust who someone seems when you meet them. Income, she argues, offers a safety net and greater possibility for independence.

> 'You intend to be very rich,' said Edmund, with a look which to Fanny's eye had a great deal of serious meaning.
>
> 'To be sure. Do not you? – Do not we all?'
>
> 'I cannot intend anything which it must be so completely beyond my power to command. Miss Crawford may chuse her degree of wealth. She has only to fix on the number of thousands a year, and there can be no doubt of their coming. My intentions are only not to be poor.'
>
> […]
>
> 'Be honest and poor by all means – but I shall not envy you; I do not think I shall even respect you. I have a much greater respect for those that are honest and rich.'
>
> 'Your degree of respect for honesty, rich or poor, is precisely what I have no manner of concern with. I do not mean to be poor. Poverty is exactly what I have determined against. Honesty, in the something between, in the middle state of worldly circumstances, is all I am anxious for your not looking down on.'
>
> 'But I do look down upon it if it might have been higher. I must look down on anything contented with obscurity when it might have been higher.'[14]

Mary does not care what it is that Edmund does, as long as it lets him be distinguished in some way. She doesn't want to live anonymously, and she would rather have a large income than a small one. She suggests that having money will help solve day-to-day issues – Edmund talks about delays, and paying the poulterers – she responds by saying that she plans to have enough money not to have to worry about that. Here, both she and Edmund agree that they don't want to be poor, but while he supports the state he knows he'll be in as a clergyman, she argues against settling for one thing when you could do better. Fundamentally, here we see that one of the biggest issues she has with the set-up she would have with Edmund is the isolation and obscurity that would come from it.

Though Fanny judges Mary harshly for her views, Austen does not.[15] She is only in the countryside in the first place because her uncle made it impossible for her to continue living in his house. In what might be Austen's most famous innuendo, Mary talks about having seen a great many '*Rears* and *Vices*' at his house – suggesting that the problematic behaviours were sexual. (Her uncle is high up in the Navy; rear and vice are both types of admiral.)[16] She is dependent on her brother for her ability to travel, on her other relatives for a place to stay, and she doesn't want to be dependent on anyone. Mary also witnessed and lived through the unhappiness of her aunt at the hands of her uncle, a 'bad school for matrimony' which has significantly impacted how she views marriage.[17] We can see this clearly in a conversation about the idea of her brother Henry eventually getting married:

> 'Oh dear – let him stand his chance and be taken in. It will do just as well. Everyone is taken in at some point or other.'
>
> 'Not always in marriage, dear Mary.'
>
> 'In marriage especially. With all due respect to such of the present company as chance to be married, my dear Mrs Grant, there is not one in a hundred of either sex, who is not taken in when they marry. Look where I will, I see that it *is* so; and I feel that it *must* be so, when I consider that it is, of all transactions, the one in which people expect most from others, and are least honest themselves.'
>
> 'Ah! You have been in a bad school for matrimony, in Hill Street.'
>
> 'My poor aunt certainly had little cause to love the state; but, however, speaking from my own observation, it is a manoeuvring business. I know so many who have married in the full expectation and confidence of some one particular advantage in the connection,

or accomplishment or good quality in the person, who have found themselves entirely deceived, and been obliged to put up with and take exactly the reverse! What is this but a take-in?'[18]

Mary isn't expecting her happiness to come from her husband. She's clearly aware of the transactional element of marriage, and that people are dishonest when they come to that particular bargaining table. If we factor that in when we think about her bluntness and openness about the expectations she has for her future lifestyle, we see that rather than being mercenary or crass (as Fanny sees it), she is actually being honest and open. She flatly refuses to 'take-in' Edmund – it would be quite easy for her to lie to him in order to marry him. She could even marry him and then attempt to change his mind afterwards. But she never pretends to be looking for a way of life that is different from what she believes that she needs to be happy. She acts in the opposite way to her declarations on the way people scheme to get into marriages; her attraction to Edmund in spite of his being the second son and not the kind of person she decided she would marry, and her insistence on discussing their financial circumstances ahead of time, indicate how genuine her attachment to him is.

In this, she demonstrates more self-knowledge than most of the characters in *Mansfield Park*. The novel's opening fable reminds us not to discount the realities of a lifestyle or way of life in determining how happy a person might be – your lifestyle must be suited to your character for you to live in it creditably.

'I am glad Bertram will be so well off. He will have a very pretty income to make ducks and drakes with, and earned without much trouble. I apprehend he will not have less than seven hundred a year. Seven hundred a year is a fine thing for a younger brother; and […] a sermon at Christmas and Easter I suppose will be the sum total of sacrifice.'

His sister tried to laugh off her feelings by saying, 'Nothing amuses me more than the easy manner with which every body settles the abundance of those who have a great deal less than themselves.

> You would look rather blank, Henry, if your menus plaisirs were to be limited to seven hundred a year.'
>
> 'Perhaps I might; but all *that* you know is entirely comparative. Birthright and habit must settle the business [...]'
>
> Miss Crawford *could* have said that there would be something to do and suffer for it, which she could not think lightly off; but she checked herself and let it pass.[19]

Henry is teasing his sister about the lower income she would have if she were to marry clergyman Edmund, but his point about comparative situations is more apt than it sounds. Fanny has got used to the calm and quiet that the financial affluence at Mansfield allows, and when she is sent home to Portsmouth she finds the noise and bustle and lack of privacy really distressing.[20] A clergyman's life might not be as affluent or high-society as Mary would like, but it is certainly more comfortable – and quiet – than Fanny's family home. Henry, meanwhile, does not have to worry about having a lower income, regardless of the person he marries, because he is in direct financial control of the income from his estates. It gives him an independence that doesn't rely on having to find another person to create the life he wants. Edmund, as a second son, doesn't have the same independence or resources, and so he needs a profession – he has already lost out on a chunk of his inheritance to pay off his brother's debts. Mary has some personal fortune, but it is one lump sum. It is not an income in the way that her brother's is. In their conversation above, she points out the practicalities of living on a lower income, and how they wouldn't suit the kind of life Henry wants. His comments about it being an admirable income to 'make ducks and drakes with' – a mocking take on setting up in modest domestic comfort – is precisely the kind of lifestyle that Fanny would like. But it's equally clear from his teasing that a small country parsonage would not suit Mary in the way that it would Fanny – and Mary is aware that this set-up will not make her happy. Indeed, she views it as requiring an active 'sacrifice'.

With Mary and Edmund, Austen demonstrates a match that would never work, because each of the participants requires something that the other is not prepared to give or give up. Though they both care for each other – almost in spite of themselves – and are drawn to each other, neither will sacrifice or concede to the other on the key point of how to live. And what we see here, through this discussion, is not so much a failed romance as a successfully avoided marital disaster. Mary refuses to follow the 'bad school for matrimony' she has been witness to; rather, she negotiates for her future openly, giving equal weight to her own requirements for happiness. Where Edmund sees a woman who will not accept the lifestyle and profession he is going to have, Mary sees a man who does not love her enough to change something that would enable them to marry. She thinks to herself that 'It was plain that he could have no serious views, no true attachment, by fixing himself in a situation which he must know she would never stoop to. She would learn to match him in indifference.'[21] She is as guilty as Edmund of viewing the situation with her own concerns and wants dominant, but it is refreshing to find a female character who is so unapologetically assertive about what her needs are for her future life – and for her not to be mocked as a result of this. What Edmund wants in a wife, ultimately, is someone who will think like him and agree with him on important points. He is generally quite inflexible in his thinking, particularly when confronted with direct opposition, and wants a wife who fits in with his intentions for how to live his life. Conveniently, Fanny wants the same thing. 'Having formed her mind and gained her affections, he had a good chance of her thinking like him', says the narrator; aside from Edmund's admiration for Mary, Fanny's tendency is to fit herself to the shape he thinks best.[22] She can't do that when he urges her to marry Henry Crawford, because Edmund himself is still unmarried and she can't give up on that dream. But Edmund has, somewhat unwittingly, groomed for himself 'the model of a woman' that he would like to marry.

If we think back to *Emma*, where the romance also has problematically familial overtones, the love story is more successful. I think a key part of this comes down to one of the central themes in *Emma*, of self-knowledge and the acceptance of flaws in each other. All of the characters in relationships are flawed, but all also seem well suited to each other. Mr Elton and his bride Augusta are of a similar turn of mind, even if that mind is very small and very obnoxious. Together they form a strongly cohesive unit, even as they irritate all the other residents of Highbury. Jane Fairfax is totally aware that Frank Churchill has flaws – is repeatedly hurt by them – but loves and accepts him in spite of them. The same is largely true of Knightley and Emma. Though Knightley argues with Emma, telling her off for her unkindness, it is her spirit that he loves. Like Edmund, he's had a hand in forming her character – after all, he has known her ever since he held her as a baby. But unlike with Edmund and Fanny, we get to see the impact that Emma has on Knightley on the page. The two of them argue, they sulk, they are jealous of each other, and disagree with their views on other people; but they are able to have those arguments, admit to their own mistakes, and love each other because they understand that they want to be 'first' with each other.[23] It's not just Emma looking to be first with him. Knightley even says that he will move in to Emma's father's house when they are married – which was very much not the normal thing to do – because he knows that she would not be happy to leave her father. It's not a small sacrifice. Emma

> was sensible of all the affection it evinced. She felt that, in quitting Donwell, he must be sacrificing a great deal of independence of hours and habits; that in living constantly with her father, and in no house of his own, there would be much, very much, to be borne with.[24]

Though it is absolutely still problematic to have a romance where the hero has known the heroine since she was a child, and says he has been in love with her since she was at least 13, we see that as an adult he treats her as someone worthy of making compromises for.[25] Though the bar may be low, Edmund Bertram would never do this.

Neither of the young men in *Emma* comes close to matching the self-awareness of *Persuasion*'s Frederick Wentworth, though. If we come full circle, back to our conversation about whether Anne was right to refuse him all those years before, Frederick comes to his own conclusions. He asks Anne whether, if he had written to her when he had first made his money, when his circumstances had changed and he had come back to England, she would have accepted him. (She absolutely would.)

> But I was proud, too proud to ask again. I did not understand you. I shut my eyes, and would not understand you, or do you justice. This is a recollection which ought to make me forgive every one sooner than myself. Six years of separation and suffering might have been spared.[26]

That the last word we have on the subject is Frederick owning his own role in their separation is a lovely reminder that the best relationships in Austen are those of mutual respect. Her characters typically have to go through a series of mishaps or misunderstandings which ultimately result in their spending a lot of time together and learning to communicate well with each other. They can go into their marriages confident that they're going to be able to live with each other well. Darcy and Elizabeth spend most of *Pride and Prejudice* being aware of each other's flaws – and very kindly pointing them out to each other. But as they get to know each other better, some of those flaws are removed, and others become less important as they begin to value different qualities in each other. The aspirational relationships of *Mansfield Park* are those that *do not* result in unions, but do involve the openness, negotiation, and disagreement of both parties involved. Not settling for a life or partner you are not compatible with is a success in its own way. In *Northanger Abbey*,

Catherine and Henry may need to wait a year before they have permission to get married, but the 'unjust interference, so far from being really injurious to their felicity, was perhaps rather conducive to it, by improving their knowledge of each other, and adding strength to their attachment'.[27] When Anne and Captain Wentworth are finally brought together at the end of *Persuasion*, Austen describes them as

> More exquisitely happy, perhaps, in their re-union, than when it had first been projected; more tender, more tried, more fixed in a knowledge of each other's character, truth, and attachment; more equal to act, and more justified in acting.[28]

Maybe Anne was right in refusing Wentworth when they were younger; maybe she was wrong. Either way, the two are able to come together finally as adults who respect and love each other. Who know exactly what – and who – they are choosing to build a future with.

There's something beautiful there, in this idea that we love people better when we know them. Love is not ultimately in our faces, or our flawlessness, or our finances. It's something that springs from trust, from mutual respect, mutual teasing. It blooms best when you're both aligned on where you want your life to grow. When we look at Austen and think about ending on a happily ever after, we see that hers are rarely fairytale perfect, for all they end in marriages. (In most ideal worlds, the 17-year-old doesn't end up marrying the man in his forties after all…) But at the root, Austen's best relationships show women valued as individuals by men who can admit to their own mistakes, and forgive their partners theirs. Men who respect their word, and who take it seriously. Who see their future partner as an equal to negotiate with, not a prize to be won or an obstacle to conquer. It's a future we must never give up negotiating for.

Conclusion

> And where the words of women are crying to be heard, we must each recognise our responsibility to seek those words out, to read them and share them and examine them in pertinence to our lives.
>
> – Audre Lorde[1]

I opened this book laughing. We had to laugh, I said, to keep from crying. Many years later that has got harder. I didn't expect to see *Roe* v. *Wade* under threat. I didn't expect to see fascism so normalised and so prevalent again. It's easy to get sucked into the belief that progress is linear, and that once we win rights and battles, they are won for good. And I got sucked in, and things have changed, and I am fearful for what comes next.

As I write this, a slogan is echoing around the internet: 'your body, my choice'. A known sex offender has been re-elected to the White House. Genocide is being loudly ignored.

My friends and I are too tired to laugh much now. Now it's much harder to get out of bed, to go on putting your care and your best into a world that feels as though it's sucking the goodness out of you. But we must keep caring. And when I see them keep caring, it is a little easier for me to keep on too.

I lost my uncle to cancer this year. When he lived with us, we'd all have dinner in the evenings, and as a result he ended up hearing a lot about my research. I can't say that eighteenth-century novels were his cup of tea, and honestly a lot of the feminism stuff was a challenge to some of his ways of thinking. Leaving school young and going straight into being a mechanic, he was a kind man who with the best will in the world called all women 'sweetheart', and struggled to understand why they might not like that. I remember his shock when I finally got through to him about just how many women I know got assaulted at university. Yes, that many. Yes, actually that many. Not in the abstract number way, but in the I-could-tell-you-so-many-stories-and-none-of-them-are-special kind of way. I remember him thinking a lot about that. And I remember the evening he came home from work and proudly told me about how he'd been in a room with people commenting on how a woman was dressed, and what was she thinking, and he told them she had the right to dress exactly how she wanted. For him, a lot of his thinking was bound up in the stories he knew about how the world worked – and now, he was learning new narratives. I definitely wasn't the first person to talk to him about this kind of thing, but I think he had finally found himself in a position to listen.

Moving forwards, I think that's what we have to look for. Finding ways and places where we can get people to understand. The world is big and bleak and full of fear, and I have no answers for how to fix it. But I think we can do some good with stories. Stories are part of how we connect the world together. They're a way to explain, to explore, and to escape. They are both a source of hope and a collection of anger. They are powerful. And we need to be using them now, to reach the uncles and the friends and the people who are not bad people but who don't understand. We need to fight against the other stories they are hearing.

We need to get away from this idea that caring about consent is a recent thing. It's not something that's new and too much, not something that is ruining fun. We need to listen to the stories that are already out there, about the tyranny that comes from one person having total financial and physical control over another. Do not put your neck into that yoke willingly. It might get painted as a relief not to do your own thinking, not to have to wrestle with the world, but there is a whole world of difference between being a housewife and being a housewife who belongs to her husband and cannot leave. Between giving up a job and having to give up a job. That world is choice. Not just choice in a moment, but choice again and again in every moment. If you do not get to disagree, then you are not free. If you cannot say no, and have that no respected in your own right, then you are not free. If you cannot change your mind, then you are not free. Keep your running-away money. Advocate for domestic labour to be recognised. Do not give in to the idea that people are property – and fight it when it creeps into your own thinking. As the inimitable feminist activist and philosopher Sara Ahmed says,

> Fighting to change the system is how we acquire an ever-deepening knowledge of the *function of inequality*: who does the work, who cleans, who cares; how wealth depends on the extraction of resources from land and from people and how inequalities are reproduced by that very extraction, the exhaustion of people's capacities. There are so many ways that power and violence work through exhaustion: the exhaustion of people's capacities to resist: the exhaustion of people's will to live their lives on their own terms; the exhaustion of having to navigate systems, including welfare systems, designed to make it harder for people to get what they need. When we are weary, because we are weary, we need to be in alliance.[2]

Like the metaphor of the choir, it's fine to take a moment to breathe as long as you don't all breathe at the same time. We must make sure we do not all breathe at the same time. We must also make sure there are enough of us to have a moment to breathe.

We need to see that we wouldn't have all these eighteenth-century writers – women who would disagree with each other about all sorts of fundamental things – all advocating for the right to meaningful consent, the right to education, the right to be considered rational people, if the good old days were all that good. We must listen even harder to the stories that we don't hear, the voices that didn't have enough privilege to write down their own stories. Those stories existed, though not as neatly bound, but they have been blanked out of our easy reach. If you imagine yourself back in time, the chances are that you would not be living at leisure in a fine house, attending balls and choosing muslins. More likely you are the servant, the tradesman, the governess, or the truth that is often shied away from, the enslaved.

We have gained ground since the eighteenth century – I would never have been able to write this book if we had not – and whatever we do, we must not give it back.

Appendix

Crime (sexual offence subtypes)	Total defendants brought to trial	Total guilty	% guilty of offence	% of sexual offences this offence	% of guilty verdicts for sexual offences this offence
Assault with intent	380	266	70%	11%	12%
Assault with sodomical intent	48	31	65%	1%	1%
Bigamy	965	837	87%	29%	39%
Indecent assault	310	173	56%	9%	8%
Keeping a brothel	59	43	73%	2%	2%
Rape	1060	568	54%	32%	26%
Sodomy	437	220	50%	13%	10%
Other	53	35	66%	2%	2%

Figure 1 Breakdown of sexual offences by type and verdict distribution

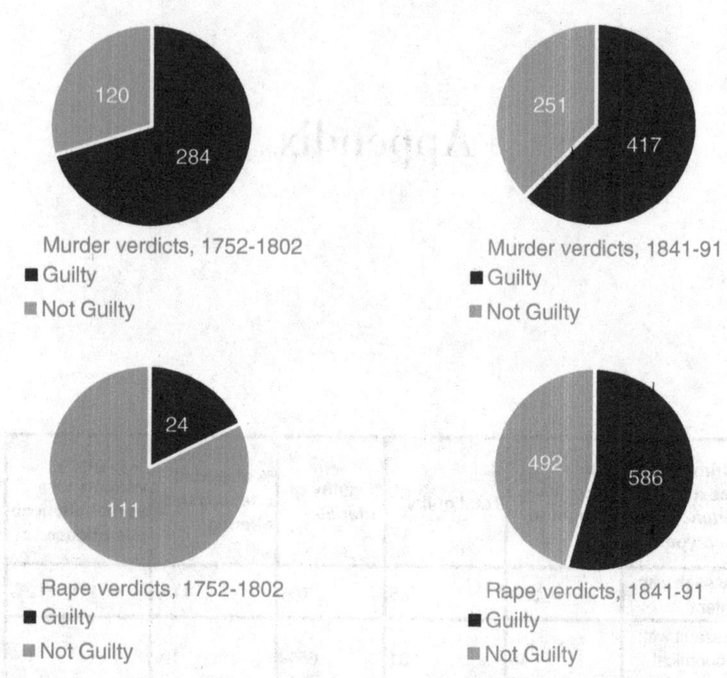

Figure 2 Comparison between rape and murder verdict distribution in the Old Bailey Proceedings for 1752–1802 and 1841–91

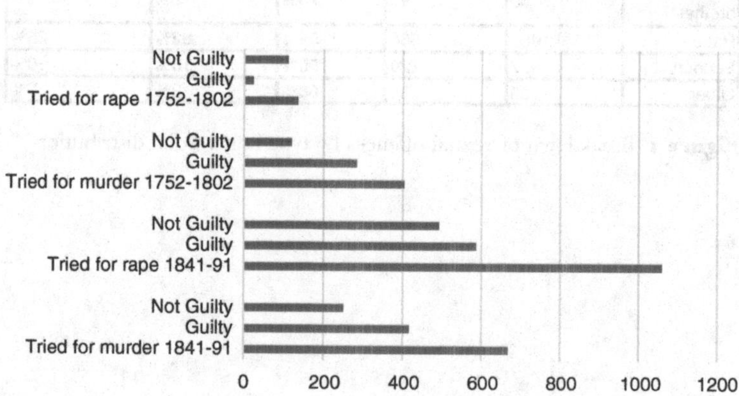

Figure 3 Comparison between rape and murder cases, 1752–1802 and 1841–91, numbers and verdicts

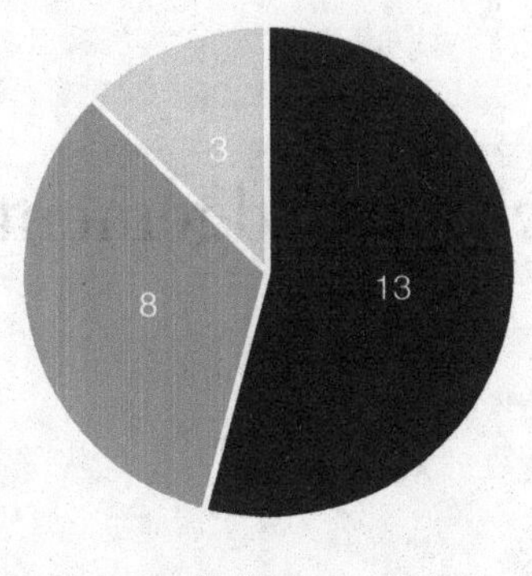

Figure 4 Actual fates of men sentenced to death for rape in the Old Bailey Proceedings, 1752–1802

Acknowledgements

I still can't quite believe that I've written a book, let alone that other people are going to read it! It doesn't seem real somehow. I'd like to thank you for joining me on this adventure – it means more than I can say.

But as with any book, this isn't just mine, and there are people I'm so grateful for who shepherded it along the way.

Firstly, to my agents Ben Clark and Sarah Stamp at The Soho Agency. You've been nothing but kind and supportive over what ended up being a very difficult time in my life. It's been a delight to work with you, and I can't thank you enough for everything you've done since you pulled me out of the slush pile.

I must also thank the entire team at Manchester University Press, without whom there would be no object in your hands. To Kim Walker, Tom Dark, Alun Richards, Becca Parkinson in particular, thank you for taking on this project and for making it happen.

Without Professor Markman Ellis, possibly the greatest PhD supervisor ever to supervise, I would never have got to this point. Markman is a gem in academia, and I couldn't have done this research without his generous support, belief, and guidance. You have, and always will have, my most sincere thanks. Thanks also go to the brilliant Professor Shahidha Bari, for encouraging me to be angrier; the wonderful Dr Katie Fleming, for keeping me sane;

and the entire Queen Mary English department for fostering such a creative and curious environment.

I've been lucky enough to have had some truly inspiring teachers along the way to this book. I can't thank them all, but I must mention a few more. Dr Ruth Abbott, Jonathan Thorpe, Jon Stubbings, and Mich Jonas – you gave me the love of the discipline that has been such an enormous part of my life, the tools to study it, and the references to help me take each step through it. The world is a better place with teachers like you in it.

My friends and colleagues have had to listen to me talk about this book a lot over the years, so it's only fair that I give them the recognition they so richly deserve. Samantha Novak-Mitchell, Zoë Willis, and Sara Abou El Ella: you've gone above and beyond to teach me about how you actually do this whole book thing, listened to my late-night wobbles, and offered all-round advice and support on the industry. You're wonderful people and I'm deeply grateful. Tori Moss, you made me feel like a real writer even more than you gave me impostor syndrome with how unbelievably competent you are. Carolyn Da Silva, my PhD co-conspirator, you drive me to be a better academic – your students are lucky to have you. Rachel Dlugatch, Em Spoor, Solly Elstein, Alex Beddell, Slavi Georgieva, and Lucy Eckersley, you inspire me to be a better human being. Thank you for making the world a softer, brighter, and braver place. Three extremely shrill cheers for the IC dance club – teammates, friends, and incredible distractions from the darker parts of life. You honestly kept me sane through a lot of this process, and I can't wait to be back competing with you again.

Shoutouts too to my Waterstones Holborn crew, Waterstones Piccadilly (especially the fabulous 2nd floor and RP gangs), and the ever-growing Illumiteam – thank you for being such phenomenal colleagues, and for believing in me and this book. I can't tell you how touched I've been by your support.

Then there's my family. My sister Cleo is someone who always believes in me, and was the very first person to buy this book. Cle,

I had you in my head a lot writing this – especially your general maxim of just telling you the interesting bits! It's easier to be brave knowing you're always rooting for me.

Ever since I can remember, I've wanted to be an author (something which stuck around longer than the thankfully short-lived desire to also be a vet). I had always planned to dedicate the first book to my parents. In the end life didn't work out that way, but this book is also for them. Without them, none of this would have been possible. Mum, Dad, you've given me absolutely everything. In return, all I can give you is my thanks and my love. And yes, I will put the kettle on.

Last but not least is Ben Biggs, a menace, a delight, and my partner in everything. You're even better than books.

Notes

Introduction

1 Adrienne Rich, *On Lies, Secrets, and Silence: Selected Prose 1966–1979* (New York: W. W. Norton, 1979), p. 30.

2 See the landmark NUS Hidden Marks survey: 'Hidden Marks' (2011), www.nusconnect.org.uk/resources/hidden-marks-2011 (accessed 3 June 2025).

3 'In the majority of cases in all incident categories surveyed, the perpetrator was known to the victim. Victims of serious sexual assault were the most likely to know their attacker (81 per cent), and conversely women subject to less serious sexual assault were least likely to know the person involved (53 per cent).' 'Nature of Sexual Assault by Rape or Penetration, England and Wales: Year Ending March 2020', p. 11, www.ons.gov.uk/peoplepopulationandcommunity/crimeandjustice/articles/natureofsexualassaultbyrapeorpenetrationenglandandwales/yearendingmarch2020 (accessed 3 June 2025).

4 Department of Justice, Office of Justice Programs, Bureau of Justice Statistics, National Crime Victimization Survey, 2010–2016 (2017), https://rainn.org/statistics/perpetrators-sexual-violence (accessed 3 June 2025).

5 Channel 4's 2018 Factcheck on the subject states that 'a man is 230 times more likely to be raped than to be falsely accused of rape', www.channel4.com/news/factcheck/factcheck-men-are-more-likely-to-be-raped-than-be-falsely-accused-of-rape (accessed 3 June 2025); see also the more recent briefing from Rape Crisis Scotland which collates surveys and studies done on this subject: www.rapecrisisscotland.org.uk/resources/False-allegations-briefing-2021.pdf (accessed 3 June 2025).

6 Mary Astell, *Reflections Upon Marriage. The third edition. To which is added a preface in answer to some objections* (London: R. Wilkin, 1706), pp. 31, 23.
7 Antje Blank, 'Charlotte Smith', in *The Literary Encyclopedia*, vol. 1.2.1.06: *English Writing and Culture of the Romantic Period, 1789–1837*, ed. Janet Todd, Daniel Cook and Daniel Robinson (2003), www.litencyc.com/php/speople.php?rec=true&UID=4112 (accessed 24 February 2025).
8 Chanel Miller, *Know My Name* (London: Viking, 2019), p. 340, quoting the Buzzfeed News post 'Here's the Powerful Letter the Stanford Victim Read to Her Attacker'.
9 Miller, *Know My Name*, p. 321.
10 Miller, *Know My Name*, p. 232.

1 Clarissa, or The Perfect Victim Myth

1 Laurie Penny, *Bitch Doctrine: Essays for Dissenting Adults* (London: Bloomsbury, 2018), p. 17.
2 Samuel Richardson, *Clarissa, or, The History of a Young Lady*, ed. Angus Ross (London: Penguin, 2004), p. 221.
3 The full original title of *Robinson Crusoe* runs to 65 words – where titles are excessively long, I've chosen to spare us all and use the abridged versions.
4 Not everything that trended as a result of a book was as decorative or pleasant – Johann Wolfgang von Goethe's book *The Sorrows of Young Werther*, published in 1778, generated a wave of copycat suicides.
5 Toni Bowers, *Force or Fraud: British Seduction Stories and the Problem of Resistance 1660–1760* (Oxford: Oxford University Press, 2011), p. 274. See also Janice Broder, 'Lady Braidshaigh Reads and Writes *Clarissa*: The Marginal Notes in her First Edition', in *Clarissa and Her Readers: New Essays for The Clarissa Project*, ed. Carol Houlihan Flynn and Edward Copeland (New York: AMS Press, 1999), vol. 9, pp. 269–308.
6 T. C. Duncan Eaves and Ben D. Kimpel, 'An Unpublished Pamphlet by Samuel Richardson', *Philological Quarterly*, 63 (1984), p. 402.
7 Bowers and I concentrate on slightly different periods of time, but there is significant overlap. That's also why you'll find later quotes from her talking about the seventeenth century where this book broadly talks about the eighteenth century.
8 Bowers, *Force or Fraud*, p. 8.
9 Bowers, *Force or Fraud*, p. 21.
10 Catherine Rottenburg, 'Sabina Nessa's Murder and the Grievability of Women's Lives', 26 September 2021, Al Jazeera, www.aljazeera.com/opinions/2021/9/26/sabina-nessas-murder-and-the-grivability-of-womens-lives (accessed 3 June 2025).

2 Cecilia, or Credit and Credibility

1 Rebecca Solnit, *Whose Story is This? Old Conflicts, New Chapters* (London: Granta, 2019), p. 51.
2 Frances Burney, *Cecilia, or Memoirs of an Heiress*, ed. Peter Sabor and Margaret Anne Doody (Oxford: Oxford University Press, 2008), pp. 181–2.
3 Sian Norris, 'Frilly Dresses and White Supremacy: Welcome to the Weird, Frightening World of "Trad Wives"', *The Guardian*, 31 May 2023, www.theguardian.com/commentisfree/2023/may/31/white-supremacy-trad-wives-far-right-feminist-politics (accessed 3 June 2025).
4 This discussion of speech acts focuses on Rae Langton, 'Speech Acts and Unspeakable Acts', *Philosophy and Public Affairs*, 22, no. 4 (1993), pp. 293–330. See also J. L. Austin, *How to do Things with Words: The William James Lectures*, ed. J. O. Urmson and Marina Sbisà (Oxford: Clarendon Press, 1962).
5 Langton, 'Speech Acts and Unspeakable Acts', pp. 320–1.
6 Burney, *Cecilia*, p. 309.
7 Burney, *Cecilia*, p. 296.
8 Burney, *Cecilia*, p. 296.
9 Zoe Williams, 'Why Did No One Speak Out about Harvey Weinstein?', *The Guardian*, 10 October 2017, www.theguardian.com/film/2017/oct/10/why-did-no-one-speak-out-about-harvey-weinstein (accessed 3 June 2025).
10 Williams, 'Why Did No One Speak Out about Harvey Weinstein?'
11 Jodi Kantor and Megan Twohey, *She Said: Breaking the Sexual Harassment Story that Helped Ignite a Movement* (London: Bloomsbury Circus, 2019), p. 177.
12 'When women do report sexual harassment, the outcomes are terrible. Over two-thirds of young women are experiencing sexual harassment in the workplace now, today. Eighty per cent of them felt unable to report it, but three-quarters of the ones who did said that nothing changed afterwards, and 16% said that the situation got worse.' Williams, quoting Laura Bates, 'Why Did No One Speak Out about Harvey Weinstein?'

3 Jane Doe, or Misreading the Room

1 Chanel Miller, *Know My Name* (London: Viking, 2019), p. 50.
2 Catherine MacKinnon, *Towards a Feminist Theory of the State* (Cambridge, MA: Harvard University Press, 1989), p. 230.
3 Amnesty International, 'Let's Talk about Yes!', 29 November 2018, www.amnesty.org/en/latest/campaigns/2018/11/rape-in-europe/ (accessed 3 June 2025).

4 Alan Duke quoting Elliot Rodger, 'Timeline to "Retribution": Isla Vista Attacks Planned Over Years', CNN, 27 May 2014, https://edition.cnn.com/2014/05/26/justice/california-elliot-rodger-timeline/index.html (accessed 3 June 2025).
5 Rodger murdered Katherine Cooper, Veronika Weiss, Cheng Yuan Hong, Weihan Wang, George Chen and Christopher Michaels-Martinez. BBC News, 'Elliot Rodger: How Misogynist Killer Became "Incel Hero"', 26 April 2018, www.bbc.co.uk/news/world-us-canada-43892189 (accessed 3 June 2025).
6 BBC News, 'Elliot Rodger: How Misogynist Killer Became "Incel Hero"'.
7 BBC News, 'Elliot Rodger: How Misogynist Killer Became "Incel Hero"'.
8 Laura Bates, *Men Who Hate Women* (London: Simon and Schuster, 2020).
9 Douglas N. Husak and George C. Thomas III, 'Date Rape, Social Convention, and Reasonable Mistakes', *Law and Philosophy*, 11, no. 1/2 (1992), pp. 95–126.
10 Douglas N. Husak and George C. Thomas III, 'Rapes Without Rapists: Consent and Reasonable Mistakes', *Law and Philosophy*, 11 (2001), pp. 86–117.
11 *Mens rea* refers to the notion of a 'guilty mind' and is used to signify whether the action taken was intentional. For the debate about the role of intention in rape cases, see, for example, Catherine MacKinnon, 'Feminism, Marxism, Method, and the State: An Agenda for Theory', *Signs*, 7, no. 3 (1982), pp. 515–44.
12 Husak and Thomas, 'Date Rape', pp. 98–9.
13 Husak and Thomas, 'Date Rape', p. 100. I also note here that Husak and Thomas use an explicitly gendered male defendant and female victim throughout their scenarios, and assume that all parties are heterosexual and cisgendered.
14 For a really excellent analysis of the gender biases in the British legal system, see Helena Kennedy, *Eve Was Framed: Women and British Justice* (London: Vintage, 1993), and Helena Kennedy, *Misjustice: How British Law is Failing Women* (London: Vintage, 2018).
15 Husak and Thomas, 'Date Rape', p. 102.
16 Husak and Thomas 'Date Rape', p. 102.
17 It is important to acknowledge that they may be compelled to by financial need, or by a dangerous working environment.
18 See, for example, Jenny Davidson, *Hypocrisy and the Politics of Politeness: Manners and Morals from Locke to Austen* (Cambridge: Cambridge University Press, 2004).
19 Frances Sheridan, *The Conclusion of the Memoirs of Miss Sidney Bidulph*, ed. Nicole Garret and Heidi Hunter (Toronto, Ont.: Broadview Press, 2013).
20 Husak and Thomas, 'Date Rape', p. 114. Schulhoefer argues for a 'yes model' of consent, also known as 'active consent' or 'affirmative consent',

which suggests that consent should not be assumed unless there is a clear positive expression of it. This is in contrast to 'no models', where consent is assumed unless it is made explicit that it is withdrawn, and to 'negotiation models', which frame the interaction as a constant series of communications establishing boundaries and willingness. See Stephen Schulhoefer, *Unwanted Sex: The Culture of Intimidation and the Failure of Law* (Cambridge, MA: Harvard University Press, 1998). For a brief retrospective on Schulhoefer's work, its relevance and significance, see Mara Wilson, '"Unwanted Sex," Twenty Years Later', *The Atlantic, Letters from the Archive*, 21 October 2018, www.theatlantic.com/letters/archive/2018/10/stephen-schulhofers-unwanted-sex-20-years-later/573241/ (accessed 22 July 2021]).

21 Husak and Thomas, 'Date Rape', p. 114.

22 Sohaila Abdulali, *What We Talk About When We Talk About Rape* (Oxford: Myriad Editions, 2018), p. 95.

23 Amnesty International, 'Let's Talk About Yes!'

24 Husak and Thomas, 'Date Rape', p. 117, discussing the work of Perper and Weis.

25 Husak and Thomas, 'Date Rape', p. 118. Let us also pass over the problem of describing any form of impending rape as 'normal circumstances'.

26 Rape Crisis England and Wales website, 'Myths vs Facts', https://rapecrisis.org.uk/get-informed/about-sexual-violence/myths-vs-realities/ (accessed 3 June 2025).

27 For more in-depth analysis of this, see Judith Herman, *Trauma and Recovery: The Aftermath of Violence – From Domestic Abuse to Political Terror* (New York: Basic Books, 2015 [1997]), and Babette Rothschild, *8 Keys To Safe Trauma Recovery: Take-Charge Strategies to Empower Your Healing* (New York: W. W. Norton, 2010).

28 See, for example, Laura Bates, *Everyday Sexism* (London: Simon and Schuster, 2014), and 'The Everyday Sexism Project', https://everydaysexism.com/ (accessed 9 August 2021). Note that these types of resources were not as prevalent when Husak and Thomas were writing, but that the information and situation are not new – the range of examples is just bigger.

29 Alan Duke quoting Elliot Rodger, 'Timeline to "Retribution": Isla Vista Attacks Planned Over Years'.

30 There are far too many instances of this to list; examples include Julie Bosman, 'A College Student Was Killed by a Man Whose Catcalls She Tried to Ignore, Say Prosecutors', *The New York Times*, 27 November 2019, www.nytimes.com/2019/11/27/us/chicago-college-student-killed-catcall.html (accessed 9 August 2021); Barney Davis and John Dunne, 'London Woman "Run Down by Moped Riding Thugs in Rainham after Ignoring Catcalls"', *The Evening Standard*, 29 September 2016,

www.standard.co.uk/news/crime/young-woman-run-down-by-moped-riding-thugs-after-ignoring-their-catcalls-a3356736.html (accessed 9 August 2021).

31 Many of the authors I discuss highlight the struggle to speak at all when faced with a sexual threat. As I shall go on to discuss in Chapter 8, Mary Hays's *The Victim of Prejudice* goes so far as to highlight the issue of post-traumatic stress disorder, and the way in which it generates a freeze response in a victim of sexual violence after the event itself.

32 Husak and Thomas, 'Rape without Rapists', p. 99.

33 I am not suggesting that every hard 'no' will result in violence. However, every hard 'no' comes with the risk of violence, and therefore will be framed within that context even should the conclusion be that the scenario is safe enough to take that risk.

34 Again, these roles are not necessarily gendered, but are framed in this way in the articles examined.

35 For a more detailed discussion of rape myths, see, for example, Kate Harding, *Asking for It: The Alarming Rise of Rape Culture – And What We Can Do About It* (Boston: Da Capo, 2015), and Peggy Reeves Sanday, *Fraternity Gang Rape: Brotherhood and Privilege on Campus* (New York: New York University Press, 2007).

36 Husak and Thomas, 'Rape without Rapists', p. 99.

4 Ophelia, or Resisting the Unknown

1 Angel Props, 'Letter 8: I Am', in *Dear Sister: Letters from Survivors of Sexual Violence*, ed. Lisa Factora-Borchers (Edinburgh: AK Press, 2014), p. 67.

2 Sarah Fielding, *The History of Ophelia*, ed. Peter Sabor (Peterborough, Ont.: Broadview Press, 2004), p. 51.

3 Fielding, *The History of Ophelia*, p. 44.

4 See, for example, *Shamela*, in Henry Fielding, *Joseph Andrews and Shamela*, ed. Judith Hawley (London: Penguin, 1999). Bowers offers an interesting reading here, suggesting that Pamela uses indirect resistance strategies to attempt to reject Mr B., and that 'the assumptions behind readings that dismiss Pamela as a hypocrite are similar to the assumptions that make it difficult for juries to understand that a woman not injured or killed in the course of a sexual assault, or who cannot show "adequate" or "convincing" physical signs of violent resistance, could have been raped.' Toni Bowers, *Force or Fraud: British Seduction Stories and the Problem of Resistance 1660–1760* (Oxford: Oxford University Press, 2011), p. 260. For more extensive discussion of the behaviour of victims of domestic violence, including their perceived inaction, see Jane Monckton Smith, *In Control: Dangerous Relationships and How They End in Murder* (London:

Bloomsbury Circus, 2021). For a contrasting view, see Helen Thompson's analysis of *Pamela* as a novel which uses compliance to demonstrate the arbitrariness of relationship power-dynamics; Helen Thompson, *Ingenuous Subjection: Compliance and Power in the Eighteenth-Century Domestic Novel* (Philadelphia, PA: University of Pennsylvania Press, 2005), ch. 3.

5 Fielding, *Ophelia*, p. 57.

6 Sandra Macpherson, 'Lovelace, LTD', *ELH*, 65, no. 1 (1998), p. 113. For more on this topic, see Sandra Macpherson, *Harm's Way: Tragic Responsibility and the Novel Form* (Baltimore, MD: Johns Hopkins University Press, 2010).

7 Helena Kennedy, *Eve Was Framed: Women and British Justice* (London: Vintage, 1993); Helena Kennedy, *Misjustice: How British Law is Failing Women* (London: Vintage, 2018).

8 Fielding, *Ophelia*, pp. 51–2.

9 It is also worth noting here that the very act of abduction on horseback heightens the presence of the sexual threat by alluding to the classical root of the word from *rapere* (to carry off), typically used in Latin to describe the actions of centaurs carrying virginal maidens into the woods to rape them.

10 Fielding, *Ophelia*, p. 86.

11 Fielding, *Ophelia*, p. 96.

12 Fielding, *Ophelia*, p. 75.

13 Fielding, *Ophelia*, p. 104.

14 Fielding, *Ophelia*, p. 76.

15 Tim Evans, Mark Alesia and Marisa Kwiatkowski, 'Former USA Gymnastics Doctor Accused of Abuse', *IndyStar*, 12 September 2016, https://eu.indystar.com/story/news/2016/09/12/former-usa-gymnastics-doctor-accused-abuse/89995734/ (accessed 17 September 2024).

16 Christina Caron, 'Gymnast Maggie Nichols Wants "Everyone to Know" About Larry Nassar's Abuse', *New York Times*, 9 January 2018, www.nytimes.com/2018/01/09/sports/maggie-nichols-abuse-larry-nassar.html (accessed 17 September 2024).

17 Rachel Denhollander in Bonni Cohen and Jon Shenk (dir.), *Athlete A*, Netflix, 24 June 2020; Evans, Alesia and Kwiatkowski, 'Former USA Gymnastics Doctor Accused of Abuse'.

18 Evans, Alesia and Kwiatkowski, 'Former USA Gymnastics Doctor Accused of Abuse'.

19 Dakota Crawford and Amy Haneline, 'Follow IndyStar's Investigation of USA Gymnastics and Larry Nassar from Start to Finish', *IndyStar*, 24 January 2018, https://eu.indystar.com/story/sports/2018/01/24/indystar-larry-nassar-usa-gymnastics-investigation/1062120001/ (accessed 17 September 2024); Caron, 'Gymnast Maggie Nichols Wants "Everyone to Know" About Larry Nassar's Abuse'.

20 Caron, 'Gymnast Maggie Nichols Wants "Everyone to Know" About Larry Nassar's Abuse'.
21 Evans, Alesia and Kwiatkowski, 'Former USA Gymnastics Doctor Accused of Abuse'.
22 Evans, Alesia and Kwiatkowski, 'Former USA Gymnastics Doctor Accused of Abuse'.
23 Mark Alesia, Tim Evans and Marisa Kwiatkowski, 'Ex-USA Gymnastics Doctor's Charges are "Tip of Iceberg"', *IndyStar*, 22 November 2016, https://eu.indystar.com/story/news/2016/11/22/larry-nassar-michigan-state-university-child-sexual-assault-usa-gymnastics-michigan-attorney-general/94280568/ (accessed 17 September 2024).
24 Crawford and Amy Haneline, 'Follow IndyStar's Investigation of USA Gymnastics and Larry Nassar from Start to Finish'. This refers to the Ingahm County case brought against Nassar – including victims from Eaton County, the total number making victim impact statements was 204.
25 Jamie R. Abrahams and Amanda Potts, 'The Language of Harm: What the Nassar Victim Impact Statements Reveal about Abuse and Accountability', *University of Pittsburgh Law Review*, 82 (2020), pp. 74–5, 85, https://lawreview.law.pitt.edu/ojs/lawreview/article/download/775/466/ (accessed 17 September 2024).
26 Chanel Miller, *Know My Name* (London: Viking, 2019).

5 Camilla and Eugenia, or What You Don't Know Can Hurt You

1 Laura Bates, *Everyday Sexism* (London: Simon and Schuster, 2014), p. 122.
2 Sara Ahmed, *The Feminist Killjoy Handbook* (London: Allen Lane, 2023), p. 137.
3 Frances Burney, *Camilla, or A Picture of Youth*, ed. Edward A. Bloom and Lillian D. Bloom (Oxford: Oxford University Press, 2009), p. 294.
4 Burney, *Camilla*, p. 705.
5 Burney, *Camilla*, p. 705.
6 Burney, *Camilla*, p. 705.
7 We might note that Edgar, who is playing with Camilla's emotions in order to decide whether she is good enough for him, does not critique himself in the same manner.
8 Burney, *Camilla*, p. 703.
9 Burney, *Camilla*, p. 721.
10 See, for example, Lionel and Claremont's teasing of Hal Westwyn for living within his means. Burney, *Camilla*, p. 600.

11 This deal is illegal because Camilla is under 21.
12 It is perhaps also worth noting at this point that *Camilla* was written when Burney herself was in need of money.
13 Take, for example, Lionel's unease about his own debts. He is planning to leave England in order to avoid being thrown into debtors' prison, and has this to say about the matter: 'I've a few debts too, of my own, that make me a little uneasy. I don't mean to trades people; they can wait well enough; our credit is good: but a man looks horrid small walking about, when he can't pay his debts of honour.' Burney, *Camilla*, p. 738. Understanding the importance of paying tradespeople is another of Burney's markers of good character.
14 Sir Hugh, as the cause of Eugenia's various ailments, feels both guilt and responsibility, and therefore makes the request that she be kept ignorant of her degree of difference in order to protect his niece – and by extension himself.
15 Burney, *Camilla*, p. 293.
16 Burney, *Camilla*, p. 312.
17 Burney, *Camilla*, p. 313.
18 Burney, *Camilla*, p. 118.
19 Burney, *Camilla*, p. 148.
20 Burney, *Camilla*, p. 153.
21 Burney, *Camilla*, p. 336.
22 Burney, *Camilla*, p. 336.
23 Burney, *Camilla*, p. 337.
24 And also in part because Burney uses the national stereotype of the sentimental Scot in the case of MacDearsy.
25 Burney, *Camilla*, p. 805.
26 Burney, *Camilla*, p. 806.
27 Burney, *Camilla*, pp. 806–7.
28 Camilla reflects that 'Whatever she had personally to bear, she constantly imagined some imprudence or impropriety had provoked; but Eugenia, while she appeared to her so blameless, that she could merit no evil, was so amiable, that willingly she would have borne for her their united portions.' Burney, *Camilla*, pp. 804–5.
29 The Marriage Act of 1753 sought to reduce the number of clandestine marriages taking place by setting out more defined rules for weddings which would ensure that marriages were properly recorded and witnessed. For more on the role of Hardwicke's 1753 Marriage Act in Burney's works, see Melissa J. Ganz, 'Clandestine Schemes: Burney's *Cecilia* and the Marriage Act', *The Eighteenth Century*, 54, no. 1 (2013), pp. 25–51.
30 For further discussion of abduction law in relation to *Camilla*, see Katherine Jane Wright, 'Flights, Fear or Fantasy: Abduction Plots in Fiction of the

Eighteenth Century 1740–1811', unpublished PhD thesis, University of Edinburgh, 2017.

6 Evelina, or The Value of Virginity

1 Claudia L. Johnson, *Equivocal Beings: Politics, Gender, and Sentimentality in the 1790s: Wollstonecraft, Radcliffe, Burney, Austen* (Chicago: University of Chicago Press, 1995), p. 15.

2 Rebecca West, *The Court and the Castle: A Study of the Intersections of Political and Religious Ideas in Imaginative Literature* (London: Macmillan, 1958), p. 136.

3 Frances Burney, *Evelina, or The History of a Young Lady's Entrance into the World*, ed. Edward A. Bloom (Oxford: Oxford University Press, 2008), p. 234.

4 Though if line of succession were the only consideration, one might have thought that this problem could more easily be solved by establishing a female line of succession instead, since this highlights the fact that a woman knows that any children she bears are hers. See also the notion of modesty as performing a practical function: 'Almost every eighteenth-century account defines modesty as a matter of utility, accounting for women's sexual modesty by the observation (for instance) that modesty allows men to be sure of their children's paternity.' Jenny Davidson, *Hypocrisy and the Politics of Politeness: Manners and Morals from Locke to Austen* (Cambridge: Cambridge University Press, 2004), p. 89.

5 Respect for the innocence of a woman lower in status than the male character (or indeed, simply respect for lower-class women in general) is often used by authors to signify the morality of that male character.

6 For a novelistic example of this, see Frances Sheridan, *Conclusion of the Memoirs of Miss Sidney Bidulph*, ed. Nicole Garret and Heidi Hutner (Peterborough, Ont.: Broadview Press, 2013).

7 For a discussion of the transition of rape from property crime to violent crime, see Cristine Varholy, 'Sexual Assault and Compulsion', in *Violence, Politics and Gender in Early Modern England*, ed. Joseph Ward (Basingstoke: Palgrave Macmillan, 2008), pp. 41–66. For a discussion of the normalisation of the abuse of working-class women, and the way in which from the 1830s, safety from sexual violence became leveraged as a means of controlling women's movements, see Anna Clark, *Women's Silence, Men's Violence: Sexual Assault in England 1770–1845* (London: Pandora Press, 1987).

8 Burney, *Evelina*, p. 147.

9 Burney, *Evelina*, p. 147.
10 Burney, *Evelina*, p. 147.
11 Burney, *Evelina*, p. 149.
12 Burney, *Evelina*, p. 150.
13 For further discussion of the role of violence-as-comedy, see Audrey Bilger, *Laughing Feminism: Subversive Comedy in Frances Burney, Maria Edgeworth, and Jane Austen* (Detroit, MI: Wayne State University Press, 1998).
14 Burney, *Evelina*, p. 152.
15 Burney, *Evelina*, p. 150. See also the note to p. 150, which indicates that Burney's italicisation of *rouge* indicates the novelty of the term, as the fashion had not migrated fully from France at this point. Love interest Orville says in relation to Evelina that 'the difference of nature and of artificial colour, seems to me very easily discerned; that of Nature, is mottled, and varying; that of art, *set*, and *too* smooth; it wants that animation, that glow, that *indescribable something* which, even now that I see it, wholly surpasses all my powers of expression'. Burney, *Evelina*, p. 81.
16 Burney, *Evelina*, p. 197.
17 Burney, *Evelina*, p. 197.
18 Burney, *Evelina*, p. 197.
19 Burney, *Evelina*, p. 197.
20 Burney, *Evelina*, p. 197.
21 Burney, *Evelina*, p. 198.
22 Burney, *Evelina*, p. 198.
23 Burney, *Evelina*, pp. 198–9.
24 Contrast Evelina's description of her own lack of control with her later description of the predicament of the Miss Branghtons, whom she abandoned in her initial flight: 'my own safety being then insured, I grew extremely uneasy for the Miss Branghtons, whose danger, however imprudently incurred by their own folly, I too well knew how to tremble for'. Burney, *Evelina*, p. 200.
25 Burney, *Evelina*, p. 198.
26 Burney, *Evelina*, p. 201.
27 Burney, *Evelina*, p. 203.
28 Burney, *Camilla*, p. 703.
29 See Abdulali here: 'Talking about "prevention" is tricky, because, if we know the fault lies with the men who rape, why should we talk with women and girls about prevention at all? If we tell our daughters (and sons) how to keep themselves safe, aren't we also saying that it's their own fault if something happens?' Sohaila Abdulali, *What We Talk About When We Talk About Rape* (Oxford: Myriad Editions, 2018), p. 182.
30 For a deeply disturbing account of behavioural consent being read into all actions, see the case of Mary Ashford from 1817, described in Clark,

Women's Silence, Men's Violence, p. 71. Ashford was raped and drowned, with clear imprints on the ground of where she was held down, and puddles of blood between the imprinted legs. Nonetheless, it was concluded that she consented, as she had willingly spent time with the man beforehand.

31 Davidson, *Hypocrisy and the Politics of Politeness*, p. 89.

32 Jean-Jacques Rousseau, quoted in Mary Wollstonecraft, *A Vindication of the Rights of Woman* (London: Vintage, 2014), pp. 131–2.

33 Wollstonecraft, *Vindication*, p. 141.

34 'Telling little girls to "just say no" is official policy on sex education curriculum on several continents. But that does no good when it turns out that that "no" won't always be respected. It's even less use in a sexual culture where "no" is one of the most erotic things a woman can say. The fetishization of female resistance – the erotics of "no" – is ancient, but it is not immutable.' Laurie Penny, *Unspeakable Things: Sex, Lies and Revolution* (London: Bloomsbury, 2014), p. 108.

35 For further discussion on the role of female suffering in constructions of male virtue and sentimentality, see Johnson, *Equivocal Beings*, p. 15: 'the spectacle of imminent and outrageous female suffering may not be the unthinkable crime which chivalric sentimentality forestalls, but rather the one-thing-needful to solicit male tears and the virtues that supposedly flow with them'.

36 Wollstonecraft, *Vindication*, p. 108.

37 Wollstonecraft, *Vindication*, p. 143.

38 I believe that profitable work could be done in thinking about the internet as a space which operates in a similar manner to eighteenth-century masquerade culture.

39 Sara Ahmed, *The Feminist Killjoy Handbook* (London: Allen Lane, 2023), p. 18.

40 Laura Bates, *Men Who Hate Women* (London: Simon and Schuster, 2020). See also Rebecca Solnit, *Whose Story is This? Old Conflicts, New Chapters* (London: Granta, 2019).

41 See also Clark, *Women's Silence, Men's Violence*, p. 7.

42 Chanel Miller, *Know My Name* (London: Viking, 2019), p. 217.

43 See, for example, Jordan Erica Webber, 'It's Frustrating to be Known as the Woman who Survived #Gamergate', *The Guardian*, 16 October 2017, www.theguardian.com/lifeandstyle/2017/oct/16/anita-sarkeesian-its-frustrating-to-be-known-as-the-woman-who-survived-gamergate (accessed 27 November 2024); Bates, *Men Who Hate Women*.

44 The limited perception of female labour is in part a result of the centring of middle- and upper-class women, who had fewer class-accepted options for labour. Female labour is largely unseen in these novels, as indeed it

is today, but opportunities for prestigious or distinguished work were certainly lacking.

7 Anon., or The Context of the Courtroom

1 Laura Bates, *Everyday Sexism* (London: Simon and Schuster, 2014), p. 15.
2 Quoted from an anonymous article of 1777 in *The Pennsylvania Evening Post*, in Susan Brownmiller, *Against Our Will: Men, Women and Rape* (New York: Fawcett Books, 1975), p. 118.
3 For a full breakdown of the methodology behind this chapter, see Zoë McGee, 'Novel Evidence: The Eighteenth-Century Courtship Novel as Advocate for Meaningful Consent', PhD thesis, Queen Mary University of London, 2021.
4 Clive Emsley, Tim Hitchcock and Robert Shoemaker, 'The Proceedings – The Value of the Proceedings as a Historical Source', *Old Bailey Proceedings Online*, www.oldbaileyonline.org/static/Value.jsp#reading (accessed 21 March 2020), quoting John Langbein, *The Origins of Adversary Criminal Trial* (Oxford: Oxford University Press, 2003).
5 See Figure 1 in the Appendix.
6 There are occasional errors when calculating case numbers from the Old Bailey Proceedings site (for example, the system occasionally logs multiple defendants involved in the same case as a single defendant). While I have checked through the rape cases individually, I have not gone over the murder cases, and therefore these figures have a slight margin for error in either direction. This does not, however, affect the substance of this point.
7 'Rape ceased to be a capital offence in 1841, and from this date the number of prosecutions, and in particular, successful prosecutions, rises dramatically. In the eighteenth century the conviction rate for rape fell as low as 5% in some decades. From the 1840s onwards this rises to approximately 50%.' Clive Emsley, Tim Hitchcock and Robert Shoemaker, 'Crime and Justice – Crimes Tried at the Old Bailey', *Old Bailey Proceedings Online*, paragraph on 'Rape' under 'Sexual Offences' heading, www.oldbaileyonline.org/static/Crimes.jsp#sexualoffences (accessed 6 June 2017).
8 See Figures 2 and 3 in the Appendix.
9 Factors such as the 1834 renaming of the Old Bailey as the Central Criminal Court, and the extension of its jurisdiction from London and Middlesex to the whole of England, would explain some of this rise in numbers, although not necessarily why murder rates did not increase on a comparative scale.
10 70% in 1752–1802, 62% in 1841–91.

11 This terminology can be used flexibly, and can be found referring to the act or the crime of rape, depending on context. See, for example, Laurie Edelstein, 'An Accusation Easily to be Made? Rape and Malicious Prosecution in Eighteenth-Century England', *The American Journal of Legal History*, 42, no. 4 (1998), p. 362. For additional thoughts on factors which could be contributing to this dark figure, see Gregory Durston, 'Rape in the Eighteenth-Century Metropolis: Part 1', *British Journal for Eighteenth-Century Studies*, 28, no. 2 (2005), p. 172.

12 See, for example, Claire Waxman, 'The London Rape Review: Reflections and Recommendations', *Official Website for the Mayor of London*, 31 July 2019, p. 2, www.london.gov.uk/sites/default/files/vcl_rape_review_-_final_-_31st_july_2019.pdf (accessed 22 July 2021). For further analysis of rape myths and their enduring relationship to the courtroom, see, for example, Kellie R. Lynch et al., 'Associations between Sexual Behaviour Norm Beliefs in Relationships and Intimate Partner Rape Judgements', *Violence Against Women*, 23, no. 4 (2017), pp. 426–51; Joan McGregor, *Is It Rape? On Acquaintance Rape and Taking Women's Consent Seriously* (Aldershot: Ashgate, 2005); Peggy Reeves Sanday, *Fraternity Gang Rape: Brotherhood and Privilege on Campus* (New York: New York University Press, 2007).

13 Anna Clark, *Women's Silence, Men's Violence: Sexual Assault in England 1770–1845* (London: Pandora Press, 1987), pp. 98–9.

14 Edelstein, 'An Accusation Easily to be Made?', pp. 370–2. See also Antony E. Simpson, 'The "Blackmail Myth" and the Prosecution of Rape and its Attempt in 18th Century London: The Creation of a Legal Tradition', *The Journal of Criminal Law and Criminology*, 77, no. 1 (1986), pp. 101–50.

15 Nineteen of the 111 Not Guilty cases share no details beyond the names of the parties and the date, so my analysis is by necessity based on those cases which do provide information.

16 Lackey (t17570420-42, 20 April 1757).

17 Antony E. Simpson, 'Popular Perceptions of Rape as a Capital Crime in Eighteenth-Century England: The Press and Trial of Francis Charteris in the Old Bailey, February 1730', *Law and History Review*, 22, no. 1 (2004), p. 57. See also, for example, Medows (t17630914-13, 14 September 1763).

18 Simpson, 'Popular Perceptions of Rape', p. 48. See also Antony E. Simpson, 'Vulnerability and the Age of Female Consent: Legal Innovation and its Effects on Prosecutions for Rape in Eighteenth-Century London', in *Sexual Underworlds of the Enlightenment*, ed. G. S. Rousseau and Roy Porter (Manchester: Manchester University Press, 1987), pp. 181–205, for further discussion of the significance of the victim's age.

19 Simpson, 'Popular Perceptions of Rape', p. 48.

20 See, for example, cases t17960217-37, p. 3; t17960914-12, p. 8.

21 See, for example, the trials of Linsey (t175000912-29, 12 September 1750) and Tankling (t17500711-25, 11 July 1750).

22 Anna Clark notes the assertions from medical professionals in the early nineteenth century stating that lacerations are 'compatible with final consent' and that 'some women will not consent without some force', including in response to the highly publicised 1817 case of Mary Ashford. In this period at the Old Bailey, however, lacerations are generally taken as evidence of non-consent. Clark, *Women's Silence, Men's Violence*, p. 71.
23 Larwell (t17780916-12, 16 September 1778).
24 Birmingham (t17530502-35, 2 May 1753).
25 Vaughan (t17870912-32, 12 September 1787).
26 '[T]he passage was so straight as hardly to receive a finger'; Earle (t17701205-39, 5 December 1770); Larwell (t17780916-12, 16 September 1778).
27 Anna Clark notes the differing presence of shame in assize depositions held in the Old Bailey courtroom in comparison with the situation for women in the north-east of England, who could make depositions before a single magistrate in his own home. Clark, *Women's Silence, Men's Violence*, pp. 26–7.
28 Scott (t17960914-12, 14 September 1796), p. 12.
29 Scott (t17960914-12, 14 September 1796), p. 1.
30 See, for example, 'in and upon Ann Thacker, did make an assault, and her the said Ann, did ravish and carnally know', in Payne (t17670909-69, 9 September 1767) and Davenport (t1796 0217-37, 17 February 1796).
31 M'kave (t17530424-59, 24 April 1753) and Brophy (t17660909-38, 9 September 1766).
32 Sheridan (17680413-30, 13 April 1768), p. 2.
33 Sarah Pollard, Briant (t17970920-12, 20 September 1797), p. 8.
34 Cole (t1789 1209-91, 9 December 1789), p. 3.
35 It must be said that there are many narratives missing from the courtroom, and that educated upper-class women were by no means the only (or indeed the most) disadvantaged group. However, they were the group most heavily involved in the production and consumption of novels, and for this reason they are my focus here.
36 Jane Austen, *Persuasion*, ed. Gillian Beer (London: Penguin, 2011), p. 220.

8 Mary, or Violating Convention

1 Marianne Kirby, 'You Don't Owe it to Anyone Else to Report', in *Dear Sister: Letters from Survivors of Sexual Violence*, ed. Lisa Factora-Borchers (Edinburgh: AK Press, 2014), p. 49.
2 Mary Hays, *The Victim of Prejudice*, ed. Eleanor Ty (Peterborough, Ont.: Broadview Press, 1998), p. 119.

3 For a fuller discussion of rape myths, their prevalence and persistence, see, for example, Susan Brownmiller, *Against Our Will: Men, Women and Rape* (New York: Fawcett Books, 1975); Kate Harding, *Asking for It: The Alarming Rise of Rape Culture – And What We Can Do About It* (Boston: Da Capo, 2015); Joan McGregor, *Is It Rape? On Acquaintance Rape and Taking Women's Consent Seriously* (Aldershot: Ashgate, 2005).
4 Matthew Lewis, *The Monk* (London: Penguin, 2012).
5 Hays, *The Victim of Prejudice*, p. 22.
6 Hays, *The Victim of Prejudice*, pp. 116–17.
7 See Rae Langton's description of both *perlocutionary frustration* and *illocutionary disablement* in 'Speech Acts and Unspeakable Acts', *Philosophy and Public Affairs*, 22, no. 4 (1993), pp. 293–330, esp. pp. 315–20.
8 During the second instance, Mary is being held captive by Osborne; she is already suffering at his hands, and is somewhat afraid of him. Shock is therefore less prevalent here than fear or dread.
9 Hays, *The Victim of Prejudice*, pp. 122–3.
10 RAINN, 'Effects of Sexual Violence', https://rainn.org/effects-sexual-violence (accessed 3 June 2025). See also, for example, Shaila Dewan, 'Why Women Can Take Years to Come Forward with Sexual Assault Allegations', *The New York Times*, 18 September 2018, www.nytimes.com/2018/09/18/us/kavanaugh-christine-blasey-ford.html (accessed 29 July 2021); Judith Herman, *Trauma and Recovery: The Aftermath of Violence – From Domestic Abuse to Political Terror* (New York: Basic Books, 2015 [1997]).
11 National Health Service, 'Symptoms – Post-Traumatic Stress Disorder', 27 September 2018, www.nhs.uk/mental-health/conditions/post-traumatic-stress-disorder-ptsd/symptoms/ (accessed 29 July 2021).
12 Indeed, even today PTSD is primarily studied as a condition that affects military veterans, with a far more limited scope of work focussed on its relationship to sexual violence, or what we might conceptualise as domestic forms of trauma.
13 Herman, *Trauma and Recovery*, p. 31.
14 Herman, *Trauma and Recovery*, p. 13.
15 Herman, *Trauma and Recovery*, p. 13.
16 Herman, *Trauma and Recovery*, p. 14.
17 Hays, *The Victim of Prejudice*, pp. 139–40.
18 Hays, *The Victim of Prejudice*, p. 148.
19 Hays, *The Victim of Prejudice*, pp. 148, 149.
20 Hays, *The Victim of Prejudice*, pp. 147, 148.
21 Hays, *The Victim of Prejudice*, p. 150.
22 Hays, *The Victim of Prejudice*, p. 161.
23 Hays, *The Victim of Prejudice*, p. 170.
24 Hays, *The Victim of Prejudice*, p. 119.

25 Soraya Chemaly, quoted in Rebecca Solnit, *Whose Story is This? Old Conflicts, New Chapters* (London: Granta, 2019), pp. 104–5.
26 Hays, *The Victim of Prejudice*, pp. 68–9.
27 Hays, *The Victim of Prejudice*, p. 69.
28 Hester Chapone, *Letters on the Improvement of the Mind. Addressed to a young lady* (Dublin: Printed for J. Exshaw, H. Saunders, W. Sleater, J. Potts, D. Chamberlain, J. Williams, and R. Moncrieffe, 1773), p. 111.
29 See, for example, More's exclamation: 'I am not sounding an alarm to female warriors, or exciting female politicians: I hardly know which of the two is the most disgusting.' Hannah More, *Strictures on the Modern System of Female Education* (London: Printed for T. Cadell Jun. and W. Davies, 1799), p. 6.
30 Hays, *The Victim of Prejudice*, p. 29.
31 More, *Strictures*, pp. 142–3.
32 For an unusual perspective on this, see Amelia Opie, *Adeline Mowbray, or The Mother and Daughter; A Tale*, ed. Anne McWhir (Peterborough, Ont.: Broadview Press, 2010), which offers a critique of specific aspects of female independence.
33 Hays, *The Victim of Prejudice*, p. 52.
34 Hays, *The Victim of Prejudice*, p. 63.
35 Hays, *The Victim of Prejudice*, p. 65.
36 Hays, *The Victim of Prejudice*, p. 141.
37 Hays, *The Victim of Prejudice*, p. 163.
38 'Your beauty and unprotected situation may, perhaps, but still further provoke the lawless attempts of our sex and oppose the sympathy of your own.' Hays, *The Victim of Prejudice*, pp. 118–19.
39 Hays, *The Victim of Prejudice*, p. 163.
40 Hays, *The Victim of Prejudice*, p. 66.
41 More, *Strictures*, p. 48
42 Hays, *The Victim of Prejudice*, p. 64.
43 More, *Strictures*, p. 48.
44 Hays, *The Victim of Prejudice*, p. 67.
45 Mary Wollstonecraft, *A Vindication of the Rights of Woman* (London: Vintage, 2014), p. 107.
46 National Sexual Violence Resource Centre, 'Statistics', www.nsvrc.org/statistics (accessed 3 June 2025).

9 Theodora and Dorothea, or The Bystander Effect

1 Frances Sheridan, *Conclusion of the Memoirs of Miss Sidney Bidulph*, ed. Nicole Garret and Heidi Hutner (Peterborough, Ont.: Broadview Press, 2013), p. 211.

2 Sheridan, *Conclusion*, p. 202.
3 Mary Wollstonecraft, *Mary, A Fiction and The Wrongs of Woman, or Maria*, ed. Michelle Faubert (Peterborough, Ont.: Broadview Press, 2012), p. 157.
4 Wollstonecraft, *The Wrongs of Woman*, p. 157.
5 *The Victim of Prejudice* came out after *The Wrongs of Woman*, so Wollstonecraft is not following Hays here.
6 Wollstonecraft, *The Wrongs of Woman*, p. 192.
7 As the people who claim that sexism has been eradicated from present-day Western society demonstrate, this issue of non-belief in significant problems because the problem appears to be too significant is still with us today. See also my earlier example of Freud's retraction of his theory that hysteria stemmed from childhood sexual trauma, as that would require a level of abuse he was not willing to believe was possible. See also Laura Bates, *Everyday Sexism* (London: Simon and Schuster, 2014), and 'The Everyday Sexism Project', https://everydaysexism.com/ (accessed 9 August 2021), as attempts to debunk this myth via the collation of evidence of the scale of the problem.
8 Wollstonecraft, *The Wrongs of Woman*, p. 193.
9 Wollstonecraft, *The Wrongs of Woman*, p. 193.
10 Wollstonecraft, *The Wrongs of Woman*, p. 194.
11 For further discussion of Hardwicke's Marriage Act and its influence in novels, see, for example, Melissa J. Ganz, 'Clandestine Schemes: Burney's *Cecilia* and the Marriage Act', *The Eighteenth Century*, 54, no. 1 (2013), pp. 25–51; Virginia M. Duff, 'Early English Women Novelists Testify to the Law's Manifest Cruelties Against Women Before the Marriage Act of 1753', *Women's Studies*, 29 (2000), pp. 583–618.
12 Sheridan, *Conclusion*, p. 211.
13 Sheridan, *Conclusion*, p. 124.
14 Sheridan, *Conclusion*, p. 125.
15 Sheridan, *Conclusion*, p. 211.
16 Sheridan, *Conclusion*, p. 124.
17 Sheridan, *Conclusion*, p. 143.
18 Sheridan, *Conclusion*, pp. 72–3.
19 Sheridan, *Conclusion*, p. 182.
20 Sheridan, *Conclusion*, p. 192.
21 Sheridan, *Conclusion* (Letter XXVII, Cecilia), p. 119.
22 Sheridan, *Conclusion* (Letter XXVIII, Sidney), p. 120.
23 Sheridan, *Conclusion* (Letter XXVIII, Sidney), p. 119.
24 Sheridan, *Conclusion*, p. 127.
25 Sheridan, *Conclusion*, p. 127.
26 Sheridan, *Conclusion*, p. 155.
27 'Yes, she was pleased to say, I had behaved extremely well; but I had no trials till now. And she hoped when I was called to one, I would not fail

in it […] Now that you are grown up to marriageable years is the test […] You have been hitherto, as you are pretty ready to plead, a dutiful child – You have indeed had no *cause* to be otherwise; no child was ever more favoured – Whether you will discredit all your past actions; whether, at a time and upon an occasion that the highest instance of duty is expected from you (an instance that is to crown all), and when you declare *your heart is free* – you will give that instance; or whether having a view to the independence you may claim […] you will break with us all and stand in defiance.' Samuel Richardson, *Clarissa, or, The History of a Young Lady*, ed. Angus Ross (London: Penguin, 1985), Letter 17, pp. 95–6.

10 Elinor, or Honouring Engagements

1 Laurie Penny, *Bitch Doctrine: Essays for Dissenting Adults*, rev. edn (London: Bloomsbury, 2018), pp. 35, 47.
2 Jane Austen, *Emma*, ed. Fiona Stafford (London: Penguin, 2009), p. 373.
3 For an interesting discussion of the duality between Colonel Brandon and Willoughby, see the section on cameos in Barbara K. Seeber, *General Consent in Jane Austen: A Study of Dialogism* (Kingston, Ont.: McGill-Queen's University Press, 2000), pp. 67–75.
4 Claudia Johnson, *Jane Austen: Women, Politics, and the Novel* (Chicago: University of Chicago Press, 1988), p. 56.
5 It must be said that we do not know the extent to which Lucy's attachment is genuine. As I will go on to discuss later, Mary Crawford makes decisions about whom she is prepared to marry based on financial circumstance, but it is simultaneously clear that she cares for Edmund. We do not have the same insight into Lucy's character as we do for Mary's – the speculations as to her actual level of attachment come from Elinor and Edward, both of whom have a vested interest in minimising them.
6 Jane Austen, *Sense and Sensibility*, ed. Ros Ballaster (London: Penguin, 2008), p. 341.
7 See, for example, the motivation behind Edgar Mandlebert's testing of Burney's *Camilla*.
8 It is also worth noting that though Elinor is better bred than Lucy, she also is not in an easy financial position.
9 Austen, *Sense and Sensibility*, p. 342.
10 Austen, *Sense and Sensibility*, p. 341.
11 It is worth noting that much of this representation is done in Elinor's voice, which impacts the way we should interpret it.
12 There are real similarities with Frank Churchill from Austen's *Emma* here: '"It is a great pleasure where one can indulge in it," said the young man, "though there are not many houses that I should presume on so far;

but in coming *home* I felt I might do anything." [... he had] professed himself to have always felt the sort of interest in the country which none but one's *own* country gives, and the greatest curiosity to visit it. That he should never have been able to indulge so amiable a feeling before, passed suspiciously through Emma's brain; but still if it were a falsehood, it was a pleasant one, and pleasantly handled.' Or here: 'Ahh! – (shaking his head) – the uncertainty of when I may be able to return! – I shall try for it with a zeal! – It will be the object of all my thoughts and cares! – and if my uncle and aunt go to town this spring – but I am afraid – they did not stir last spring – I am afraid it is a custom gone for ever.' Austen, *Emma*, pp. 179–80, 241. In both cases, the male character has the ability to travel but chooses not to, in contrast to the female characters who lack this autonomy.

13 Seeber, *General Consent*, p. 35.

14 Austen, *Sense and Sensibility*, p. 342.

15 Austen, *Sense and Sensibility*, pp. 298–9.

16 Austen, *Sense and Sensibility*, pp. 299–300.

17 Austen, *Sense and Sensibility*, pp. 176–7.

18 Austen, *Sense and Sensibility*, p. 300.

19 Austen, *Sense and Sensibility*, p. 305.

20 Austen, *Sense and Sensibility*, p. 306.

21 Austen, *Sense and Sensibility*, p. 306.

22 Austen, *Sense and Sensibility*, p. 306.

23 Austen, *Sense and Sensibility*, p. 307.

24 Austen, *Sense and Sensibility*, p. 307.

25 Austen, *Sense and Sensibility*, p. 301.

26 Though the fact that Willoughby can leave Devonshire knowing that 'I had reason to believe myself secure of my present wife, if I chose to address her' (Austen, *Sense and Sensibility*, p. 302) indicates that his womanising behaviour is a pattern, and therefore that there may well be other women beside Eliza – and indeed, possibly even other bastard children.

27 That Mrs Smith ultimately does forgive Willoughby is also due to his conduct towards women – in this case his wife. By her 'stating his marriage with a woman of character, as the source of her clemency', she causes Willoughby to believe that 'had he behaved with honour towards Marianne, he might at once have been happy and rich' (Austen, *Sense and Sensibility*, p. 352). Though his conduct towards Eliza is forgiven here, the emphasis falls on the idea that Willoughby's aunt would forgive him provided that he subsequently behaved with honour – and therefore ultimately it would not have mattered which of the women he had married.

28 Austen, *Sense and Sensibility*, p. 300.

29 See, for example, Lovelace in *Clarissa*: 'I may do what I will, and plead violence of *passion*; which, they will have it, makes violence of *action*

pardonable with their sex; as well as an allowed extenuation with the unconcerned of both sexes.' Samuel Richardson, *Clarissa, or, The History of a Young Lady*, ed. Angus Ross (London: Penguin, 1985), p. 702.

30 Sandra Macpherson, *Harm's Way: Tragic Responsibility and the Novel Form* (Baltimore, MD: Johns Hopkins University Press, 2010), p. 91.

31 Austen, *Sense and Sensibility*, p. 301.

32 It is interesting to consider this in the context of Elinor's situation. If Willoughby's indifference to Eliza is not grounds for his abandonment of her, then indifference to Lucy would not be grounds for Edward abandoning her either – though of course the form of 'abandonment' differs.

33 Austen, *Emma*, p. 227.

34 Austen, *Emma*, p. 213.

35 Austen, *Emma*, p. 205.

36 Austen, *Emma*, p. 345.

37 Austen, *Emma*, p. 350.

38 Austen, *Emma*, p. 349.

39 Austen, *Emma*, p. 349.

40 Jane compares the 'governess-trade' to the slave trade, describing it as being 'widely different certainly as to the guilt of those who carry it on; but as to the greater misery of the victims, I do not know where it lies'. There are very significant differences between the situations of the victims of slavery and of women working as governesses, both at individual and national levels regarding the scale of the oppression, destruction, and dehumanisation. The two are categorically not the same. The point that women in the position of governess were the victims of many kinds of abuse, and at scales which we might now discount as being unrealistic, is nonetheless an important one to recognise. The fact that Austen gives this comment to Jane Fairfax, a character who is not prone to exaggeration, suggests that we should take the problem of governess treatment seriously, even as we reject the slavery comparison. Austen, *Emma*, p. 280.

41 Austen, *Emma*, p. 385. That Harriet does arrive at the wrong conclusions based on observing Mr Knightley's behaviour is not seen as fault in him for behaving that way – it simply evidences the way in which judging by behaviour is an inexact science.

11 Fanny, or The Price of Refusal

1 Jane Monckton Smith, *In Control: Dangerous Relationships and How They End in Murder* (London: Bloomsbury Circus, 2021), pp. x–xv.

2 Helena Kennedy, *Misjustice: How British Law is Failing Women* (London: Vintage, 2018), p. 104.

3 Jane Austen, *Mansfield Park*, ed. Katherine Sutherland (London: Penguin, 2011), p. 352.

4 Austen, *Mansfield Park*, p. 362.

5 Rebecca West, *The Court and the Castle: A Study of the Intersections of Political and Religious Ideas in Imaginative Literature* (London: Macmillan, 1958), p. 136.

6 Laurie Penny, *Unspeakable Things: Sex, Lies and Revolution* (London: Bloomsbury, 2014), p. 1.

7 Austen, *Mansfield Park*, p. 70.

8 Joan Klingel Ray describes Fanny as 'Jane Austen's insightful characterisation of the "Battered Child Syndrome"' in 'Jane Austen's Case Study of Child Abuse: Fanny Price', *Persuasions: Journal of the Jane Austen Society of North America*, 13 (1991), pp. 16–26. Particularly interesting in relation to this quotation is Ray's citation of Bernard J. Paris. Paris quotes Maslow's hierarchy of needs, stating that 'Apprehensiveness, fear, dread and anxiety, tension, nervousness, and jitteriness are all consequences of safety-need frustration', pointing out that Fanny is therefore unable to achieve 'self-actualisation' because her safety need is unmet.

9 Austen, *Mansfield Park*, p. 204.

10 Austen, *Mansfield Park*, pp. 258–9.

11 Austen, *Mansfield Park*, p. 288.

12 Austen, *Mansfield Park*, p. 269.

13 Austen, *Mansfield Park*, p. 269.

14 Austen, *Mansfield Park*, p. 270.

15 Barbara Seeber comes to the same conclusion, writing that 'Fanny's love for Edmund is the result of her abuse'. Seeber then goes on to an interesting discussion focused on the incestuous elements of the relationship. Barbara K. Seeber, *General Consent in Jane Austen: A Study of Dialogism* (Kingston, Ont.: McGill-Queen's University Press, 2000), p. 113.

16 Austen, *Mansfield Park*, p. 275.

17 Austen, *Mansfield Park*, p. 277.

18 Austen, *Mansfield Park*, pp. 227–8.

19 Austen, *Mansfield Park*, p. 278. Note here a rare instance of Fanny's feeling as though she does not deserve the ill-treatment she is met with – though of course, the fact that this action comes from someone outside the family is significant.

20 Jane Austen, *Pride and Prejudice*, ed. Vivien Jones (London: Penguin, 2008), p. 106.

21 Austen, *Mansfield Park*, pp. 278, 279, 290.

22 Samuel Richardson, *Clarissa, or, The History of a Young Lady*, ed. Angus Ross (London: Penguin, 1985), Letter 17, pp. 95–6.

23 '[…] since the designing and encroaching, finding out what we most fear to forfeit, direct their batteries against these weaker places and, making

an artillery, if I may so phrase it, of our hopes and fears, play it upon us at their pleasure.' Richardson, *Clarissa*, Letter 19, p. 105.

24 Austen, *Mansfield Park*, p. 290.

25 'And such-like *consenting negatives*, as I may call them, and yet not intend a reflection upon my sister; for what can any young creature in the like circumstances say, when she is not sure but a too ready consent may subject her to the slights of a sex that generally values a blessing either more or less as it is obtained with difficulty or ease?' Richardson, *Clarissa*, Letter 2, p. 44.

26 Austen, *Mansfield Park*, pp. 291–2.

27 I place here this quotation from Chanel Miller's *Know My Name* to highlight the way in which the form of this conversation has endured: 'I was thankful to have Lucas. But it bothered me that having a boyfriend and being assaulted should be related, as if I, alone was not enough. At the hospital it had never occurred to me that it was important I was dating someone; I had only been thinking of me and my body. It should have been enough to say, *I did not want a stranger touching my body*. It felt strange to say, *I have a boyfriend, which is why I did not want Brock touching my body*. What if you're assaulted and didn't already belong to a male? Was having a boyfriend the only way to have your autonomy respected?' Chanel Miller, *Know My Name* (London: Viking, 2019), p. 66. Miller highlights here the way in which her stated lack of interest was not understood as a suitable reason for rejecting the attentions of Brock Turner, and how her being in a relationship with another man was seen as giving credibility to that lack of interest. Her boyfriend was seen as legitimising her lack of interest.

28 Austen, *Mansfield Park*, p. 292. For another example of Sir Thomas's wilful belief, see his conversation with Maria prior to her marriage to Mr Rushworth.

29 Austen, *Mansfield Park*, p. 293.

30 Austen, *Persuasion*, ed. Gillian Beer (London: Penguin, 2011), p. 220.

31 Austen, *Mansfield Park*, pp. 272–3.

32 'I do not censure her *opinions*; but there certainly *is* impropriety in making them public.' Austen, *Mansfield Park*, pp. 60–1.

33 Jenny Davidson, *Hypocrisy and the Politics of Politeness: Manners and Morals from Locke to Austen* (Cambridge: Cambridge University Press, 2004), p. 146.

34 Seeber, *General Consent*, p. 113.

35 Austen, *Mansfield Park*, p. 355.

36 For a discussion of the violence of *Mansfield Park*, and specifically of Sir Thomas as a perpetrator of child abuse, see Seeber, *General Consent*, pp. 95–115.

37 Austen, *Mansfield Park*, p. 299.

38 Austen, *Mansfield Park*, pp. 293–4.

39 Austen, *Mansfield Park*, p. 259.
40 Austen, *Mansfield Park*, p. 259. This idea is reinforced in *Persuasion* in a kind of inversion: there, Anne chooses to refuse Captain Wentworth's hand because she listens to the advice of her mother-figure Lady Russell. She gives way to what she believes is her familial duty, and sound advice, even though it goes against her own inclinations. Frederick Wentworth resents her for being too easily persuadable, and talks about the importance of women knowing and maintaining their own opinions of men when he reappears in the novel. Because of this, he is too proud to seek her out again himself. Yet what Anne does is what Fanny is not doing here – giving way to the counsels of people she feels a duty towards. There is no conflict of ethics as there is with Fanny, because not marrying a person does not carry the same problems as marrying a person one does not love. It is worth noting this trope, as it echoes through many of the earlier novels of the period as well – the question of whether obedience and persuadabilty, or independence and resolution, are more desirable is usually easy to answer based on which course requires the character to act in the way the person judging their behaviours wants them to.
41 '"She does not like to be dictated to; she certainly has a little spirit of secrecy, and independence, and nonsense, which I would advise her to get the better of." As a general reflection on Fanny, Sir Thomas thought nothing could be more unjust, though he had been so lately expressing the same sentiments himself.' Austen, *Mansfield Park*, p. 298.
42 Austen, *Mansfield Park*, p. 295.
43 Austen, *Mansfield Park*, p. 295.
44 Austen, *Mansfield Park*, p. 305. Consider also this comment from the narrator, once Fanny has been sent away to Portsmouth: 'though Sir Thomas, had he known all, might have thought his niece in the most promising way of being starved, both mind and body, into a much juster value for Mr Crawford's good company and good fortune, he would probably have feared to push his experiment farther, lest she might die under the cure.' Austen, *Mansfield Park*, pp. 383–4.
45 Austen, *Mansfield Park*, p. 301.
46 Austen, *Mansfield Park*, p. 301.
47 Toni Bowers, *Force or Fraud: British Seduction Stories and the Problem of Resistance 1660–1760* (Oxford: Oxford University Press, 2011), p. 9.
48 Austen, *Mansfield Park*, p. 302.
49 '[…] when force is at once gendered and eroticized, when sexual arousal and satisfaction are routinely linked with men's domination of women, a stable distinction between seduction and rape, like the idea of straightforward consent and resistance that distinction relies on, becomes problematic […] For when it is one person's unquestioned right to pursue and the other's job to resist or consent, the answering voice will remain secondary and

subordinate, her "choice" pre-emptively limited to the narrow options "yes" or "no."' Bowers, *Force or Fraud*, pp. 20–1.

50 Austen, *Mansfield Park*, p. 302. Consider also: 'In essence, males and females learn a cultural language and an interpretive framework for understanding their sexual interactions and for shaping their expectations about those interactions – a hegemonic cultural framework woven into the fabric of male–female sexual interactions, a framework through which sexual violence is legitimated and reproduced.' Gregory M. Matoesian, *Reproducing Rape: Domination Through Talk in the Courtroom* (Cambridge: Polity, 1993), pp. 13–14.

51 Austen, *Mansfield Park*, pp. 304–5.

52 Austen, *Mansfield Park*, p. 316.

53 Austen, *Mansfield Park*, p. 331.

54 Austen, *Mansfield Park*, p. 317.

55 Austen, *Mansfield Park*, pp. 322–3.

56 Austen, *Mansfield Park*, p. 322.

57 Austen, *Mansfield Park*, pp. 322, 327.

58 Austen, *Mansfield Park*, p. 327.

59 For a reading of their relationship as an idealised model of equality available via the sibling bond, see Margaret Kirkham, 'Feminist Irony and the Priceless Heroine of *Mansfield Park*', in *Jane Austen's Mansfield Park*, ed. Harold Bloom (New York: Chelsea, 1987), p. 129; for a mixture of the fraternal and erotic that is broadly characterised as successful, see Glenda Hudson, *Sibling Love and Incest in Jane Austen's Fiction* (New York: St. Martin's Press, 1992); for a reading of the relationship as incestuous, see Seeber, *General Consent*, pp. 95–115.

12 Anne, or Negotiating the Future

1 Jane Austen, *Pride and Prejudice*, ed. Vivien Jones (London: Penguin, 2008), p. 356.

2 Jane Austen, *Persuasion*, ed. Gillian Beer (London: Penguin, 2011), p. 198.

3 Austen, *Persuasion*, p. 27.

4 Austen, *Persuasion*, p. 26.

5 Austen, *Persuasion*, p. 29.

6 Austen, *Persuasion*, p. 229.

7 Austen, *Persuasion*, pp. 230–1.

8 Jane Austen, *Mansfield Park*, ed. Katherine Sutherland (London: Penguin, 2011), p. 195.

9 Austen, *Mansfield Park*, p. 436.

10 'I have no jealousy of any individual. It is the influence of the fashionable world altogether that I am jealous of. It is the habits of wealth that I fear.

Her ideas are not higher than her own fortune may warrant, but they are beyond what our incomes united could authorise. There is comfort, however, even here. I could better bear to lose her, because not rich enough, than because of my profession. That would only prove her affection not equal to sacrifices, which, in fact, I am scarcely justified in asking; and if I am refused, *that*, I think, will be the honest motive.' Austen, *Mansfield Park*, p. 391.

11 Austen, *Pride and Prejudice*, p. 209.

12 Austen, *Pride and Prejudice*, p. 228.

13 Respectively: Austen, *Pride and Prejudice*, p. 24; Austen, *Mansfield Park*, pp. 197, 44.

14 Austen, *Mansfield Park*, pp. 197–8.

15 Fanny's disregard for her own consequence, and her admiration for Edmund, lead to her finding Mary's requirements excessive, and proof of her character flaws. When overthinking a letter from Mary discussing her interactions with Edmund in London, Fanny generally concludes: 'that Miss Crawford, after proving herself cooled and staggered by a return to London habits, would yet prove herself in the end too much attached to him, to give him up. She would try to be more ambitious than her heart would allow. She would hesitate, she would teaze, she would condition, she would require a great deal, but she would finally accept. This was Fanny's most frequent expectation. A house in town! – *that* she thought must be impossible. Yet there was no saying what Miss Crawford might not ask. The prospect for her cousin grew worse and worse.' Austen, *Mansfield Park*, p. 387.

16 Austen, *Mansfield Park*, p. 57.

17 Austen, *Mansfield Park*, p. 44.

18 Austen, *Mansfield Park*, p. 44.

19 Austen, *Mansfield Park*, pp. 209–10.

20 Though there are aspects of Portsmouth, such as her ability to subscribe to the library, that she enjoys.

21 Austen, *Mansfield Park*, p. 211.

22 Austen, *Mansfield Park*, p. 61.

23 Jane Austen, *Emma*, ed. Fiona Stafford (London: Penguin, 2009), p. 389. Seeber makes an interesting comparison between Harriet Smith's precarity and Fanny's, suggesting that Harriet's indecisiveness arises from this as much as Fanny's submissiveness does – and that it causes both of them to be overlooked. See Barbara K. Seeber, *General Consent in Jane Austen: A Study of Dialogism* (Kingston, Ont.: McGill-Queen's University Press, 2000), pp. 43–6.

24 Austen, *Emma*, pp. 419–20.

25 Austen, *Emma*, p. 432.

26 Austen, *Persuasion*, p. 231.

27 Jane Austen, *Northanger Abbey*, ed. Marilyn Butler (London: Penguin, 2011), p. 235.
28 Austen, *Persuasion*, p. 225.

Conclusion

1 Audre Lorde, *Your Silence Will Not Protect You* (London: Silver Press, 2017), p. 5.
2 Sara Ahmed, *The Feminist Killjoy Handbook* (London: Allen Lane, 2023), p. 219.

Bibliography

Abbey, Antonia, 'Sex Differences in Attributions for Friendly Behaviour: Do Males Misperceive Females' Friendliness?', *Journal of Personality and Social Psychology*, 42, no. 5 (1982), pp. 830–8

Abdulali, Sohaila, *What We Talk About When We Talk About Rape* (Oxford: Myriad Editions, 2018)

Abrahams, Jamie R., and Amanda Potts, 'The Language of Harm: What the Nassar Victim Impact Statements Reveal About Abuse and Accountability', *University of Pittsburgh Law Review*, 82 (2020), https://lawreview.law.pitt.edu/ojs/lawreview/article/download/775/466/ (accessed 17 September 2024)

Ahmed, Sara, *The Feminist Killjoy Handbook* (London: Allen Lane, 2023)

—— *Living a Feminist Life* (Durham, NC: Duke University Press, 2017)

—— *What's the Use? On the Uses of Use* (Durham, NC: Duke University Press, 2019)

Amnesty International, 'Let's Talk About Yes!', 29 November 2018, www.amnesty.org/en/latest/campaigns/2018/11/rape-in-europe/ (accessed 3 June 2025)

Anderson, Michelle J., 'All-American Rape', *St. John's Law Review*, 79, no. 3 (2005), pp. 625–44

—— 'Negotiating Sex', *Southern California Law Review*, 78 (2005), pp. 1401–38

—— 'Prostitution and Trauma in U.S. Rape Law', *Journal of Trauma Practice*, 2 (2003), pp. 75–92

Anderson, Scott A., 'Sex Under Pressure: Jerks, Boorish Behaviour, and Gender Hierarchy', *Res Publica*, 11 (2005), pp. 349–69

Anonymous, *Girl A: My Story* (London: Ebury Press, 2013)

Anonymous, *The Woman of Colour: A Tale*, ed. Lyndon J. Dominique (Peterborough, Ont.: Broadview Press, 2008)

Archard, David, '"A nod's as good as a wink" – Consent, Convention, and Reasonable Belief', *Legal Theory*, 3 (1997), pp. 273–90

—— *Sexual Consent* (Boulder, CO: Westview Press, 1998)

—— 'The Wrong of Rape', *The Philosophical Quarterly (1950–)*, 57, no. 228 (2007), pp. 374–93

Armstrong, Nancy, *Desire and Domestic Fiction* (New York: Oxford University Press, 1987)

Astell, Mary, *Reflections Upon Marriage. The third edition. To which is added a preface in answer to some objections* (London: R. Wilkin, 1706)

—— *A Serious Proposal to the Ladies*, ed. Patricia Springborg (Peterborough, Ont.: Broadview Press, 2002)

Austen, Jane, *Emma*, ed. Fiona Stafford (London: Penguin, 2009)

—— *Love and Freindship and Other Youthful Writings*, ed. Christine Alexander (London: Penguin, 2014)

—— *Mansfield Park*, ed. Katherine Sutherland (London: Penguin, 2011)

—— *Northanger Abbey*, ed. Marilyn Butler (London: Penguin, 2011)

—— *Persuasion*, ed. Gillian Beer (London: Penguin, 2011)

—— *Pride and Prejudice*, ed. Vivien Jones (London: Penguin, 2008)

—— *Sanditon, with Lady Susan and the Watsons*, ed. Margaret Drabble (London: Penguin, 2019)

—— *Selected Letters*, ed. Vivien Jones (Oxford: Oxford University Press, 2009)

—— *Sense and Sensibility*, ed. Ros Ballaster (London: Penguin, 2008)

—— *The Oxford Illustrated Jane Austen: Minor Works*, ed. R. W. Chapman (Oxford: Oxford University Press, 1988)

—— *Volume the First*, ed. Katherine Sutherland (Oxford: Bodleian Library, 2015)

—— *Volume the Second*, ed. Katherine Sutherland and Joan Strasbaugh (New York: Abbeville Press, 2014)

—— *Volume the Third*, ed. Katherine Sutherland and Joan Strasbaugh (New York: Abbeville Press, 2014)

Austin, J. L., *How to do Things with Words: The William James Lectures*, ed. J. O. Urmson and Marina Sbisà (Oxford: Clarendon Press, 1962)

Baker, Katie J. M., 'Here is the Powerful Letter the Stanford Victim Read Aloud to her Attacker', *Buzzfeed News*, 3 June 2016, www.buzzfeed.com/katiejmbaker/heres-the-powerful-letter-the-stanford-victim-read-to-her-ra?utm_term=.ds8VWY2bW#.fsDa24oO2 (accessed 3 June 2016)

Banyard, Kat, *The Equality Illusion: The Truth About Women and Men Today* (London: Faber and Faber, 2011)

—— *Pimp State: Sex, Money and the Future of Equality* (London: Faber and Faber, 2016)

Barker-Benfield, G. J., *The Culture of Sensibility: Sex and Society in Eighteenth-Century Britain* (Chicago: University of Chicago Press, 1992)

Barker, Hannah, and Elaine Chalus, *Women's History: Britain 1700–1850, An Introduction* (Abingdon: Routledge, 2005)

Batchelor, Jennie, *Dress, Distress and Desire: Clothing the Female Body in Eighteenth-Century Literature* (Basingstoke: Palgrave Macmillan, 2005)

BIBLIOGRAPHY

Batchelor, Jennie, and Cora Kaplan, *Women and Material Culture 1660–1830* (New York: Palgrave Macmillan, 2007)

Bates, Laura, *Everyday Sexism* (London: Simon and Schuster, 2014)

—— *Men Who Hate Women* (London: Simon and Schuster, 2020)

Bay-Chen, Laina Y., and Rebecca K. Eliseo-Arras, 'The Making of Unwanted Sex: Gendered and Neoliberal Norms in College Women's Unwanted Sexual Experiences', *The Journal of Sex Research*, 45, no. 4 (2008), pp. 386–97

BBC World News, 'Elliot Rodger: How Misogynist Killer Became "Incel Hero"', 26 April 2018, www.bbc.co.uk/news/world-us-canada-43892189 (accessed 3 June 2025)

Benn, Melissa, *What Should We Tell Our Daughters? The Pleasures and Pressures of Growing Up Female* (London: John Murray, 2013)

Beres, Melania A., '"Spontaneous" Sexual Consent: An Analysis of Sexual Consent Literature', *Feminism and Psychology*, 17, no. 1 (2007), pp. 93–108

Bilger, Audrey, *Laughing Feminism: Subversive Comedy in Frances Burney, Maria Edgeworth, and Jane Austen* (Detroit, MI: Wayne State University Press, 1998)

Binhammer, Katherine, 'The Economics of Plot in Burney's *Camilla*', *Studies in the Novel*, 43, no. 1 (2011), pp. 1–20

Blackstone, William, *Commentaries on the Law of England: A Facsimile of the First Edition of 1765–1769* (Oxford: Oxford University Press, 2011)

—— *Blackstone's Commentaries on the Laws of England*, ed. Wayne Morrison, 4 vols (London: Cavendish Publishing, 2001)

Blank, Antje, 'Charlotte Smith', in *The Literary Encyclopedia, vol. 1.2.1.06: English Writing and Culture of the Romantic Period, 1789–1837*, ed. Janet Todd, Daniel Cook and Daniel Robinson (2003), www.litencyc.com/php/speople.php?rec=true&UID=4112 (accessed 24 February 2025)

Bosman, Julie, 'A College Student Was Killed by a Man Whose Catcalls She Tried to Ignore, Say Prosecutors', *The New York Times*, 27 November 2019, www.nytimes.com/2019/11/27/us/chicago-college-student-killed-catcall.html (accessed 9 August 2021)

Bourke, Joanna, *Rape: A History from 1860 to the Present* (London: Virago, 2008)

Bowers, Toni, *Force or Fraud: British Seduction Stories and the Problem of Resistance 1660–1760* (Oxford: Oxford University Press, 2011)

Breitenberg, Mark, *Anxious Masculinity in Early Modern England* (Cambridge: Cambridge University Press, 1996)

Broder, Janice, 'Lady Bradshaigh Reads and Writes *Clarissa*: The Marginal Notes in her First Edition', in *Clarissa and Her Readers: New Entries for The Clarissa Project*, ed. Carol Houlihan Flynn and Edward Copeland (New York: AMS Press, 1999), vol. 9, pp. 97–118

Brown, Martha G., 'Fanny Burney's "Feminism": Gender or Genre?', in *Fetter'd or Free? British Women Novelists 1670–1815* ed. Mary Anne Schofield and Cecilia Macheski (Athens, OH: Ohio University Press, 1987), pp. 29–39

Brownmiller, Susan, *Against Our Will: Men, Women and Rape* (New York: Fawcett Books, 1975)

Burgess-Jackson, Keith, 'A Crime Against *Women*: Calhoun on the Wrongness of Rape', *Journal of Social Philosophy*, 31, no. 3 (2000), pp. 286–93

—— *Rape: A Philosophical Investigation* (Brookfield, Vancouver: Dartmouth Publishing, 1996)

Burney, Frances, *Camilla, or A Picture of Youth*, ed. Edward A. Bloom and Lillian D. Bloom (Oxford: Oxford University Press, 2009)

—— *Cecilia, or Memoirs of an Heiress*, ed. Peter Sabor and Margaret Anne Doody (Oxford: Oxford University Press, 2008)

—— *Evelina, or The History of a Young Lady's Entrance into the World*, ed. Edward A. Bloom (Oxford: Oxford University Press, 2008)

Butler, Judith, *Gender Trouble: Feminism and the Subversion of Identity* (Abingdon: Routledge, 2006)

Byrne, Paula, *Jane Austen and the Theatre* (London: Hambledon Continuum, 2002)

Cameron, Deborah, 'On Banter, Bonding and Donald Trump', *debuk*, 9 October 2016, https://debuk.wordpress.com/2016/10/09/on-banter-bonding-and-donald-trump/ (accessed 9 October 2016)

Campbell, Ann, 'Clandestine Marriage and Frances Burney's Critique of Matrimony in *Cecilia*', *Eighteenth-Century Life*, 37, no. 2 (2013), pp. 85–103

Cardwell, M. John, 'The Rake as Military Strategist: *Clarissa* and Eighteenth-Century Warfare', *Eighteenth Century Fiction*, 19, no. 1 & 2 (2006), pp. 153–80

Caron, Christina, 'Gymnast Maggie Nichols Wants "Everyone to Know" About Larry Nassar's Abuse', *New York Times*, 9 January 2018, www.nytimes.com/2018/01/09/sports/maggie-nichols-aqbuse-larry-nassar.html (accessed 17 September 2024)

Castle, Terry, 'The Culture of Travesty: Sexuality and Masquerade in Eighteenth-Century England', in *Sexual Underworlds of the Enlightenment*, ed. G. S. Rousseau and Roy Porter (Manchester: Manchester University Press, 1987), pp. 156–80

Channel 4, Factcheck (2018), www.channel4.com/news/factcheck/factcheck-men-are-more-likely-to-be-raped-than-be-falsely-accused-of-rape (accessed 3 June 2025)

Chapone, Hester, *Letters on the Improvement of the Mind, Addressed to a Young Lady*, 2 vols (Dublin: Printed for J. Exshaw, H. Saunders, W. Sleater, J. Potts, D. Chamberlaine, J. Williams, and R. Moncrieffe, 1773)

Chico, Tita, *Designing Women: The Dressing Room in Eighteenth-Century English Literature and Culture* (Lewisberg, PA: Bucknell University Press, 2005)

Clark, Anna, *Women's Silence, Men's Violence: Sexual Assault in England 1770–1845* (London: Pandora Press, 1987)

Cohen, Bonni, and Jon Shenk (dir.), *Athlete A*, Netflix, 24 June 2020

Cole, William, 'Jane Austen Museum Launches BLM-inspired "Interrogation" of Author's Love for Drinking Tea and Wearing Cotton due to Slave Trade Links', *Mail Online*, 19 April 2021, www.dailymail.co.uk/news/article-9486419/Jane-Austen-museum-launches-BLM-inspired-interrogation-authors-love-drinking-tea.html (accessed 15 June 2021)

Cowart, Monica R., 'Understanding Acts of Consent: Using Speech Act Theory to Help Resolve Moral Dilemmas and Legal Disputes', *Law and Philosophy*, 23, no. 5 (2004), pp. 495–525

Crawford, Dakota, and Amy Haneline, 'Follow IndyStar's Investigation of USA Gymnastics and Larry Nassar from Start to Finish', IndyStar, 24 January 2018, https://eu.indystar.com/story/sports/2018/01/24/indystar-larry-nassar-usa-gymnastics-investigation/1062120001/ (accessed 3 June 2025)

Crawford, Katherine, *European Sexualities, 1400–1800* (Cambridge: Cambridge University Press, 2007)

Csengei, Ildiko, *Sympathy, Sensibility, and the Literature of Feeling in the Eighteenth Century* (Basingstoke: Palgrave Macmillan, 2012)

Cutting, Rose Marie, 'Defiant Women: The Growth of Feminism in Fanny Burney's Novels', *Studies in Eighteenth Century Literature, 1500–1900*, 17, no. 3 (1977), pp. 519–33

Dabhiowala, Faramerz, *The Origins of Sex: A History of the First Sexual Revolution* (London: Penguin, 2015)

Davidson, Jenny, *Hypocrisy and the Politics of Politeness: Manners and Morals from Locke to Austen* (Cambridge: Cambridge University Press, 2004)

Davis, Barney, and John Dunne, 'London Woman "Run Down by Moped Riding Thugs in Rainham after Ignoring Catcalls"', *The Evening Standard*, 29 September 2016, www.standard.co.uk/news/crime/young-woman-run-down-by-moped-riding-thugs-after-ignoring-their-catcalls-a3356736.html (accessed 9 August 2021)

Defoe, Daniel, *Roxana, the Fortunate Mistress*, ed. John Mullan (Oxford: Oxford University Press, 2008)

Dewan, Shaila, 'Why Women Can Take Years to Come Forward with Sexual Assault Allegations', *New York Times*, 18 September 2018, www.nytimes.com/2018/09/18/us/kavanaugh-christine-blasey-ford.html (accessed 29 July 2021)

Dickson, Rebecca, 'Misrepresenting Jane Austen's Ladies', in *Jane Austen in Hollywood*, ed. Linda Troost and Sayre Greenfield (Lexington, KY: University Press of Kentucky, 1998), pp. 44–57

The Digital Panopticon, 'John Sullivan, Life Archive ID obpt17620714-34-defend312', www.digitalpanopticon.org/life?id=obpt17620714-34-defend312 (accessed 12 September 2018)

—— 'William Caswell, Life Archive ID obpt17620714-34-defend314', www.digitalpanopticon.org/life?id=obpt17620714-34-defend314 (accessed 12 September 2018)

—— 'William Fitzgerald, Life Archive ID obpt17620714-34-defend316', www.digitalpanopticon.org/life?id=obpt17620714-34-defend316 (accessed 12 September 2018)

Dragiewicz, Molly, 'Women's Voices, Women's Words: Reading Acquaintance Rape Discourse', in *Feminist Interpretations of Mary Daly: Re-reading the Canon*, ed. Sarah L. Hoagland and Marilyn Frye (University Park, PA: Penn State University Press, 2000), pp. 194–221

Dripps, Donald, 'Beyond Rape: An Essay on the Difference Between the Presence of Force and the Absence of Consent', *Columbia Law Review*, 92, no. 7 (1992), pp. 1780–1809

Duff, Virginia M., 'Early English Women Novelists Testify to the Law's Manifest Cruelties Against Women Before the Marriage Act of 1753', *Women's Studies*, 29 (2000), pp. 583–618

Duke, Alan, 'Timeline to "Retribution": Isla Vista Attacks Planned Over Years', CNN, 27 May 2014, https://edition.cnn.com/2014/05/26/justice/california-elliot-rodger-timeline/index.html (accessed 3 June 2025).

Durston, Gregory, 'Rape in the Eighteenth-Century Metropolis: Part 1', *British Journal for Eighteenth-Century Studies*, 28, no. 2 (2005), pp. 167–79

Eaves, T. C. Duncan, and Ben D. Kimpel, 'An Unpublished Pamphlet by Samuel Richardson', *Philological Quarterly*, 63 (1984), pp. 401–9

Edelstein, Laurie, 'An Accusation Easily to be Made? Rape and Malicious Prosecution in Eighteenth-Century England', *The American Journal of Legal History*, 42, no. 4 (1998), pp. 351–90

Edgeworth, Maria, *Belinda*, ed. Katheryn J. Kirkpatrick (Oxford: Oxford University Press, 2008)

Emsley, Clive, Tim Hitchcock and Robert Shoemaker, 'Crime and Justice – Crimes Tried at the Old Bailey', *Old Bailey Proceedings Online*, www.oldbaileyonline.org/static/Crimes.jsp#sexualoffences (accessed 6 June 2017)

—— 'The Proceedings – The Value of the Proceedings as a Historical Source', *Old Bailey Proceedings Online*, www.oldbaileyonline.org/static/Value.jsp#reading (accessed 21 March 2020)

Emsley, Sarah, *Jane Austen's Philosophy of the Virtues* (Basingstoke: Palgrave Macmillan, 2005)

Evans, Tim, Mark Alessia and Marisa Kwiatkowski, 'Former USA Gymnastics Doctor Accused of Abuse', IndyStar, 12 September 2016, https://eu.indystar.com/story/news/2016/09/12/former-usa-gymnastics-doctor-accused-abuse/89995734/ (accessed 17 September 2024)

The Everyday Sexism Project, https://everydaysexism.com/ (accessed 9 August 2021)

BIBLIOGRAPHY

Factora-Borchers, Lisa (ed.), *Dear Sister: Letters from Survivors of Sexual Violence* (Edinburgh: AK Press, 2014)

Fausto-Sterling, Anne, *Sexing the Body: Gender Politics and the Construction of Sexuality* (New York: Basic Books, 2000)

Fenwick, Eliza, *Secresy, or The Ruin on the Rock*, ed. Isobel Grundy (Peterborough, Ont.: Broadview Press, 1994)

Fergus, Jan S., 'Sex and Social Life in Jane Austen's Novels', in *Jane Austen in a Social Context*, ed. David Monaghan (Totowa, NJ: Macmillan, 1981), pp. 66–85

Ferguson, Frances, 'Rape and the Rise of the Novel', *Representations*, no. 20, special issue: 'Misogyny, Misandry, and Misanthropy' (1987), pp. 88–112

Fielding, Henry, *Joseph Andrews and Shamela*, ed. Judith Hawley (London: Penguin, 1999)

Fielding, Sarah, *The History of Ophelia*, ed. Peter Sabor (Peterborough, Ont.: Broadview Press, 2004)

Fraiman, Susan, *Unbecoming Women: British Women Writers and the Novel of Development* (New York: Columbia University Press, 1993)

Friedman, Marilyn, *Autonomy, Gender, Politics* (Oxford: Oxford University Press, 2003)

Fulford, Tim, *Romanticism and Masculinity: Gender Politics and Poetics in the Writings of Coleridge, Cobbett, Wordsworth, De Quincey, and Hazlitt* (Basingstoke: Macmillan, 1999)

Gallagher, Catherine, *Nobody's Story: The Vanishing Acts of Women Writers in the Marketplace 1670–1820* (Berkeley, CA: University of California Press, 1994)

Ganz, Melissa J., 'Clandestine Schemes: Burney's *Cecilia* and the Marriage Act', *The Eighteenth Century*, 54, no. 1 (2013), pp. 25–51

Gay, Penny, *Jane Austen and the Theatre* (Cambridge: Cambridge University Press, 2002)

Gilbert, Sandra M., and Susan Gubar, *The Madwoman in the Attic: The Woman Writer and the Nineteenth-Century Literary Imagination*, 2nd edn (New Haven, CT: Yale University Press, 2000)

Grundy, Isobel, 'Seduction Pursued by Other Means? The Rape in *Clarissa*', in *Clarissa and Her Readers: New Entries for The Clarissa Project*, ed. Carol Houlihan Flynn and Edward Copeland (New York: AMS Press, 1999), vol. 9, pp. 255–68

Haag, Pamela, *Consent: Sexual Rights and the Transformation of American Culture* (Ithaca, NY: Cornell University Press, 1999)

Hamilton, Elizabeth, *Memoirs of Modern Philosophers*, ed. Claire Grogan (Peterborough, Ont.: Broadview Press, 2000)

Harding, D. W., *Regulated Hatred and Other Essays on Jane Austen* (London: Athlone Press, 1998)

Harding, Kate, *Asking for It: The Alarming Rise of Rape Culture – And What We Can Do About It* (Boston: Da Capo, 2015)

BIBLIOGRAPHY

Harvey, Arnold D., *Sex in Georgian England: Attitudes and Prejudices from the 1720s to the 1820s* (London: Phoenix, 2001)

Harvey, Karen, *Reading Sex in the Eighteenth Century: Bodies and Gender in English Erotic Culture* (Cambridge: Cambridge University Press, 2004)

Hays, Mary, *The Victim of Prejudice*, ed. Eleanor Ty (Peterborough, Ont.: Broadview Press, 1998)

Haywood, Eliza, *The History of Miss Betsy Thoughtless*, ed. Christine Blouch (Peterborough, Ont.: Broadview Press, 1998)

Herman, Judith, *Trauma and Recovery: The Aftermath of Violence – From Domestic Abuse to Political Terror* (New York: Basic Books, 2015 [1997])

Hinton, Laura, *The Perverse Gaze of Sympathy: Sadomasochistic Sentiments from Clarissa to Rescue 911* (New York: State University of New York Press, 1999)

Hudson, Glenda, *Sibling Love and Incest in Jane Austen's Fiction* (New York: St. Martin's Press, 1992)

Hughes, Derek, *The Theatre of Aphra Behn* (Basingstoke: Palgrave Macmillan, 2001)

Husak, Douglas N., and George C. Thomas III, 'Date Rape, Social Convention, and Reasonable Mistakes', *Law and Philosophy*, 11, no. 1/2 (1992), pp. 95–126

—— 'Rapes Without Rapists: Consent and Reasonable Mistake', *Law and Philosophy*, 11 (2001), pp. 86–117

Johnson, Claudia, L., *Equivocal Beings: Politics, Gender, and Sentimentality in the 1790s: Wollstonecraft, Radcliffe, Burney, Austen* (Chicago: University of Chicago Press, 1995)

—— *Jane Austen: Women, Politics, and the Novel* (Chicago: University of Chicago Press, 1988)

—— 'What Became of Jane Austen? *Mansfield Park*', *Persuasions: Journal of the Jane Austen Society of North America*, 17 (1995), pp. 59–70

Johnson, Katherine, *Sexuality: A Psychosocial Manifesto* (Cambridge: Polity, 2015)

Jones, Hazel, *Jane Austen and Marriage* (London: Continuum, 2009)

Jordan, Meghan, 'Marriage and Matrimony in Frances Burney's *Cecilia*', *SEL Studies in English Literature 1500–1900*, 55, no. 3 (2015), pp. 559–78

Kahn, Madeline, *Narrative Transvestism: Rhetoric and Gender in the Eighteenth-Century English Novel* (Ithaca, NY: Cornell University Press, 1991)

Kantor, Jodi, and Megan Twohey, *She Said: Breaking the Sexual Harassment Story that Helped Ignite a Movement* (London: Bloomsbury Circus, 2019)

Kappeler, Susanne, *The Pornography of Representation* (Cambridge: Polity, 1986)

Kazan, Patricia, 'Sexual Assault and the Problem of Consent', in *Violence Against Women: Philosophical Perspectives*, ed. Stanley French, Wanda Teays and Laura Purdy (Ithaca, NY: Cornell University Press, 1998)

Kennedy, Helena, *Eve Was Framed: Women and British Justice* (London: Vintage, 1993)

—— *Misjustice: How British Law is Failing Women* (London: Vintage, 2018)

Kipnis, Laura, *Unwanted Advances: Sexual Paranoia Comes to Campus* (London: Verso, 2018)

Kirkham, Margaret, 'Feminist Irony and the Priceless Heroine of *Mansfield Park*', in *Jane Austen's Mansfield Park*, ed. Harold Bloom (New York: Chelsea, 1987), pp. 117–33

Klekar, Cynthia, '"Her Gift Was Compelled": Gender and the Failure of the "Gift" in *Cecilia*', *Eighteenth Century Fiction*, 18, no. 1 (2005), pp. 107–26

Knafla, Louis A., *Crime, Gender and Sexuality in Criminal Prosecutions* (Westport, CT: Greenwood Press, 2002)

Knellwolf, Claudia, *A Contradiction Still: Representations of Women in the Poetry of Alexander Pope* (Manchester: Manchester University Press, 1998)

Langbein, John H., *The Origins of Adversary Criminal Trial* (Oxford: Oxford University Press, 2003)

Langton, Rae, 'Speech Acts and Unspeakable Acts', *Philosophy and Public Affairs*, 22, no. 4 (1993), pp. 293–330

Laqueur, Thomas, *Making Sex: Bodies and Gender from the Greeks to Freud* (Cambridge, MA: Harvard University Press, 1990)

Lennox, Charlotte, *Euphemia*, ed. Susan Kubica Howard (Peterborough, Ont.: Broadview Press, 2008)

—— *The Female Quixote*, ed. Margaret Dalziel (Oxford: Oxford University Press, 1998)

Lewis, Matthew, *The Monk* (London: Penguin, 2012)

Locke, John, *Second Treatise of Government and A Letter Concerning Toleration*, ed. Mark Golde (Oxford: Oxford University Press, 2016)

Lorde, Audre, *Your Silence Will Not Protect You* (London: Silver Press, 2017)

Lubey, Kathleen, 'Sexual Remembrance in *Clarissa*', *Eighteenth-Century Fiction*, 29, no. 2 (2016–17), pp. 151–78

Lynch, Kellie R., et al., 'Associations Between Sexual Behaviour Norm Beliefs in Relationships and Intimate Partner Rape Judgements', *Violence Against Women*, 23, no. 4 (2017), pp. 426–51

MacDonagh, Oliver, *Jane Austen: Real and Imagined Worlds* (New Haven, CT: Yale University Press, 1991)

MacKinnon, Catherine A., *Are Women Human? And Other International Dialogues* (Cambridge, MA: Harvard University Press, 2006)

—— 'Feminism, Marxism, Method, and the State: An Agenda for Theory', *Signs*, 7, no. 3 (1982), pp. 515–44

—— *Feminism Unmodified: Discourses on Life and Law* (Cambridge, MA: Harvard University Press, 1987)

—— *Toward a Feminist Theory of the State* (Cambridge, MA: Harvard University Press, 1989)

—— *Women's Lives, Men's Laws* (Cambridge, MA: Harvard University Press, 2005)

BIBLIOGRAPHY

Macpherson, Sandra, *Harm's Way: Tragic Responsibility and the Novel Form* (Baltimore, MD: Johns Hopkins University Press, 2010)

—— 'Lovelace, LTD', *ELH*, 65, no. 1 (1998), pp. 99–123

Marlowe, Christopher, 'Hero and Leander', in *The Collected Poems of Christopher Marlowe*, ed. Patrick Cheney and Brian J. Striar (Oxford: Oxford University Press, 2006), pp. 193–219

Matoesian, Gregory M., *Reproducing Rape: Domination Through Talk in the Courtroom* (Cambridge: Polity, 1993)

Mazzeno, Laurence, *Jane Austen: Two Centuries of Criticism* (New York: Camden House, 2011)

McCrea, Brian, *Frances Burney and Narrative Prior to Ideology* (Newark, DE: University of Delaware Press, 2013)

McGee, Zoë, 'Novel Evidence: The Eighteenth-Century Courtship Novel as Advocate for Meaningful Consent', PhD thesis, Queen Mary University of London, 2021

McGregor, Joan, *Is It Rape? On Acquaintance Rape and Taking Women's Consent Seriously* (Aldershot: Ashgate, 2005)

McLynn, Frank, *Crime and Punishment in Eighteenth-Century England* (London: Routledge, 1989)

McMaster, Juliet, 'The Talkers and Listeners of *Mansfield Park*', *Persuasions: Journal of the Jane Austen Society of North America*, 17 (1995), pp. 77–89

Miller, Chanel, *Know My Name* (London: Viking, 2019)

Miller, Michael E., 'All-American Swimmer Found Guilty of Sexually Assaulting Unconscious Woman on Stanford Campus', *The Washington Post*, 31 March 2016, www.washingtonpost.com/news/morning-mix/wp/2016/03/31/all-american-swimmer-found-guilty-of-sexually-assaulting-unconscious-woman-on-stanford-campus/ (accessed 31 March 2016)

Monckton Smith, Jane, *In Control: Dangerous Relationships and How They End in Murder* (London: Bloomsbury Circus, 2021)

More, Hannah, *Strictures on the Modern System of Female Education* (London: Printed for T. Cadell Jun. and W. Davies, 1799)

Morgan, Susan, *In the Meantime: Character and Perception in Jane Austen's Fiction* (Chicago: University of Chicago Press, 1980)

Moulton, Ian Frederick, *Before Pornography: Erotic Writing in Early Modern England* (Oxford: Oxford University Press, 2000)

National Health Service, 'Dissociative Disorders', 10 August 2020, www.nhs.uk/conditions/dissociative-disorders/ (accessed 10 August 2020)

—— 'Symptoms – Post-Traumatic Stress Disorder', 27 September 2018, www.nhs.uk/mental-health/conditions/post-traumatic-stress-disorder-ptsd/symptoms/ (accessed 29 July 2021)

National Sexual Violence Resource Centre, 'Statistics', www.nsvrc.org/statistics (accessed 3 June 2025)

National Union of Students, 'Hidden Marks' (2011), www.nusconnect.org.uk/resources/hidden-marks-2011 (accessed 3 June 2025)

Norris, Sian, 'Frilly Dresses and White Supremacy: Welcome to the Weird, Frightening World of "Trad Wives"', *The Guardian*, 31 May 2023, www.theguardian.com/commentisfree/2023/may/31/white-supremacy-trad-wives-far-right-feminist-politics (accessed 3 June 2025)

Nussbaum, Felicity, *Torrid Zones: Maternity, Sexuality, and Empire in Eighteenth-Century English Narratives* (Baltimore, MD: Johns Hopkins University Press, 1995)

Office for National Statistics, 'Nature of Sexual Assault by Rape or Penetration, England and Wales: Year Ending March 2020', 18 March 2021, www.ons.gov.uk/peoplepopulationandcommunity/crimeandjustice/articles/natureofsexualassaultbyrapeorpenetrationenglandandwales/yearendingmarch2020 (accessed 3 June 2025)

O'Malley, Ida Beatrice, *Women in Subjection: A Study of the Lives of Englishwomen Before 1832* (London: Duckworth, 1933)

Opie, Amelia, *Adeline Mowbray, or The Mother and Daughter; A Tale*, ed. Anne McWhir (Peterborough, Ont.: Broadview Press, 2010)

—— *The Father and Daughter with Dangers of Coquetry*, ed. Shelley King and John B. Pierce (Peterborough, Ont.: Broadview Press, 2003)

O'Toole, Emer, *Girls Will Be Girls: Dressing Up, Playing Parts and Daring to Act Differently* (London: Orion, 2015)

Peakman, Julie, *Lascivious Bodies: A Sexual History of the Eighteenth Century* (London: Atlantic Books, 2004)

Penny, Laurie, *Bitch Doctrine: Essays for Dissenting Adults*, rev. edn (London: Bloomsbury, 2018)

—— *Unspeakable Things: Sex, Lies and Revolution* (London: Bloomsbury, 2014)

Pepe, Victoria, with Rachel Holmes, Amy Annette, Alice Stride and Martha Mosse, *I Call Myself a Feminist: The View from Twenty-Five Women Under Thirty* (London: Virago, 2015)

Perry, Ruth, 'Clarissa's Daughters: Or, The History of Innocence Betrayed', in *Clarissa and Her Readers: New Entries for The Clarissa Project*, ed. Carol Houlihan Flynn and Edward Copeland (New York: AMS Press, 1999), vol. 9, pp. 119–42

Pineau, Lois, 'Date Rape: A Feminist Analysis', *Law and Philosophy*, 8 (1989), pp. 217–43

Price, Fiona L., and Scott Masson, *Silence, Sublimity, and Suppression in the Romantic Period* (New York: The Edwin Mellen Press, 2002)

Pugh, Brandie, and Patricia Becker, 'Exploring Definitions and Prevalence of Verbal Sexual Coercion and its Relationship to Consent to Unwanted Sex: Implications for Affirmative Consent Standards on College Campuses', *Behavioral Sciences*, 8, no. 69 (2018), pp. 1–28

Radcliffe, Ann, *The Mysteries of Udolpho* (London: Penguin, 2010)

RAINN, 'Perpetrators of Sexual Violence: Statistics', https://rainn.org/statistics/perpetrators-sexual-violence (accessed 3 June 2025)

Rape Crisis Scotland, 'False Allegations Briefing 2021', www.rapecrisisscotland.org.uk/resources/False-allegations-briefing-2021.pdf (accessed 3 June 2025)

Ray, Joan Klingel, 'Jane Austen's Case Study of Child Abuse: Fanny Price', *Persuasions: Journal of the Jane Austen Society of North America*, 13 (1991), pp. 16–26

Reitan, Eric, 'Date Rape and Seduction: Towards a Defence of Pineau's Definition of "Date Rape"', *Southwest Philosophy Review*, 20 (2004), pp. 99–106

Rich, Adrienne, *On Lies, Secrets, and Silence: Selected Prose 1966–1979* (New York: W. W. Norton, 1979)

Richardson, Leslie, '"Who shall restore my lost credit?": Rape, Reputation and the Marriage Market', *Studies in Eighteenth-Century Culture*, 32 (2003), pp. 19–44

Richardson, Samuel, 'Answer to the Letter of a Very Reverend and Worthy Gentleman, Objecting to the Warmth of a Particular Scene in *The History of Clarissa*', in *Samuel Richardson's Published Commentary on Clarissa 1747–65*, ed. Thomas Keymer (London: Pickering and Chatto, 1998), vol. 1, pp. 121–39

—— *Clarissa, or, The History of a Young Lady*, ed. Angus Ross (London: Penguin, 1985)

—— *Pamela; or, Virtue Rewarded*, ed. Thomas Keymer and Alice Wakely (Oxford: Oxford University Press, 2008)

Robinson, Mary, *A Letter to the Women of England and The Natural Daughter*, ed. Sharon M. Setzer (Peterborough, Ont.: Broadview Press, 2003)

Rothschild, Babette, *8 Keys To Safe Trauma Recovery: Take-Charge Strategies to Empower Your Healing* (New York: W. W. Norton, 2010)

Rottenburg, Catherine, 'Sabina Nessa's Murder and the Grievability of Women's Lives', 26 September 2021, Al Jazeera, www.aljazeera.com/opinions/2021/9/26/sabina-nessas-murder-and-the-grivability-of-womens-lives (accessed 3 June 2025)

Ruderman, Anne C., *The Pleasures of Virtue: Political Thought in the Novels of Jane Austen* (Lanham, MD: Rowman and Littlefield, 1995)

Rudolph, Julia, 'Rape and Resistance: Women and Consent in Seventeenth-Century English Legal and Political Thought', *Journal of British Studies*, 39 (2000), pp. 157–84

Sanday, Peggy Reeves, *Fraternity Gang Rape: Brotherhood and Privilege on Campus* (New York: New York University Press, 2007)

Schwartz, Joan I., 'Eighteenth Century Abduction Law and *Clarissa*', in *Clarissa and Her Readers: New Entries for The Clarissa Project*, ed. Carol Houlihan Flynn and Edward Copeland (New York: AMS Press, 1999), vol. 9, pp. 269–308

Schulhoefer, Stephen, *Unwanted Sex: The Culture of Intimidation and the Failure of Law* (Cambridge, MA: Harvard University Press, 1998)

Searle, John, *Expression and Meaning: Studies in the Theory of Speech Acts* (Cambridge: Cambridge University Press, 1985)

Seeber, Barbara K., *General Consent in Jane Austen: A Study of Dialogism* (Kingston, Ont.: McGill-Queen's University Press, 2000)

Shelley, Mary, *Mathilda*, ed. Michelle Faubert (Peterborough, Ont.: Broadview Press, 2017)

Sheridan, Frances, *Conclusion of the Memoirs of Miss Sidney Bidulph*, ed. Nicole Garret and Heidi Hutner (Peterborough, Ont.: Broadview Press, 2013)

—— *The Memoirs of Miss Sidney Bidulph*, ed. Heidi Hutner and Nicole Garret (Peterborough, Ont.: Broadview Press, 2011)

Sheridan, Richard Brinsley, *The Rivals* (London: New Mermaids, 2004)

Simpson, Antony E., 'The "Blackmail Myth" and the Prosecution of Rape and its Attempt in 18th Century London: The Creation of a Legal Tradition', *The Journal of Criminal Law and Criminology*, 77, no. 1 (1986), pp. 101–50

—— 'Popular Perceptions of Rape as a Capital Crime in Eighteenth-Century England: The Press and Trial of Francis Charteris in the Old Bailey, February 1730', *Law and History Review*, 22, no. 1 (2004), pp. 27–70

—— 'Vulnerability and the Age of Female Consent: Legal Innovation and its Effects on Prosecutions for Rape in Eighteenth-Century London', in *Sexual Underworlds of the Enlightenment*, ed. G. S. Rousseau and Roy Porter (Manchester: Manchester University Press, 1987), pp. 181–205

Smith, Charlotte, *Desmond*, ed. Antje Blank and Janet Todd (Peterborough, Ont.: Broadview Press, 2001)

Sobba Green, Katherine, *The Courtship Novel 1740–1820: A Feminized Genre* (Lexington, KY: University Press of Kentucky, 1991)

Solnit, Rebecca, *Men Explain Things to Me* (London: Granta, 2014)

—— *The Mother of All Questions: Further Feminisms* (London: Granta, 2017)

—— *Whose Story is This? Old Conflicts, New Chapters* (London: Granta, 2019)

Springbord, Patricia, 'Mary Astell (1666–1732), Critic of Locke', *The American Political Science Review*, 89, no. 3 (1995), pp. 621–33

'St John Street: Introduction; West Side', in *Survey of London: Volume 46, South and East Clerkenwell*, ed. Philip Temple (London, 2008), pp. 203–21

Stewart, Ann Marie, *The Ravishing Restoration* (Selinsgrove, PA: Susquehanna University Press, 2010)

Tandon, Bharat, *Jane Austen and the Morality of Conversation* (London: Anthem Press, 2003)

Thompson, Emma, *Sense and Sensibility: The Screenplay and Diaries* (London: Bloomsbury, 1995)

Thompson, Helen, *Ingenuous Subjection: Compliance and Power in the Eighteenth-Century Domestic Novel* (Philadelphia, PA: University of Pennsylvania Press, 2005)

Thornhill, Randy, and Craig T. Palmer, *A Natural History of Rape: Biological Bases of Sexual Coercion* (Cambridge, MA: MIT Press, 2000)

Traver, John C., 'The Inconclusive Memoirs of Miss Sidney Bidulph: Problems of Poetic Justice, Closure, and Gender', *Eighteenth-Century Fiction*, 20, no. 1 (2007), pp. 35–60

Trumbach, Randolph, *Sex and the Gender Revolution, Volume I: Heterosexuality and the Third Gender in Enlightenment London* (Chicago: University of Chicago Press, 1998)

van Dernoot Lipsky, Laura, and Connie Burk, *Trauma Stewardship: An Everyday Guide to Caring for Self While Caring for Others* (Oakland, CA: Berret-Koehler, 2009)

Varholy, Cristine, 'Sexual Assault and Compulsion', in *Violence, Politics and Gender in Early Modern England*, ed. Joseph Ward (Basingstoke: Palgrave Macmillan, 2008), pp. 41–66

Vickery, Amanda, *Behind Closed Doors: At Home in Georgian England* (New Haven, CT: Yale University Press, 2009)

—— *The Gentleman's Daughter: Women's Lives in Georgian England* (New Haven, CT: Yale University Press, 1999)

Waxman, Claire, 'The London Rape Review: Reflections and Recommendations', *Official Website for the Mayor of London*, 31 July 2019, www.london.gov.uk/sites/default/files/vcl_rape_review_-_final_-_31st_july_2019.pdf (accessed 22 July 2021)

Webber, Jordan Erica, 'It's Frustrating to be Known as the Woman who Survived #Gamergate', *The Guardian*, 16 January 2024, www.theguardian.com/lifeandstyle/2017/oct/16/anita-sarkeesian-its-frustrating-to-be-known-as-the-woman-who-survived-gamergate (accessed 27 November 2024)

West, Rebecca, *The Court and the Castle: A Study of the Intersections of Political and Religious Ideas in Imaginative Literature* (London: Macmillan, 1958)

Wikipedia, 'Gaslighting', https://en.wikipedia.org/wiki/Gaslighting (accessed 13 March 2020)

Williams, Zoe, 'Why Did No One Speak Out About Harvey Weinstein?', *The Guardian*, 10 October 2017, www.theguardian.com/film/2017/oct/10/why-did-no-one-speak-out-about-harvey-weinstein (accessed 3 June 2021)

Wilson, Mara, '"Unwanted Sex," Twenty Years Later', *The Atlantic, Letters from the Archive*, 21 October 2018, www.theatlantic.com/letters/archive/2018/10/stephen-schulhofers-unwanted-sex-20-years-later/573241/ (accessed 22 July 2021)

Wollstonecraft, Mary, *Mary, A Fiction and The Wrongs of Woman, or Maria*, ed. Michelle Faubert (Peterborough, Ont.: Broadview Press, 2012)

—— *A Vindication of the Rights of Woman* (London: Vintage, 2014)

Woodworth, Megan, '"If a man dared act for himself": Family Romance and Independence in Frances Burney's *Cecilia*', *Eighteenth-Century Fiction*, 22, no. 2 (2009–10), pp. 355–70

Wright, Katherine Jane, 'Flights, Fear or Fantasy: Abduction Plots in Fiction of the Eighteenth Century 1740–1811', unpublished PhD thesis, University of Edinburgh, 2017

Yeazell, Ruth Bernard, *Fictions of Modesty: Women and Courtship in the English Novel* (Chicago: University of Chicago Press, 1991)

Zonitch, Barbara, *Familiar Violence: Gender and Social Upheavals in the Novels of Frances Burney* (Newark, DE: University of Delaware Press, 1997)

EU authorised representative for GPSR:
Easy Access System Europe, Mustamäe tee 50,
10621 Tallinn, Estonia
gpsr.requests@easproject.com

www.ingramcontent.com/pod-product-compliance
Lightning Source LLC
LaVergne TN
LVHW041943100826
845152LV00008B/157/J

* 9 7 8 1 5 2 6 1 8 8 8 5 4 *